THE RULE OF THUMB 2

WRITTEN BY
STEVE & JO DEW-JONES

Dear Rob,

thanks for supporting us. Hope you like the book.

Love Steve & Jo x

INTREPID BOOKS

First edition, published in July 2016 by
Intrepid Books, London, W3
www.theruleofthumb2.wordpress.com

Printed in the UK by Sarum Colourview
www.colourview.co.uk

ISBN 978-0-9567162-1-7

DRAWINGS BY PHILIPPE NASH

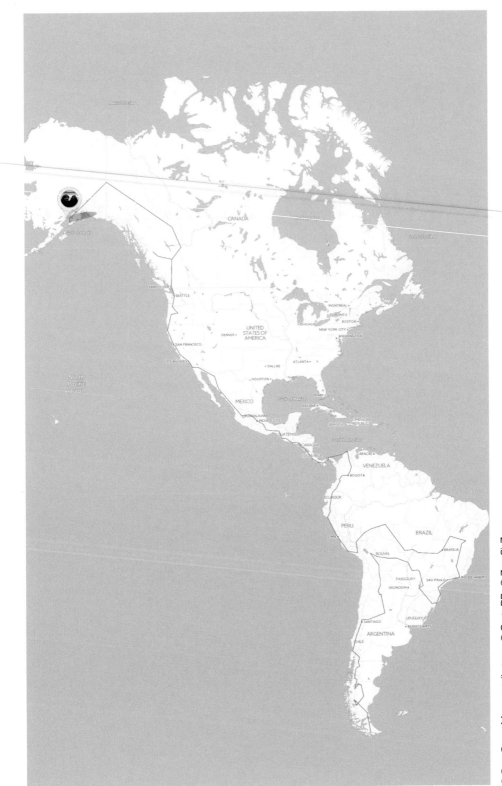

CONTENTS

PROLOGUE

SUNDAY 16TH MARCH 2014, 04.34
AIR EUROPA FLIGHT TO BUENOS AIRES, BRAZILIAN AIRSPACE

STEVE

Five years have passed since Will Jackson and I returned from Malaysia at the end of our six-month-long hitchhike from England. Now, here I sit, alongside my wife Jo, at the onset of a new adventure – hitchhiking from the southern tip of Argentina to Alaska. England to Malaysia represented about as far as you can go overland from west to east; this one is the furthest possible south to north.

We expect the journey to take eight or nine months. Beyond that, our only definitive plan at this moment is to arrive in Brazil in time for the 2014 World Cup, which begins in three months. We will touch down in Buenos Aires in a little over four hours, before heading on to Ushuaia, Argentina's southernmost city, the next day.

Despite my best efforts, I was unable to persuade my erstwhile travelling companion to join us for this next adventure, which we conceived together in Malaysia. Five years on, and without Will by my side, this journey promises to be a different affair. At 27, I have a few more years under my belt, and travelling as a couple, rather than just a couple of friends, is a different proposition.

It would be fair to say that not all of our friends and family have been entirely thrilled by the idea, but I am convinced that it remains as true now as it was in 2009 that the world is filled with good people, and that they vastly outnumber those who would wish to do us harm. Perhaps my greatest goal is to prove that the Malaysia hitch was no fluke and that truly, wherever one goes, one can rely on the kindness of strangers.

MONDAY 17TH MARCH 2014, 17.46
SEAT 29D, AEROLINEAS ARGENTINAS FLIGHT FROM BUENOS AIRES TO USHUAIA

Jo

If this were a bigger plane, seat 29D would be somewhere near the wing, firmly stationed in the centre of the action. However, it is not, and thus Steve and I find ourselves one side each of the aisle on the very back row, increasingly perfumed by the smell of the adjacent toilets and variously bumped by bags or bottoms as passengers negotiate their way past.

We are flying to Ushuaia, the so-called "End of the World", which sounds rather dramatic and by all accounts should be. We hear rumours of vast glaciers and jagged, lofty mountains that run into the sea: a fitting backdrop for the end of civilisation.

Recent discussions about the coming days have left me feeling ever more overwhelmed. Our challenge is immense and with myriad unknowns (the worst kind of scenario for my personality): nothing is certain; there is no end in sight; everything is flexible. When I consider the day ahead or certain specific locations, I feel flickers of excitement, but as soon as time and space loom larger, fear muscles its way back in. America is currently my arbitrary beacon of hope – on a very distant horizon.

THE RULES

1 NEVER PAY FOR TRANSPORT

2 NEVER SAY NO TO AN OFFER

THE THUMB

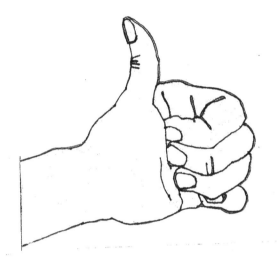

TO OUR DRIVERS - 392 REASONS
FOR THINKING BETTER OF THE
HUMAN RACE.

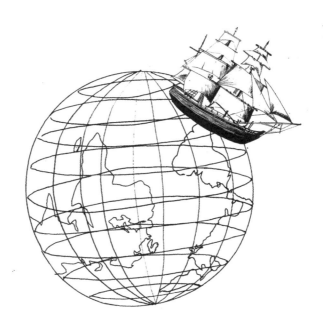

1. BEGINNING AT THE END

DAY 2: THURSDAY 20TH MARCH 2014, 20.49
HOSTEL PIONEROS DEL VALLE, EL CHALTÉN, SANTA CRUZ, PATAGONIA, ARGENTINA

STEVE

A gale is still blowing outside as Jo and I take stock after a whirlwind first 36 hours. Yesterday morning, at long last, the waiting ended and the adventure began.

We were on the road by 10.45. And by "on the road", I mean that we had wandered away from Ushuaia's Hostal Malvinas (that's Argentinian for "Falklands") and taken residence at a roundabout at the start of Route 3.

"This could be fun!" I joked, as a silver Ford Fiesta approached, sporting a badly crumpled left-hand side and a wobbly front-left wheel.

As if in response, the struggling chassis stopped and a pony-tailed 22-year-old named Fabrizio wound down the window and asked us where we were going. We had found our first ride.

Fabrizio took us around 20km out of Ushuaia, and deposited us by the side of the road at another roundabout. Roundabouts are usually good hitching spots because they afford one the opportunity to elect an exit, and then to stand beside it, leaving drivers with no uncertainty over the direction one wishes to travel.

In this case, we wanted to continue north on Route 3 in the direction of Río Grande, San Sebastian, the Chilean border and then the ferry crossing from Tierra del Fuego ("Land of Fire") to the mainland.

After leaving Fabrizio's car, a few droplets of rain began to fall, forcing us to slip on the rain covers over our backpacks for the first time. But barely had we done so, when, for the second time that morning, I uttered the words: "This could be fun!"

On this occasion the fun that I predicted did not relate to the dilapidated state of the approaching vehicle, but the fact that the black Mitsubishi Lancer had tinted windows, a loud spoiler and was travelling apace – all the signs of a boy racer.

The car duly answered my call, stopping beside us and unveiling its driver as the heavily tattooed Daniel, a 29-year-old tattooist on his way to Río Grande because, he told us, "I like the drive".

This was good news. Río Grande is some 200km from Ushuaia, over fairly mountainous beginnings, and this represented our first significant lift.

Daniel, whose breath was rather pungent, certainly lived up to his billing. For the next two hours, we were treated to the very finest rally driving, complete with daredevil overtaking, some impressive tailgating and fine use of the racing line.

To a soundtrack of '90s anthems, we saw breathtaking peaks and were certainly left gasping for breath by the boy racer in the driving seat. Daniel informed us that he liked to play driving games on his PlayStation. I informed him that driving on the PlayStation involves less risk of actual death. He laughed.

I must admit that, to my shame, after first speaking to Daniel through the passenger window, I had whispered to Jo, "I'm not so sure about this guy."

This was our signal to say: let's make sure we enter the car with our bags in hand, and that I enter first. These security protocols are to be our way of ensuring that a driver can neither leave with our belongings, nor my wife.

However, we are learning that it is not always easy to follow such steps and, for the second time in as many lifts, the size of our baggage forced the driver, out of kindness, to offer his boot. We accepted – both for fear of offending our new acquaintance, and for a lack of alternatives. And, as with Fabrizio, our hesitancy was to prove completely unfounded.

After an entirely fitting rendition of "Take My Breath Away", as we descended from snow-capped mountains to sun-scorched plains, we arrived in Río Grande, where Daniel left us in a perfect spot, on the exit road towards San Sebastian.

For the third time in a row, we were to wait for barely a minute before a driver pulled over and asked us where we were going. This time it was the gap-toothed Federico, 23, who was on his way home to an *estancia*, or farm, 20km north of Río Grande. We accepted his kind offer of a ride but were soon to regret our decision.

After 20 minutes practising our Spanish, we arrived at the turn-off to his *estancia* and parted company, both receiving a kiss on the cheek. (Apparently it's the custom here, regardless of gender.) The problem was that Federico's *estancia* lay in the middle of nowhere – not a good place to find a ride. To make matters worse, the surrounding area was very flat and a foul wind was blowing. Federico had been the second of our three drivers to explain that, in Patagonia, this southern region of Argentina, it is always extremely windy and perfectly possible to experience all four seasons in one day.

At that moment it was the first of these factors that was our chief concern, as we battled to stay on our feet. But after a little over 30 minutes, during which time we saw precious few vehicles, along came our saviours, Flor, 28, and her mother Marta.

We have been with them ever since.

Jo

As soon as we left our hostel in Ushuaia yesterday, my nervousness abated. All that was needed to lift my spirits was a sense of action: finally, we were on the road, and thinking, speculating and agonising were of no use. It didn't take long for rides to begin slotting into place, and now we've travelled just over 1,000km in two days. It has been an encouraging and auspicious start.

This progress has brought with it the realisation that Patagonia is, unquestionably, the windiest place on earth. As we waited on the unprotected plain beyond Federico's *estancia*, I half expected myself to be sent cartwheeling away with the tumbleweed; every time a truck roared past I had to clutch onto Steve, while the subsequent gusts bullied our meagre forms. It was humbling, really – in the ego fight between man and nature, man was barely getting a look in.

When Flor and Marta pulled over, we began making our way to their car, but our progress was so impeded by the wind that Flor saw fit to reverse the vehicle to meet us. Thereupon we discovered that Flor speaks excellent English; Marta doesn't (though her character needs no translation – Steve has already adopted her as his first surrogate mother of the trip); and Flor is addicted to a strange, bitter, tea-like drink called *mate*.

So began our initiation into what we are told is the beverage of choice for the true Argentinian. Partaking of *mate* (pronounced "mattay") is a deeply social occupation: Flor would pour hot water into a cup filled with green leaves; the vessel was then passed around, each of us in turn sipping the bitter liquid through a perforated metal straw. The well-prepared traveller carries a set comprising the *mate* (cup), *yerba* (leaves) and a flask full of hot water at a specially regulated *mate* temperature – a commendable commitment to a hot drink. (I suspect that Flor may take this commitment to higher levels than most: she admitted that she was carrying one kilogram of *yerba* for her two-week holiday, the equivalent of 500 teabags.)

Last night Steve and I put our tent to the test, camping in Flor's Aunt Mónica's garden in Río Gallegos. It was an important experiment with some significant findings: 5°C was a struggle for the insulating capacity of our double sleeping bag, so we will not be testing it to its stated lower threshold of -9°C; camping in gusts of 30mph is not to be advised; everyone will be happier if the tent stays packed away for the time being.

It was an invaluable trial, no doubt, notwithstanding the lack of successful sleep, which left Steve translucent with tiredness and me with bags under my eyes the size of the mountains we saw on our journey here to El Chaltén. Still, a shower and a power-nap later, we're back on track.

DAY 4: SATURDAY 22ND MARCH 2014, 19.26
LA LECHUZA RESTAURANT, EL CALAFATE, SANTA CRUZ, PATAGONIA, ARGENTINA

STEVE

The last few days have merged into one – partly through a lack of sleep; partly because of consistent company. We finally parted with Flor and Marta this afternoon after a full three days together.

You join me now in El Calafate, a tourist haven by the side of the vast Lago Argentino and the closest city to Perito Moreno, a glacier which attracts thousands of visitors each day – even on a wet and windy one like today.

We bade farewell to our new friends this afternoon, but only after they had transported us from one natural wonder to the next. Yesterday it was Mount Fitzroy in El Chaltén; today Perito Moreno.

How best to describe two ladies who adopted us as their own and whose kindness seemed effortless? Flor and Marta were more like a pair of best friends than a mother and daughter. Throughout our journey, we were treated to a soundtrack of Flor's favourite Argentinian music, which, naturally, included the archetypal Argentinian dance step, tango.

"Tango" became a kind of catchword for me over the course of our time with them – my best way of interacting with Marta, who spoke Spanish too quickly for us. All I had to do to make her smile was to interject the word "tango" every so often, accompanied with the raising of my arms as if ready to launch myself into the dance.

You see, if Flor enjoyed tango, for Marta it seemed to represent her very being. As soon as a tango track began, Marta would close her eyes and twirl her left hand beside her cheek in time with the music. Marta, I discovered, was an excellent tangoist.

The time for our first tango together, which had been in the offing ever since we met, was our second night, at a party in El Chaltén. After leaving Aunt Mónica's house at around 11am on Thursday morning, we had continued our journey north in a diagonal line towards the Andean mountain range in the west.

The 450km drive to El Chaltén lasted around five hours. During the journey the two most common words spoken were, without question, "tango" and "wow". Patagonia is a truly beautiful part of the world. To our English eyes, the sight of mile upon mile of landscape dotted with only a few wild animals was mind-boggling. As Marta put it, in Patagonia, there is *todo nada* – nothing at all – for vast stretches. We saw not one petrol station, nor roadside diner, for over 650km of road, during which time the only attractions were yellow earth, a few gigantic lakes, guanacos (llama-like creatures), rheas (similar to ostriches), *estancias* and a lone *gaucho* (cowboy).

"*Solo como guanaco macho* [Alone like a male guanaco]," as Flor put it. (Apparently this simile is a favourite of Patagonians.)

That evening, my opportunity to dance with Marta finally arrived. After dinner, I needed only to say one word.

"Tango?" I asked, for at least the tenth time that day.

And this time, at long last, the response was not only laughter, but action. On came the music and off went the tables and chairs, as space was created for my new second mother to tutor me in the classic dance.

The only problem was that the success of the tango, as with many dances, is almost entirely dependent upon the proficiency of the man at leading. This I had not anticipated, and it put paid to my ambitions of relying on Marta to transform me into a tango master. Marta tried her level best to help, but regardless of how complimentary she was, the sad truth was that I was a lost cause.

"*Es muy difícil* [It's really difficult]," she said, repeatedly. And didn't I know it.

Another of the highlights of our time with the Moreno family was the chance to meet a kindred spirit in the shape of Flor's younger brother, Facundo, 26. This young man, who boasted a thick beard that made me extremely jealous, is on an adventure similar to ours, just over a greater length of time. Facundo has been on the road for two years so far and, in that time, has hitchhiked from Río Grande to Venezuela, before returning to El Chaltén to make money working at a hotel. He flies back to Venezuela in a few months, from where he plans to carry on towards Alaska.

As Facundo and I swapped hitchhiking stories, he reassured me that, despite what we may have heard, we are unlikely to die in Colombia.

"I think people speak too much about the things they don't know," he said. "You'll be fine in Colombia. It's a great country and really easy to hitchhike."

"It seems to me," I said, "that you can choose to see the world in two ways. Either you trust people, or you believe that the world is a scary place in which everyone is out to get you."

"I totally agree," said my new best friend. "And if you choose the second option, you'll never do anything or go anywhere. You'll just stay in your town."

I was very encouraged by our conversation, although there was one caveat to Facundo's optimism.

"Venezuela," he said, "is different. They have signs in the bars saying: 'No guns allowed', because of a law passed in 2012. That means that before 2012, it was OK to take your gun into a bar."

Facundo said that he thought it "completely possible" that you could be robbed in Venezuela. It was the one country in which he had chosen not to hitchhike.

This was distressing news. Our current intention is to make our way north to Venezuela from Manaus in Brazil. This route would see us cross into southern Venezuela and then skirt along the southern side of the notorious capital, Caracas, before entering northern Colombia.

When I told Jo about Facundo's comments, or at least the gist of them (I may have left out the bit about guns), she went quiet. I didn't help matters by saying that it seemed to me to be against the very essence of Facundo's and my philosophy to avoid a country out of fear.

"But you can't just go to a country to prove a point!" Jo snapped.

I decided not to push the conversation any further at this stage. Venezuela is still a long way off and we are of the belief that if it is meant to be, it will be.

Jo

I think it's fair to say that our first week has been a commendable success, and much credit must be given to Flor and family, who remained in our lives until a mere three hours ago.

Facundo delighted in my ability to pronounce the rolled Spanish letter "erre" – and equally in Steve's inability to do so – and rewarded my efforts with the teaching of a Spanish *trabalengua* (tongue-twister):

> *Erre con erre cigarro,*
> *Erre con erre barril.*
> *Rápido corren los carros,*
> *Cargados de azúcar del ferrocarril.*

This translates as follows:
> "R" with "r" cigar,
> "R" with "r" barrel,
> Quickly run the cars
> Loaded with the railroad's sugar.

Helpful.

DAY 5: SUNDAY 23RD MARCH 2014, 15.30
HOSTAL EL OVEJERO, EL CALAFATE, SANTA CRUZ, PATAGONIA, ARGENTINA

STEVE

Today has been just the sort of relaxed day we needed. Jo asked me yesterday whether I thought our stamina would increase, as after only a week away from home, we were feeling exhausted.

But this is where Sundays will come into their own, for we decided at the start of the trip to use them to relax, refresh and to find a local church. This last bit should be fairly easy in Catholic-dominated South America and Evangelical North America.

Tomorrow we will continue our journey north, taking our place on the side of the road for the first time since leaving Tierra del Fuego. Facundo raved about southern Chile and, in particular, a place called Chile Chico, which lies just a few hundred kilometres north of El Chaltén. It is to there that we will attempt to hitch tomorrow, although we are always open to a change of direction, and may well end up somewhere completely different. That will all depend upon the people we meet.

From what we have heard and seen of this remote part of the world, we will need to carry supplies, for in southern Patagonia it is possible to find oneself completely isolated, waiting for an indeterminate length of time for the next vehicle to pass. It is a fine balance between travelling light and carrying enough to survive.

DAY 6: MONDAY 24TH MARCH 2014, 19.38
YPF PETROL STATION, GOBERNADOR GREGORES, SANTA CRUZ, PATAGONIA, ARGENTINA

STEVE

The sun is setting in Gobernador Gregores, the midway point between El Calafate and Perito Moreno (a town not to be confused with the glacier of the same name) on Route 40. You find us in a petrol station on the outskirts of the town, where we have been for a couple of hours, ever since bidding farewell to Miguel, the truck driver who brought us most of the way here.

The sky is painted pink and yellow, which seems fitting, for, throughout our journey (around 350km), there were rarely more than a couple of colours in sight. Patagonia is like nowhere else I have been. I doubt we passed more than 20 vehicles on our journey to Gob. Gregores. We stopped for a toilet break at the one petrol station we passed, but otherwise there was no sign of human habitation beyond a few *estancias*, miles apart.

The distinct feeling was that we were in the middle of nowhere, which brought a certain sense of vulnerability, but at least our minds could occupy themselves with the landscape. As with elsewhere in Patagonia, our eyes were transfixed by the contrast of yellow and grey earth, speckled with the very occasional patch of deep red, or a glimpse of vegetation. Counter-intuitively, the lack of variety in scenery is part of the reason why Patagonia is so engaging.

We were slower to leave this morning than planned, but soon made up for it. In a way that no longer surprised us, we were passed by just a scattering of cars on the exit road from El Calafate before Rodrigo and his partner, Monica, arrived in their cream VW Gol. This middle-aged couple were on their way back to Ushuaia after a brief holiday. They dropped us at the turn-off to Route 40, around 80km east.

On the short stretch out of El Calafate, we saw maybe a dozen other hitchhikers, scattered at intervals. I don't think I've ever seen so many in one stretch, nor was it to be the last we would see of them.

Barely five minutes after waving farewell to Rodrigo and Mónica, three French girls bundled out of a car, wandered over to us and explained that they were hitching to El Chaltén. We had just enough time to discuss hitchhiking etiquette (i.e. that we were there first) before another couple joined us. The latter pair decided to carry on walking (I didn't quite follow their logic because the only sign suggested the next landmark, a hotel, was 78km away), while the French girls took a spot 100 metres along.

When Miguel pulled over in his ageing truck, the Frenchies nodded to us and we wished them luck, as we climbed aboard for what would be a five-hour opportunity to practise our Spanish.

These are the things we understood from our time together: Miguel had been in the lorry-driving business for some time; Miguel had a wife and two children; Miguel was on his way to Perito Moreno but was stopping for the night somewhere east of Gob. Gregores; Miguel liked to smoke; Miguel had a cup, half-filled with water, in which he would place his cigarette butts; Miguel said this cup had never before fallen over, despite the often bumpy terrain; Miguel was not always right.

Much to Miguel's surprise, on one particularly jarring patch of road, the cup proceeded to topple over and drench my only pair of trousers in a putrid grey liquid.

I forgave Miguel, partly because I was still feeling guilty about an incident in the middle of our journey together. During our brief loo stop, he had left his engine running as Jo and I popped to the toilet, with our bags in his trailer. At first I had attempted to stay with him until the engine was turned off, but it seemed that was not going to happen, so off I trotted, fretting all the while. As we reappeared, not only was Miguel's truck still parked outside, but he had four oranges in his hands (part of his load) and gave them to me with a grin that said: "What on earth were you so worried about?"

Jo

In our quiet corner of this service station, Steve and I have just watched a glorious sunset. The days are long: when we arrived in Gobernador Gregores at 5.30pm, we could have happily continued without compromising our rule never to hitchhike in the dark. After regrouping, however, we observed that most vehicles seemed to be travelling only locally, so we have stayed put. We have since enjoyed delicious fresh *empanadas* (the Argentinian equivalent of the Cornish pasty), confirmed that we can camp behind the building, and I have just been bitten by a mosquito. Shame about the last one.

There are various travelling discomforts I assume to be of an equal burden whether one is male or female. The inconvenience of being desperate for the loo while also very thirsty, for example, or the way that unpleasant smells accumulate around the armpits and socks: these are not obviously gender-specific. However, I am adamant that, in the end, girls have it harder, and it will take a persuasive man to convince me otherwise.

While male travellers embrace their beardy and unkempt masculinity, we girls generally degenerate into distinctly unfeminine specimens. As a female traveller, it might be more practical, and certainly more sensible, to avoid tight-fitting clothes, but I can't shake the feeling of mild injustice that boys, apparently, need not adapt in the slightest. And there is absolutely no male equivalent to hitchhiking at one's time of the month, with all the associated paraphernalia and process. It's not ideal, that's all I'm saying.

DAY 7: TUESDAY 25TH MARCH 2014, 20.58
SALÓN ITURRIOZ, PERITO MORENO, SANTA CRUZ, PATAGONIA, ARGENTINA

STEVE

A lot can happen in 24 hours.

This time yesterday we were sipping coffees and munching *empanadas* in the service station in Gob. Gregores, preparing mentally for a second night in our tent. Roll on one hour and we had been invited back to the home of our new friend Margoth, the Bolivian lady in charge of the service station.

The next morning – this morning – after a night on a mattress in the lounge (much preferable to the tent), we were treated to breakfast (more croissants, known as *medialunas* – "half-moons" – and coffee), and then shipped back to the service station, where Margoth could start work and we could recommence our hitchhike north.

This last part did not prove easy. For the first time in Argentina, we were left frustrated as a trickle of vehicles passed us by (one every five minutes or so) on what we were fairly sure was the main road out of town.

Now this was different from the problems one can face while hitchhiking in other countries, where a steady stream of traffic can pass without much recognition of one's presence. This time, every driver acknowledged us, but each presented his or her own reason – through the cunning use of finger-pointing or twirling – why we could not travel with them, and looked at us with much sympathy, as if to say: "If only I were going in your direction!"

We found the finger-pointing perturbing, not only because we hadn't been picked up after one hour, but because we couldn't understand why. Miguel had told us that this was the right direction. Margoth had confirmed his view. So why were all these drivers, who were going our way, unable to help us?

We decided that action was required. Waiting for more than a few minutes simply did not happen in Argentina. Picking up our weighty loads, we began to traipse out of town in the direction which, a sign confirmed, would lead eventually to Perito Moreno.

We must have walked for about an hour before we saw any sign of deviation in the very straight road. Up ahead was a warehouse, where we were soon surrounded by a host of familiar faces. It transpired that all the finger-pointers were either parked outside the warehouse or running back and forth between there and the town.

The warehouse lay beside the first turn in the road and a sign that read "*DESVÍO*" (diversion). We waited there for a while, more to have a break than because it felt like a good spot, before, at midday, I approached the warehouse's security guard to enquire again whether this really was the main road to Perito Moreno.

This was a good move. The security guard informed me that in just 300 metres, the road bent again to the right, and that there lay the end of the *desvío* and the beginning of the new road to Perito Moreno. It was reassuring to arrive at what was, indisputably, the perfect spot, especially because it confirmed to us that all the finger-pointing had been genuine.

But after an hour in our "perfect spot", just one bus had turned onto our road. No cars.

We shared a sandwich and I blabbered, as I do, about why we should remain positive.

"Don't worry, darling," I said. "This really is the perfect spot and someone is bound to come along soon … But even if they don't, we'll be in the perfect spot to hitch tomorrow … We must have just missed the morning rush …"

This did little to help Jo's state of mind, which seemed tortured. It was bright and windy, so we were suffering both sunstroke and a chill. Moreover, Jo's tendency to worry about the future is only compounded by my tendency to discuss possible futures. It's a viscious circle.

When, after a further hour, a black pick-up truck finally indicated in our direction, we leapt to our feet and waved frantically.

Possibly as much out of surprise as compassion, the driver, Jorge, pulled over and signalled that we could join him.

Jorge lived at an *estancia* 70km north, he said, and was travelling with a colleague, Claudio. Given that *estancias* represent pretty much the only habitations between Gob. Gregores and Perito Moreno, we were delighted for the opportunity to travel with them this relatively short distance.

The downside in our plan became apparent soon after we arrived at the turn-off to Estancia La Verde, the intersection between Routes 29 and 40. While in our previous spot we had at least known the comfort of well-wishers at the warehouse, after two hours in our new position, just six vehicles had passed in our direction, and each one had sped by. There was usually a gesture – either to indicate that their car was full, or to suggest that we were crazy.

When I started to enthuse about the beautiful tranquility of our latest spot, and to discuss the contrast between our current isolation and living in London, Jo cried.

My assertions that, once again, this represented another good camping location – "Look, there's a lake where we can get water and even some shelter from the wind over there!" – did little to cheer her mood.

So it was with enormous relief that we welcomed the arrival of Juan, 28, and his travelling companion, 11-year-old Luciano.

Juan was driving his blue van to Las Heras and, to our sheer delight, would first pass through Perito Moreno.

The next few hours passed in a blur of *mate* and dance music – Armand Van Helden was a particular favourite of Juan's. When we arrived at a guesthouse, we exhaled at length and in unison. It has been a long day.

Jo

I am sorry to say that my attitude has suffered something of a setback, and I am forced to concede that I am not warming to hitchhiking as much as I thought.

Despite the wonderful turn of events that led to us staying with Margoth last night, the positive impact faded all too soon. I sunk into a sulk, and it wasn't only the long waits that were responsible; it was also our decreasing proximity to habitation – that, and the incessant wind buffeting my brain cells and will power.

We weren't actually that isolated in our three hitching spots, as we inched away from Gobernador Gregores. Even at our third, 70 kilometres from significant population, Jorge's *estancia* was on the horizon (although it would have been a fair walk), and there was a lake nearby if we needed it. We had food in our bags and a tent at our disposal. Clearly, I couldn't just blame isolation for my concern. More influential, perhaps, was my uneasiness about this constant lack of a discernible plan, which caused my mind to entertain various "worst case" scenarios: what if no-one comes and we have to camp, which would mean we'd have to eat our only sandwich, which would mean that if the same happened tomorrow then we wouldn't be very well equipped with food, and I THINK THE WIND IS GETTING TO ME.

Since these emotional doldrums, we have reached our intended destination, and at a very reasonable hour too, but I am already apprehensive about what tomorrow may hold. Hopefully, though, it's just a matter of experience. Today was surely a taster of what is to come – the waiting, the unknown – so the sooner I accept these inevitabilities the better.

POLICIA DE INVESTIGACIONES
CONTROL MIGRATORIO

2

CHILE
PASO LOS LIBERTADORES

2. CHECKING INTO CHILE

DAY 8: WEDNESDAY 26TH MARCH 2014, 15.39
YAMILY Y BEATRIZ RESTAURANT, CHILE CHICO, REGIÓN DE AYSÉN, PATAGONIA, CHILE

STEVE

Bienvenido a Chile! And welcome to Chile Chico, a little border town (*chico* literally means "small") on the shores of the second biggest lake in South America, which lies in Chilean and Argentinian territory and is known by two names: Lago General Carrera in Chile, Lago Buenos Aires in Argentina.

My brain is fried. I think it's the heat, which has stepped up a notch in intensity in the 600km or so north of El Calafate. Tiredness may also be a factor. We have been on the road for only eight days, but feel in desperate need of a rest. Perhaps we will slow down at some stage, but we discussed our progress last night and agreed that it is rather difficult to assess how we are doing at this point, given the scale of what lies ahead.

David, our driver from Perito Moreno to the Chilean border (at an average of 180kmph), was an encouragement. His wife of 30 years, Patricia, and he agreed that we had been "*muy rápido*" thus far. Not as *rápido* as if David had driven us the whole way, I thought, although I doubt we'd have made it in one piece.

Our entire journey today (around 70km) took less than two hours, including the navigation of two border posts. This feels rather difficult to believe, as we relax with a coffee to escape from the mid-afternoon sun, given that at 1pm, after an hour beside a petrol station on the outskirts of Perito Moreno, I was in the middle of suggesting alternative routes.

But then David pulled over. His manner was so nonchalant that at first we were not sure if he had stopped for us or simply for a rest. This uncertainty was heightened by what had gone before – nothing but a few finger-pointers making their way, at five-minute intervals, to the nearby supermarket.

This part of the world is a strange blend of friendliness and emptiness – at once the best and the worst place to hitchhike.

The combination of a late start and mild sunstroke have convinced us to remain in Chile Chico this evening. Tomorrow we plan to join the Carreterra Austral (Southern Highway), a supposedly beautiful but empty road, which, once we have rounded the lake, will lead us north.

Jo

On our way to the Chilean border, Patricia praised us for our Spanish proficiency. This is ironic, because only this morning we had laughed at Steve's latest attempts to ascertain directions. His halting half-sentences roughly translated as,

"Where round? The road? Round on the road? Where is? Near? You know the round? ... Jo, what is the word for roundabout?"

I, on the other hand, have been confident of my proficiency ever since a conversation on the flight to Ushuaia:

Lady with the long plait: *Saying something very fast, possibly about the view, followed by a broad smile.*

Me: "Er ... Si."

Lady with the long plait: *Increased rapidity and no discernible word separation; tone implies a rhetorical question.*

Me: "... Mmm."

Lady with the long plait: *Something else and then the word* "comer".

Me: [Thinking " *'Comer'*! I know that word! 'To eat'! I am excited! ... Too excited – I have no idea what she said next."] "... Ah, si."

Lady with the long plait: *Slightly puzzled and disappointed expression.*

End of conversation.

14

Patricia's assertion that our Spanish is "very good" may have been overgenerous, but on the whole we are not doing so badly; our sentence formation leaves something to be desired, but our vocabulary increases daily.

Now, though, we have regional differences to consider. Argentina posed certain additional challenges for the Spanish learner – the "s" is dropped all over the place, the double "l" sounds like the French "j" instead of the "y" in "yet", and so on – but having just about mastered these characteristics, we have now arrived in Chile, no doubt with its own idiosyncrasies. Oh, the woes of the novice linguist!

DAY 9: THURSDAY 27TH MARCH 2014, 14.43
ROADSIDE, CARRETERRA AUSTRAL, COCHRANE, REGIÓN DE AYSÉN, PATAGONIA, CHILE

STEVE

They say that waiting is the hardest part. Well, at this moment it doesn't seem so bad. Granted, we've been here, on the outskirts of Cochrane, for only half an hour, but it's hard to feel aggrieved when before us lies a picture-perfect view. Tall pine trees stand below us and mountains surround us.

There is not much traffic here, but we've become used to that. And, having made it here from Chile Chico this morning (almost 200km away), it would seem churlish to complain …

DAY 9 (CONTINUED): 18.09
SERGIO Y ALICIA'S CABAÑA, LAGO CHACABUCO, REGIÓN DE AYSÉN, PATAGONIA, CHILE

STEVE

I was right not to complain. Perhaps it was a premonition, for at that moment a silver pick-up truck rounded the bend by which we stood and pulled over.

"*¿Adónde vas?* [Where are you going?]" I asked, as the driver wound down the window on the passenger side.

"*Mi casa* [My house] …" came his reply. This was met with a round of hearty laughter from his three travelling companions.

"And where is that?" I enquired.

"*Treinta kilometros allá!* [Thirty kilometres that way!]" he said, pointing to the road ahead.

This was good enough for me. I nodded to Jo and we dumped the bags in the back of the truck. I joined them there. There was room inside the car for only one other person and, being a gentleman, I offered this to Jo. Well, to be honest, my logic was probably half chivalry and half that I had longed for a ride in the back of a pick-up truck since we'd started.

Soon the wind was blowing through my hair as I perched on top of our bags and gazed over the vehicle, my sunglasses providing necessary protection from the debris shooting up from the gravel track below.

With every breath the fresh air seemed to cleanse me from five years of London smog. There was also the small matter of stunning scenery to enjoy, as we wound our way past more pine-tree-covered hills and aquamarine lakes. Despite being out of earshot of the other passengers, I couldn't stop talking.

"Wow!"

"Amazing!"

"This is awesome!"

Prone to superlatives, I announced grandly to myself that this was "possibly my favourite hitch *ever!*", as I reflected on the parallels between this ride and those in the back of pick-up trucks in Thailand or on the top of a lorry riding across the breadth of Pakistan.

Forty-five minutes later, the car pulled over beside a gate and, as one of the other passengers went to unlock it, Jo jumped out to share some thoughts.

"I *think*," she said, "that they've invited us to stay with them tonight ... I *think*."

I nodded in elated approval, and soon the gate was opened and on we travelled down a winding track through another forest. The road became distinctly bumpier and then we stopped. Quite why we had stopped was not immediately apparent because we seemed only to have travelled deeper into the forest. But we were told that this was as far as the truck could go and that we must walk from there.

Out stepped Sergio and Alicia, the retired couple whose holiday home we were about to visit; their son Mauricio, 36, who has Down's syndrome; and their friend, 37-year-old Lenin – "Like the dictator", I quipped. He smiled, patiently, and nodded.

Behind me now, as I sit on the jetty on the shores of Lake Chacabuco, Lenin is adding a new coat of varnish to their entirely isolated log cabin, while Alicia prepares an apple strudel. Sergio is keeping Lenin company and I'm not sure about Mauricio, but I'm sure he's happy, wherever he is. It's in his nature.

We are feeling decidedly smug.

"This is why we do what we do!" I announced, moments ago, to Jo, who sits beside me.

She smiled.

"Are you having a nice time?" I asked.

No answer.

Jo is of course very grateful for the many acts of kindness we have already received. However, there is a fundamental tension between our approaches that did not exist with Will and me. It all comes back to Jo's desire for structure and a plan. Secretly, I am hoping that in time she will come to learn to take each day as it comes. Perhaps this is solely a selfish desire for her to become more like me, but I genuinely believe the philosophy to be freeing.

... Aha! Sergio has just called us in for dinner. I wonder what's on the menu tonight.

DAY 10: FRIDAY 28TH MARCH 2014, 11.24
LAGO CHACABUCO, REGIÓN DE AYSÉN, PATAGONIA, CHILE

Jo

If I was in control of our Spanish language progression, I would have us take the useful real-life experience accrued in the past 10 days into the comfy confines of the classroom; there, I would create a learning environment perfect for nurturing grammar improvement, increased knowledge of idioms and further pronunciation practice, before a carefully monitored reintegration into society.

Reality offers no such luxury, and yesterday I was plunged into the discomfiting position of having to muddle through a series of conversations – a perfectionist's nightmare. While Steve was revelling in the hitching highlight of his life, my brain barely had time to compute the surroundings, as I attempted – and mostly failed – to respond to not just one but four Spanish speakers.

This was the first time I had been in a car without Steve's gung-ho linguistic approach, and I realised with new insight the usefulness of his "speak first, perfect later" technique. I, however, am not accustomed to this, and instead alternated between soliloquy and silence, depending on whether I had any idea what was being said. Actually, I thought I'd done fairly well on the subjects of our adventure, jobs and even football (an easy win); it was only in the evening, when we returned to these matters at greater length and with a measure of confusion relating to the details, that it became clear I had been speaking some form of gobbledygook.

Still, our time at this soul-restoring lakeside retreat has proven that a common language is not imperative. I don't know how obvious it was that during most conversations we lost the thread here and there (it probably wasn't difficult to tell) but even so, we covered topics including the Falklands, nuclear energy, border conflicts between Argentina and Chile, the dangers of hitchhiking in Colombia and Venezuela (we're well versed on that one) and Christianity around the world. Not bad for beginners.

Yesterday afternoon I sat with Alicia in the *cabaña* while the menfolk were off and about. We began to discuss family life, and as I asked about her other son, Alicia's tone changed. Her voice strained and her face clouded as she explained that she doesn't see him or her grandchild often, and that, for reasons Alicia did not divulge, her son's wife does not care for this to change.

"*Somos tres* [We are three]," Alicia said, referring to Sergio, Mauricio and herself.

It was such a sad moment, and not knowing much by way of sympathetic phrases in Spanish, I let silence convey my empathy instead.

STEVE

"*Silencio!*" whispered Sergio this morning, as we stepped outside the cabin to gaze once more upon the natural beauty of our surroundings.

"*Total!*" Alicia added.

Oh how my soul has longed for this. Total silence. Blissful peace. The precise opposite, in my mind, to London life.

We have yet to formulate a plan for today, but it seems likely that, at some point, Sergio will take us back through the forest to the main road running south to Caleta Tortel, or north to Coyhaique.

"Maybe we should just get in with the first person who pulls over, in whichever direction they are going?" I suggested to Jo.

While it would seem a shame to miss the opportunity to see Caleta Tortel, an apparently otherwordly village of floating pathways just 100km away, I am attempting to appease Jo's desire for progress by suggesting alternatives.

If it were up to me, we'd head to Tortel, but I wouldn't mind so much if we were to achieve a ride all the way to Coyhaique – some seven hours north – or back to Cochrane, from where we could continue to Coyhaique tomorrow.

If and when we do arrive in Coyhaique, we have an invitation awaiting us from our first driver yesterday. Walter, 44, who lives in the nearby town of Puerto Aysén, has invited us for an *asado*, the South American term for a barbecue.

We liked Walter from the moment he took us under his wing, whisking us away from the misery of 90 minutes of finger-pointers in Chile Chico. We had arisen early, at 7am, on the advice that this represented our only chance of a significant lift. We were on the road by 8.15, so when 9.30 came and went, we were feeling unjustly cheated of sleep. But then Walter arrived.

After heaving our bags into the back of his Tata 4x4, we hopped in and began to relay the story of our adventure, using a script that is becoming very familiar.

When we told him our aim, Walter burst out laughing (he wasn't the first) and clapped his hands together in delight. The conversation then moved on to our other staples: our jobs; that, yes, we really are married; that no, we don't yet have children, despite being married for four years; my trip to Malaysia; the first book; the second book; and who is going to win the World Cup.

The answer to this last question is always the same: Brazil. Argentina, Spain and Germany are usually mentioned in despatches, and occasionally Uruguay and even Chile. Never England, until I bring them up, alongside the words "no" and "chance".

Walter, who works in construction, was driving to Cochrane on business. He will return to Chile Chico tomorrow to watch the eldest of his three sons compete in a motorcross race. Then on Monday he will return home, where we hope to join him for our very first *asado*.

DAY 10 (CONTINUED): 18.53
Restaurante Lago Brown, Cochrane, Región de Aysén, Chile

Jo

Steve and I are marking the end of the day's hitching exertions with a *pisco sour*, a popular citrusy *aperitivo* with a curious, though not unpleasant, white froth floating atop the cloudy liquid. We are the sole occupants of this restaurant, discounting the highly trained and not at all melodramatic soap actors invading the silence via the prominently placed television.

Yesterday, as we were driving towards Cochrane (for the first time), we passed an area of scorched land, still smouldering, being tackled by a team of firemen. We watched as a helicopter collected water from a lake and released it onto the smoking grass below.

We wouldn't have thought much more about this had we not stayed with Alicia and family last night. Sergio had a two-way radio and was keeping up with the forest fire's progress, partly for interest and partly because being so cut off could be a problem if the fire came our way. As the night drew in, we could even see the glow of flames reflecting off the clouds far on the horizon. There was no real risk of it reaching us, as the wind was blowing in the opposite direction and the distance it would have needed to travel was vast, but we might see the effects as we travel north again tomorrow.

Being a relative newcomer to hitchhiking, I have been receiving a steady initiation into drivers' gestures and their meanings. They generally fall into the following categories:

- <u>Simple hand wave:</u> this usually indicates "Sorry, the car is full", but also sometimes "Yes I see you and thus acknowledge you, but I will not take you".

- <u>The finger-point:</u> "I'm only going *there*"; sometimes (depending upon our mood) interpreted as "Oh sorry, I'm only going 150km in the direction you want to go. What a shame I'm not going to take you!"

- <u>Drawing a circle in the air:</u> my personal favourite, signifying "It is such a pity, but today I'm just heading to the nearest roundabout so that I can spend a few hours driving round and round".

Sometimes the "wobbly hand" is the gesture of choice. At the moment, I can only think that it means "maybe I will, maybe I won't … no I won't": I think I still have some training to do.

DAY 12: SUNDAY 30TH MARCH 2014, 10.15
HOSPEDAJE KOI AIKE, COYHAIQUE, REGIÓN DE AYSÉN, CHILE

STEVE

In the end, we left the southern strip of the Carreterra Austral without visiting Caleta Tortel. It was mid-afternoon by the time we departed Lago Chacabuco and, with Sergio already taking Lenin back to Cochrane, we remembered that Alaska lay somewhere slightly farther in the same direction and decided to join them.

After a second sleepless night camping in Patagonia, we made another early start yesterday, hitting the road by 8am with the hope of catching a ride all the way to Coyhaique.

At 9.30, having been passed by only another squadron of finger-pointers (is there an alliance?), and a host of firefighters off to tackle the continuing blaze, we were again feeling unnecessarily robbed of sleep until Maite, 67, pulled to a stop in her red Mitsubishi 4x4.

This groovy granny, wearing a woollen jumper which matched the colour of her car, was on her way to Coyhaique airport, from where she would fly to visit family in Santiago. Maite said she was glad to have company on the treacherous road over the mountains that surround Lago General Carrerra – we weren't sure whether to feel honoured or scared.

Suddenly our decision to wake early didn't seem like such a bad idea, particularly when we proceeded to pass hitchhiker after hitchhiker attempting to secure a ride in the same direction. The sheer number of hitchers may have even surpassed the number we saw leaving El Calafate. Competition adds a whole new challenge to hitchhiking.

After six hours practising Spanish and singing along to songs spanning Maite's seven decades, we approached a T-junction and our time together came to an abrupt end.

Maite was running late, so she bade us a hasty farewell and we tried to recover from the shock of leaving her warm car for the cold emptiness of the road in front of us.

There was a sign a little way along the road, which, with squinting eyes, I read as "COYHAIQUE 12".

Traffic being thin on the ground, we decided to wait for one vehicle and, if it didn't stop, to proceed on foot. Twelve kilometres, we figured, should take only a few hours, and we had four hours before dark.

When Mario screeched to a halt, waved us in and proceeded to drive us past a sign that read "COYHAIQUE 42", we were grateful for the ride. When our new driver invited us to his home in Coyhaique for Patagonian lamb and two bottles of the finest Chilean red, gratefulness turned to joy. If it weren't for our splitting headaches – we'd missed our morning coffee-fix in our haste to hit the road – we would have been in heaven. As it was, after a couple of hours meeting and greeting Mario's extended family, his daughter Daniella, 27, who is training as an English teacher, noticed the bags under our eyes and asked if we would like to be taken to a hostel. Later that evening, she would pick us up to show us around the city.

This hitchhiking lark certainly has its perks.

Jo

Our second attempt at camping on Friday night was approximately as successful as our first. The temperature was preferable to that of our Argentinian experience, the wind was insignificant and the tent proved waterproof in the rain. But there was no quiet-hour for the local stray dogs, and the multitudinous chickens had a "roost-off" for three hours straight, starting at 5am. The tent has been packed away again.

An odd eventuality when hitchhiking is that the parting of ways can come about very suddenly. Our drive with Maite took the best part of the day, all the while learning about her life and times, and then there we were, pulling over at a junction to bid farewell. Within 40 minutes we were sitting in Mario's kitchen, eating roast lamb and drinking red wine. Breakfast had been a handful of Pringles and lunch a packet of ham-flavoured crispy bites (nutrition is not always the principal consideration on hitching days), so this feast was a wonder to behold. But it was a struggle to adjust to forging a new friendship so soon after turning our backs on the last one.

DAY 14: TUESDAY 1ST APRIL 2014, 21.02
HOSPEDAJE DE MARIO Y GLADYS, VILLA SANTA LUCIA, REGIÓN DE LOS LAGOS, PATAGONIA, CHILE

STEVE

In two weeks we have hitched more than 3,000km, but still we find ourselves just one third of the way through Chile, officially the longest country in the world.

If we had travelled in a straight line, we could have covered three quarters of the length of Chile's slightly less lengthy neighbour, Argentina. But speed is not our chief ambition. We would not trade any of the sights we have seen, nor the people we have met, for an extra 2,000km towards our end goal.

Last night, Walter's promise of an *asado* was fulfilled, at his home in Puerto Aysén. In the charming and spacious house he and his wife, Claudia, designed and built five years ago, we enjoyed fine Patagonian ribs in the company of their two youngest sons, Joaquin, 17, and Benjamin, five, and Walter's father, Walter Snr.

The younger Walter and his wife treated us to a free night in their hostel, before wishing us all the best as off we set towards the Argentinian border.

Jo

Today, for the first time, we suffered the city syndrome of blank expressions in place of gestured excuses as we waited on the edge of Puerto Aysén. The situation was righted when Leonardo, 32, drew up and took us 13km beyond his fly-fishing destination to the road leading north.

As we arrived, we spied another hitcher in residence. Ready to respect the unwritten rules, we had a short chat before making to move farther up the road, but there was no need. As we took a step, Erez from Israel flagged down a car with space for us all and companions we became.

The road was excellent. In contrast with the Andean passes – spectacular yet perilous – this route was positioned far enough from any precipices that I could fully absorb myself in the passing terrain. Alberto, our grey-haired chauffeur, was in no particular rush and we stopped several times: once to squint at condors gliding far, far above; later to stand hushed before a magnificent glacial lake.

For a time our car was a hitchhiker taxi. We dropped Erez near a national park and substituted him for Cadir from Switzerland; Alberto seemed accustomed to the popularity of the hitching trail and happy to oblige us all. We remained with him for a further five hours, during which conversation was constant – partly because Steve and Alberto discussed international football at astounding length. This predominantly involved saying the name of a player in an English accent and then finding out what it was in a Spanish accent, or vice versa. Fun for all.

Alberto also took mischievous pleasure in referring to Steve as *gordito* (chubby) and tapping his belly to signify this fact. By the end of the journey, Alberto had ordered Steve to "drink less beer and do more sit-ups" and had given him four new nicknames: *Gordito*; *Huevón* (a slang word for a man's testicles); *Flojo* (lazy); and something that sounded like "*Chaspurriado*" and was defined as someone who is bad at Spanish. Steve took it well.

3. SUPERSTITIOUS MINDS

DAY 15: WEDNESDAY 2ND APRIL 2014, 18.23
CHOCOLATE & CAFÉ, ESQUEL, CHUBUT, PATAGONIA, ARGENTINA

STEVE

And so it is that we arrive back in Argentina on *Día de Malvinas*, a national day of remembrance for those lost in the Falklands War (or, as the Argentinians would know it, the war for the Malvinas).

We were reminded of this fact by a border guard and I think I overestimated his sense of humour when I chirped: "It happened before we were born, so you can't blame us!" This line, in my mind, seemed a perfectly reasonable way to break the ice, but he wasn't amused.

Behind gritted teeth, the guard wished us *"buen viaje"* (a good journey).

As we made good our escape, we decided henceforth to refer to ourselves as Welsh. Possessing the surname "Jones" has its advantages in a country in which the remnants of an ancient Welsh community still survives, not least in Trevelin, the first town after the border, which is home to the Jhon Daniel Evans Hospital. We weren't sure what happened to the spelling of "John". Perhaps it's Welsh.

Two Chilean grannies transported us over the border. Evita and Betty, whose ages I dared not ask, caused us to question afresh our proficiency in

Spanish. Their high-pitched accents, and the rate at which they spoke, left us scratching our heads. Even grasping Betty's name proved challenging. After three attempts to understand her, I thought she was telling us her name was "Javier". When, finally, she scribbled "Betty" on a piece of paper, I was perplexed.

After arriving in Trevelin and wandering half the length of the town's entirely straight main road, we were picked up by Miguel, 67, who lives here in Esquel, a town 30km northeast of the border.

He has invited us to see him again tomorrow morning at the bus terminal where he works. We aren't quite sure why, but hope it has more to do with his English-speaking daughter, Florencia, 24, than his profession.

Jo

It has happened. I have become a criminal. I didn't mean to, honest! One moment I wasn't, and the next I just ... was.

It was the apple in my bag that did it. I couldn't bring myself to throw it away, that innocent little thing, so it ended up coming with us over the border from Chile back to Argentina – which, according to the many, many posters, is no journey for fresh produce to be undertaking.

This morning was our last in Chile for the time being, and we awoke to a thick shroud of mist hovering in the valley. As we savoured a final breakfast of freshly baked bread with jam, we heard about a strong earthquake that had occurred farther north that morning, and the subsequent risk of a tsunami. Steve and I exchanged raised eyebrows. There was no risk to us – we were 75km away and heading eastward anyway – but it was a brief reminder of our vulnerability. Taking care on the road is one thing, but avoiding natural disasters is quite another.

It was reassuring to cross back into a country we've already visited (notwithstanding my apprehension that Argentinian Customs officials would soon be bearing down upon me and my apple). Our return to Argentina promises *medialunas* for breakfast, much improved coffee, ruby Malbec and Argentina's breed of Spanish, mercifully spoken at a slower rate than that of the breakneck, slang-filled Chilean version.

DAY 19: SUNDAY 6TH APRIL 2014, 10.21
HOSTERÍA SUR, BARILOCHE, RÍO NEGRO, PATAGONIA, ARGENTINA

Jo

Over the last couple of days, our knowledge of the etiquette of drinking *mate* has vastly increased, thanks to our stay with friend-of-a-friend Miguel and his father, José Luis, in Lago Puelo.

The intricacies are various. The server should drink the first cup as it is the most bitter; serving it to someone else is a deliberate insult. Partakers must fully consume the liquid in the *mate* before returning it; slurping is acceptable to ensure that this has been carried out. Time is of the essence: anyone nursing the *mate* for too long may be told to "hand back the microphone". Never refuse an offer of *mate*, unless you can provide a legitimate excuse, such as recently having partaken, and say "thank you" only when you've had your fill, because after this is spoken you won't be offered the *mate* again.

The more we learn about such cultural practices, the more I realise how many times we must have demonstrated our ignorance through unwitting blunders. Mercifully, the Argentinians seem to be an accommodating race, and willing to turn a blind eye to our many gaffes.

STEVE

Arriving in Bariloche from the south, you could be forgiven for wondering why it is so highly regarded here in Argentina, where it is a popular honeymoon destination and, in winter, ski resort. The journey from Lago Puelo to Bariloche was certainly beautiful, and we enjoyed our time with our driver, Christian, 40, who was passing through Bariloche on his way some five hours farther northeast to the city of Neuquen. But as he drove us through the grotty outskirts of Bariloche, we started to question our logic in rejecting the opportunity of a more substantial lift.

Before all that, we had a farewell banquet at the Galdiz family home, during which José Luis became the latest person to warn us of the perils of Venezuela. José Luis's advice was at odds with that of his son, who told us that Venezuela is a beautiful place and that the current political strife would be very unlikely to affect us.

In reply, I said I had learnt not to take warnings too seriously. In every country it's the same story: the next country is full of bandits (this was José Luis's line on Chile) and even some places in *this* country are worth avoiding.

Nonetheless, I felt strangely ill at ease as, after lunch, José Luis took us to the start of the road to Bariloche. Despite my efforts to shrug aside these latest warnings, my unguarded optimism had been sullied.

So it was that, after 40 minutes of waiting, I was very relieved when Christian pulled over. It felt reassuring simply to be on the move again and, once more, to find ourselves well looked after by an accommodating Argentinian.

We will soon leave behind fair Patagonia, but not before we have spent a couple of days here in Bariloche, including Jo's birthday tomorrow.

Bariloche, it turns out, is more pleasant the closer to the centre one travels, boasting majestic views of the gigantic Lago Nahuel Huapi and a bustling city centre full of chocolate shops. But, to be honest, it's not really my kind of place. The sheer number of tourists seems to have squeezed the charm out of the city.

DAY 20: MONDAY 7TH APRIL 2014, 17.48
HOSTERÍA SUR, BARILOCHE, RÍO NEGRO, PATAGONIA, ARGENTINA

STEVE

As I glance out of the window at the cathedral opposite, my mind wanders back to yesterday's service. Unfortunately, our limited Spanish, paired with the priest's thick accent and our ignorance of Catholicism, meant we were unable to understand much of the goings-on. But one thing caught my eye and continues to puzzle me today: a poster of the Virgin Mary hovering over Lago Nahuel Huapi in a manner that seemed to be suggesting she was, in some way, the Lady of the Lake.

I may not have thought twice about the poster were it not for our conversation with Miguel on Saturday.

"South America," Miguel said, "is the only place where Mary is more important than Jesus."

This took me by surprise. It is well recognised that Catholics place more emphasis than Protestants on Mary's role, but I had never considered that any Catholic would exalt her so highly.

Miguel told me that the reason for this is steeped in history.

"When the Catholics came to South America, they built churches on top of the shrines and cemeteries of the indigenous tribes," he said. As intercessor between man and God, Mary was promoted as a way of bridging the gap between Christianity and the tribal religions.

My understanding of the link is incomplete, but I wonder whether it has any influence on the multiple superstitions that exist here. Many of our drivers, the vast majority of whom identify themselves as Catholics, have been very superstitious. One of the more interesting notions we have encountered relates to a mythical figure known as Gauchito (literally "little cowboy") Gil.

Gil is said to have been an Argentinian Robin Hood, stealing from the rich to feed the poor, and in so doing earning a reputation as a lovable rogue. This reputation was enhanced, we learnt, by the manner of his death. As Gil was on his way to the hanging post, he is said to have told a policeman that, if he was set free, he would heal the policeman's dying son. The policeman, unaware that his son was ill, rejected Gil's offer, but when he returned home to find his son dying, he prayed to Gil's spirit to save his son. He survived.

Today, hundreds of red crosses litter the roadsides in Argentina – shrines to the healing spirit of Gauchito Gil and prayers for safety while travelling.

Quite how Gil became linked with crosses, a distinctly Christian symbol, is a mystery to me, but most people here seem more certain of the existence of a general spiritual realm than they do of the Christian God. The majority of our drivers have had crosses hanging from their rear-view mirrors, but we have heard more from them about Gauchito Gil than Christianity.

DAY 22: WEDNESDAY 9TH APRIL 2014, 11.27
CAFÉ PALACE, VALDIVIA, REGIÓN DE LOS RIOS, CHILE

JO

On Monday I celebrated my twenty-seventh birthday, and, all things considered, it was a very British affair. Rain fell steadily all day, the celebrated view from a nearby peak was marred by a dense fog and we had to resort to cake and Bariloche's famed hot chocolate to warm our souls. It was just like home.

Despite a three-night rest stop, a day later we were exhausted again; the continuing miserable weather and traversing another border had taken their toll. Our spirits were further dampened by an unexpected spot of bother: no-one seemed compelled to pick us up while in view of Customs.

We had reached the Argentinian-Chilean border with relative ease, passed through Customs, and proceeded to wander beyond the exit checkpoint.

As we did so, Steve requested from the guard something along the lines of, "You [polite, plural]. Say drivers. Two Englands to Alaska".

It was unclear whether this served to help or hinder our case, but either way, the drivers who passed by intermittently over the next hour paid us no heed.

Meanwhile, the rain descended. At least we were equipped, clad head to toe in waterproofs, which was more than could be said for the Chilean chap who wandered past to wait beyond us. He wore only a light jacket, and looked completely miserable.

STEVE

A sustained period of waiting in the cold and damp transformed my typically mild manner into rage.

"Why aren't people stopping?" I fumed, as we stood, helplessly, beside the hut on the far side of Customs. "We must have been passed by more than 10 cars now and most of them had easily enough room for us. Why wouldn't they take us? We're clearly cold, wet and in need. You have to be a pretty terrible person not to lend us a hand."

Jo shrugged and did her best to defend the guard, whom I suggested must have been behind the whole operation, saying nasty things about us and ordering drivers not to help us.

When we saw another couple of would-be hitchers wandering our way, we felt sorry for them, until they informed us they had already arranged for a "*camionero*" (trucker) to pick them up.

"It generally helps if you talk to drivers at Customs and tell them you'll wait for them on the other side," the gentleman of the couple informed us.

I feigned a smile and resisted the nagging urge to tell our adviser that I was in fact an expert at hitchhiking and that it had generally proved so easy in these parts that a lack of success had seemed unthinkable, thank you very much! But after watching our competitors climb into their truck and wave us goodbye, we took their advice, and were rewarded handsomely.

Not only did our new driver (another Miguel) take us the 17km to Chilean Customs; he proceeded to drive us for more than five hours all the way to the coastal city of Valdivia.

Our passage over the Andes led to a complete shift in scenery. In place of mountain grandeur, we were met by rolling hills and lush vegetation. Farm life was in full flow in Región de Los Lagos. It felt like a piece of England.

It was 10pm by the time we parted with Miguel, a gregarious character who will be best remembered for his long list of superstitions.

As we passed through Chilean Customs, Jo asked Miguel whether she need worry about the orange in her bag. At this, Miguel pointed to a tiny apple tucked into one of the crevices on the dashboard.

"I always take an apple with me through Customs and they never find it," he said. "I'm lucky."

The "lucky" apple became something of a shared joke between us, although the apple was by no means our driver's only talisman. Miguel showed us a further five objects: a piece of quartz, two pieces of purple cloth, a crucifix and a mini horseshoe. He also said something about being from a Catholic family, although I missed the connection.

By the time it came for us to part, Miguel had very kindly taken us to Valdivia, despite it not being on his route home, and given us a guided tour. Our parting was a rather strange affair. In my attempts to tell him that we really didn't mind where we ended the night – "We don't have a plan" – I seemed to confuse Miguel. Several times he asked: "So, what do you want to do?"

Twice during our last moments together I felt sure we had understood one another, only for him to ask us the question again. The first came when we took the turn-off to Valdivia: surely a clear sign this was to be where we would spend the night. Then, after taking us to the beer factory on the edge of town, he posed the question again and mentioned something about his house.

Right, that settled it, didn't it? We were all going back to his place.

I thanked him for the tour – "At least we got a taste of Valdivia," I chirped – and prepared for the hour's drive to his home. But five minutes later we were back in the city centre and the question was posed again. This time, he turned to Jo and asked her if she was tired.

She nodded.

Miguel didn't say anything. Were we supposed to be taking a hint? Confused and exhausted, I asked Jo what she thought we should do.

"Shall we just get out here?" she replied.

I shrugged and nodded.

All parties seemed pleased with the eventual outcome, though to compound our tiredness, we were then interrogated, and kissed, by two homeless fellows speaking words that we didn't understand. It was too late for that. We apologised, waved them off and trudged to the nearest restaurant in the hope it was still serving food.

DAY 22 (CONTINUED): 19.05
SKY BAR, HOTEL DREAMS, VALDIVIA, REGIÓN DE LOS RIOS, CHILE

JO

The luck of Miguel's various charms didn't stretch to cover me, as became apparent during "The Incident of the Apple and the Orange".

As we approached the Chilean border, me with an Argentinian orange in my backpack, Miguel's comments temporarily reassured me that there was no cause for concern. We carried out the requisite paperwork (in which I declared that I did not have any fresh produce), and then we pulled up for inspection.

Within moments, the sniffer dog was dancing a merry jig around my bag, and out came the orange – this time, my criminality was not to go unnoticed. A murmured discussion took place between two guards, after which I was led into a room to fill in my paperwork again. As I ticked "yes" in the appropriate box, I learned that false declaration was usually an infraction worth $200; for an orange picked up for free at breakfast, this would have been a princely sum! I shall endeavour to curtail such heinous misconduct in future.

Valdivia has proven itself a charming host. The German heritage of this area makes it feel as if we have sidestepped into Europe; Steve has taken to pointing to every other passerby and declaring that they are "one hundred per cent German". His confidence persists despite having been as convinced about our hostel owner, only to be assured otherwise. He does have a point, though – at breakfast this morning we could just as well have been in Berlin if it wasn't for the Spanish being spoken.

Meanwhile, a high proportion of the afternoon was spent in thrall at the local sea lion population. So captivating, and yet so, so ugly.

DAY 23: THURSDAY 10TH APRIL 2014, 17.26
PASEO ARAUCO, CHILLÁN, REGIÓN DE BÍO BÍO, CHILE

STEVE

This morning we may well have broken the record for the shortest hitch of all time.

Having walked out of Valdivia, we had set our bags down at a set of traffic lights, beside a sign to Santiago. Within two minutes, we were bundling into the back of Camilla's car. Sixty seconds later, we were retrieving them again.

Camilla, you see, had hurried us into her car, traffic lights being no place to linger, and it was only after we were in that we learned she was heading in the opposite direction to us.

We took the next left, and Camilla pulled over.

"Here," she said, "is a good place to *dedo* [literally "finger", but also Chilean and Argentinian for hitchhiking]. Where you were was … How do I say? The *worst* place."

"Ah, OK … Thanks!" we said, and hopped out of the vehicle.

We soon had our next ride, courtesy of David and Myrtha's red Chevrolet pick-up. David was taking his wife to work at a lake on the other side of the motorway (Ruta 5) – essentially the opposite side of the country in this especially narrow nation. He dropped us at a toll on Ruta 5, from which we hoped to secure a longer ride.

Sure enough, barely had we time to analyse whether our new position would work, before another red 4X4 pulled over.

Four hours later, we were in Chillán, a city in the centre of Chile, and the prospective new home of Hugo, 30, and girlfriend Kahrin, 28. This couple, who currently live in Valdivia, are spending a long weekend here to do up Kahrin's old family home, which lies empty after the death of her grandmother. When Kahrin, who has the blonde locks and pale skin befitting her German descent, asked if we'd like to stay with them, it was a no-brainer: never refuse an offer.

DAY 25: SATURDAY 12TH APRIL 2014, 10.26
EL BIÓGRAFO, BARRIO LASTARRIA, SANTIAGO, REGIÓN METROPOLITANA DE SANTIAGO, CHILE

STEVE

Hola from Santiago, the heart of Chile and where nearly half the population resides. We arrived yesterday afternoon, which marked an upturn in fortunes, for our journey didn't get off to the best start.

Hugo and Kahrin, in their attempts to help us on our way, drove us out of Chillán, but after taking a wrong turn we found ourselves unexpectedly on the motorway, and, in a panic, our friends took the next exit and unwittingly deposited us in a dreadful place.

In hitchhiking terms, the hard shoulder of a motorway constitutes pretty much the worst possible spot. The only exception to this is if you just happen to be beside an entry ramp from which you can hope to find a driver passing slowly enough to see you.

We *were* near a ramp, but it was on a bend and the few drivers using it saw us only at the very last minute, at the same time as they were gathering pace (and their senses) before entering the chaos of the motorway.

We waited for 30 minutes there. I spent the majority of this time standing precariously close to the inside lane, waving my arms in the hope that some fool would be willing to slam on the brakes. No-one was.

Deciding that enough was enough, I approached a nearby farm, asking a man whether there was a better place to *dedo* nearby. The man assured me that we might have better luck farther down the road. My lack of comprehension meant that I missed the reason why, but we figured it could hardly be worse.

But after only a kilometre or so of wandering along the hard shoulder, we saw that sight we dread the most: another group of hitchhikers. There were three of them, arms flapping wildy at passing cars as they stood but a foot from the oncoming traffic.

"Idiots," I muttered to Jo, as we approached them with a wave. "What do they think they're going to achieve hitchhiking there?"

We passed them with a feigned show of mutual respect and appreciation and, yes, I mentioned my elite status as a hitchhiking champion.

Soon a truck-stop loomed on the horizon and we were feeling smug.

"Idiots," I said again, this time with a touch of sympathy, as a trucker ushered us in.

"*Hola*!" shrieked the enthusiastic Luis, a middle-aged man with greying hair. He seemed particularly pleased to hear we were from England.

"That was a very bad place to *dedo*," he bellowed. "I'll take you to a better position."

"*Gracias*," we said to our bubbly new friend as he dropped us at a service station – the perfect spot.

Here we were, I reflected, surely about to secure a ride to Santiago, while our *amigos* down the road were suffering.

"Idiots," I said a third time, shaking my head.

Another truck soon pulled over ... But what was this? A familiar head – that of a pretty young lady with messy hair and a beaming smile – peered out of the passenger window and grinned at us.

"It's one of the hitchers from earlier!" Jo said.

"Wow ..." I mumbled, feeling suddenly sheepish. "I bet the other two are in there as well."

They were. And more, it transpired that it had been at their behest the driver had stopped, despite an already crammed cabin. Our Bohemian *compadres* graciously made space for us – Jo squeezed in alongside them on the bed behind our driver Rodolfo, 35, while I was afforded the luxury of the passenger seat.

"What lovely people," I thought guiltily, as I helped myself to a large dose of humble pie.

Our new companions were Pax, 25, the girl with the smile, and her two hippie friends from university in Concepción: Andrés, 24, and Cristóbal, 23.

Conversations with our driver were a lost cause, such was the speed at which he spoke and the strength of his accent. We did our best to laugh and smile in all the right places, but most of the journey passed in an awkward silence. Outside the window, vineyards gave way to mountains, as the Andes edged closer and joined the Cordillera de la Costa (Coastal Range) to create the "hole" in which Santiago is said to sit. Not good for pollution, apparently.

When, after five hours, we arrived in what we were told was the centre of Santiago, disaster struck. Rodolfo was just pulling over to drop us off, when his front-right tyre hit the curb and we heard an explosion.

Rodolfo wore the expression of a man who had been punched in the stomach. Our driver was stopping in Santiago only to load the truck. He had a full five or six hours of driving ahead of him to return to Los Ángeles in the south.

The six of us stood beside the truck for a while and occasionally Andrés and Cristóbal attempted to lend a hand in the tyre change, but it was clear only Rodolfo had the foggiest idea what to do.

After a painful 10 minutes, the hippies were off and invited us to join them. We felt bad for leaving Rodolfo, but we could be of little assistance.

"We're sorry," we said, and hugged him goodbye.

"Don't worry," he replied, and wished us a "*buen viaje*", as we took our first steps into the concrete jungle that is Santiago.

Jo

It feels like there is noise everywhere around us in Chile, and I think it is getting to me. The constant presence of television screens and music is one factor, background clatter is another. Yesterday morning there was decorating work taking place in the apartment; this morning, construction clangs from the block opposite. Our motorway walk – with massive trucks hurtling past, spurting out fumes and roaring their authority – was not calming.

All in all, my capacity for coping with life's vagaries is suffering. Not long ago I burst into tears when my breakfast transpired to be a piece of lemon meringue pie, when all I wanted was a simple croissant. It happens to be a time when I am trying to redress my biological composition (currently two parts human to three parts complex carbohydrate), but really, this was not the kind of situation that justified a grown woman crying.

This aside, early impressions of Santiago are positive. We covered a swathe of the city during yesterday's hour-long walk to the hostel and marvelled at a variety of impressive buildings. It was early enough in the day not to feel concerned at how conspicuous we were with our backpacks; even a cry of "*Gringos!*" (typically an insult reserved for unwelcome Americans) sounded more observational than aggressive. Now, the bags are stowed away for a couple of days, and we shall step out among the masses descending upon the capital city for the weekend.

DAY 26: PALM SUNDAY, 13TH APRIL 2014, 18.21
COCKTEL BAR MAMBOLETA, BARRIO LASTARRIA, SANTIAGO, REGIÓN METROPOLITANA DE SANTIAGO, CHILE

STEVE

Today is Palm Sunday, marking the beginning of Holy Week. Today is also the day that Colo Colo, one of the Chilean capital's most popular football teams, won the national league. To be in Santiago today is to be aware of these two events.

Palm leaves are selling like hot cakes as Christians mark the day, a week before Easter, that Jesus rode into Jerusalem on a donkey. Yesterday, the approach of Holy Week was celebrated with grand processions. Hundreds of Catholics, young and old, marched through the streets, waving palm leaves and singing songs.

Today it is the fans of Colo Colo who celebrate. Flags are waving, horns honking and chanting still rings through the streets this evening.

The uglier side of football has also been on show. As we returned from lunch at the Central Market, we witnessed at close quarters fans throwing stones at riot police.

"They just won. What do they have to complain about?" remarked our new friend Federico, 34, a Colombian student currently in charge of our hostel in Barrio Lastarria, a trendy district of Santiago.

Emotions of every kind are running high in Santiago today, as the country's two great passions compete for affection.

If it weren't for football, Catholicism would be the undisputed ruler of Chile. Such is its power, we were told by Hugo and Kahrin, that the Church was once able to stop an Iron Maiden concert from taking place, owing to the band's perceived Satanic leanings. Hugo told us the Church's influence has lessened in recent years, but there is still no denying its potency.

DAY 27: MONDAY 14TH APRIL 2014, 21.58
HOTEL MANUEL RODRIGUEZ, LOS ANDES, REGIÓN DE VALPARAÍSO, CHILE

JO

Over our delicious seafood lunch at Santiago's Central Market yesterday, Federico told us that, in his opinion, people from the United States have engineered a sneaky steal by adopting the collective term "American" to denote people from their nation alone. As far as he was concerned, it should cover everyone from across the two continents.

Having never considered this oversight before, we admitted that apart from the rather wordy "people from the United States", "American" is indeed the only adjective English-speakers have at their disposal. I have since calculated that the Spanish term *estadounidenses* (equivalent to "United States-ers") is just as many syllables, so maybe they need an alternative too.

Our next destination was set to be the port city of Valparaíso, 100km from Santiago, so we were shocked when we learned last night of a huge forest fire that has forced 10,000 people to be evacuated from the area and has already destroyed hundreds of homes. The news was on in the hostel as we ate breakfast this morning, and we discussed the matter with the staff. We nodded gravely as one lady, Inés, wistfully praised "beautiful" Valparaíso.

Some way into our conversation, Inés's face grew puzzled, and she asked if Steve and I had understood the sentence she had just uttered. We had assumed so. Inés looked amused and explained that, in fact, she had changed topics: it was me she had been complimenting.

"Yes, yes," we had been agreeing, forlornly. "So beautiful."

STEVE

This morning provided perhaps our greatest challenge yet – trying to hitch a ride out of a capital city – as we turned our attention towards Mendoza, Argentina's wine capital. Our task was made even stiffer by virtue of the scorching sun. Our giant leap north over the past week has led to a significant shift in temperature and we did not help ourselves by starting as late as 11am.

Navigating our path out of the city centre towards the start of the road north took just 30 minutes, but we were still some way from the outskirts and had no knowledge at that stage whether the drivers passing us were likely to be going any distance.

An hour passed as we waited at a set of traffic lights. In this time, buses and taxis were the most frequent passing vehicles, and only a handful of drivers acknowledged us. Our apparent invisibility seemed to me to confirm that we must be in a capital city.

But not long after, our prayers for a ride out of the centre were answered by a retired policeman named Luis. Our new friend, who had been forced to quit his job due to a problem with his leg, drove us to the periphery of the city, leaving us well placed to catch a ride north.

Minutes later, we were on our way, thanks to a ride with a well-dressed thirtysomething named Hugo. He had splashed himself with aftershave and was smelling sweet, but dropped us in a rotten spot. We were with Hugo for only 15 minutes or so, until the town of Colina. As he deposited us by the motorway exit, and with no entry ramp in sight, we realised with horror that, as had happened after our previous ride with a man named Hugo, our only remaining option was going to be to attempt to hitch a ride on the motorway.

"This is a dreadful spot," I lamented. "Either we wait here, or we walk indeterminately in the hope of finding an entry ramp."

I had just declared confidently that no fool would be stupid enough to pull over on the hard shoulder when someone did just that.

Vayron, 26, was on his way to work, processing table grapes at a vineyard in Panquehue, a small town slightly west of the road to Mendoza. Despite being out of the way, when Vayron asked if we would like to see him at work, we were glad to accompany him.

Our young friend asked if we were hungry and, having missed lunch, we nodded. Vayron dropped us at a restaurant and told us he would come back within the hour. And then he left, with our bags still in the back of his car.

This was no accident on our part. We were well aware of the fact, but it would have felt rude, and distrusting, to ask to remove them. We did trust Vayron. And it was just as well, for we soon realised that, despite this trust, we were in for an anxious wait.

I had not taken Vayron's number, so there was nothing we could do but hope our friend returned.

"And now the waiting begins!" I declared, after we had downed some soup.

Then right on cue, in walked Vayron, who proceeded to pay the bill, buy us ice creams and take us on a tour of the beautiful vineyard where he works.

"Welcome to Chile!" he said, with a smile. "But be careful! You left your bags in my car. You know, not everyone can be trusted!"

I find it rather ironic that the people who show us the most kindness tend to be the ones most worried about the dangers posed by others.

There's a high likelihood that we'll be checking out of Chile tomorrow (given that we're spending the night in the last major town before the border) and, as I reassured Vayron, we will leave with the impression that the people here have been some of the most hospitable we have ever met.

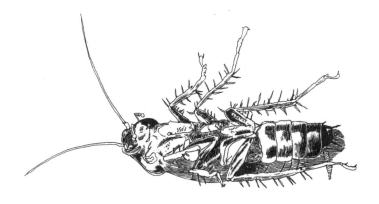

4. COCKROACHES IN CORDOBA

DAY 28: TUESDAY 15TH APRIL 2014, 20.06
DÜN KEN CAFÉ, PLAZA INDEPENDENCIA, MENDOZA, ARGENTINA

STEVE

"Welcome to the International Capital of Wine!" This was the sign that greeted us as we arrived in the city of Mendoza two hours ago.

Quite a statement. I know a few Frenchmen who would disagree. Some Chileans too. Nevertheless, we are happy to be here and, yes, we do have two glasses of the good stuff in front of us as we write.

We said farewell to the Andes today. They have been an almost constant companion, but we have now left them behind, with no immediate plans to return as we journey northeast towards Bolivia and then Brazil.

Our journey today reminded me why I love hitchhiking. First there was the enlivening trek to the edge of the city (in this case, Los Andes), then the satisfaction of watching as only the second car pulled over. Angelo, a soldier in this thirties, was on his way to his post halfway between Los Andes and the border. This charming young man left us in what he understood to be a good place to secure a ride.

Not everyone agreed. Soon we were on our way again, taking our position on the second row of seats in a truck's cabin (I've never seen the like before), as we set off to what our new driver, Eliseo, said would be a much "better place" to *dedo*.

We had been in our new, improved position by the side of a police checkpoint just a few minutes before our third and final drivers arrived. Hugo, 60, was on his way to Mendoza with his wife, Yolanda, for the Easter holidays. We travelled with them in their silver Hyundai for more than six hours, during which we sat back, enjoyed the ride and almost forgot we were hitchhiking.

It is in these moments that hitchhiking is surely the best way to travel. There is no need to worry about driving or navigation; nor to concern yourself with the state of the vehicle or the cost of the journey. Throw in a detailed commentary on the landscape, a free meal and a lift to the city centre, and you have a picture of our day.

The ride over the Andes was majestic, with views of peculiar rock formations painted different shades of red and brown. It was like being back in Patagonia, with just a few colours on show, the grey asphalt and blue sky offsetting the earthy mountainsides. But then we arrived in Argentina and all was green, apart from the faintest touches of autumn.

It feels strange to think we may never return to Chile. We loved our time there, but it is a long way from home. Perhaps we'll have to move there.

Jo

Chile must be a favourable country for the graffiti artist, I have deduced, for there was evidence of their work everywhere – not just on the bus stops and park benches, but also on houses, churches, monuments. Even today, as we travelled over the border, we noticed an array of tags sprayed onto the mountainsides. I grudgingly acknowledged the commitment of these people, who had thought in advance to equip themselves with the requisite spray-paint, and had then driven miles away from habitation to leave their mark. I was pleased to note, however, that the mountains' height, magnitude and splendour more than exposed these spindly signatures for what they were.

Once into Argentina we stopped for lunch. Steve and I already had sandwiches with us, and, to avoid the risk of smuggling fresh goods again, had eaten them in the car at around midday. Hugo and Yolanda must have assumed that this was our mid-morning snack, for by 2pm we were drawing up to a restaurant and being invited to share a *parrilla* (an alternative name for an *asado*). There was to be no backing out owing to lack of hunger. We were soon presented with a mountainous pile of meat (delicious meat at that) and I resigned myself to the impossibility of maintaining a balanced diet on hitching days.

We have now entered the most populous corridor of this part of South America. Santiago, Mendoza and Córdoba (our next destination) are on similar latitudes, and with less than 1,000km between the three, it has made it an obvious route. City visits are tiring, what with the traffic, ceaseless noise and extra caution required, but we profit from the amenities available and the likelihood of finding a cheap hotel. These are the cost-benefit analyses involved in adventure economics!

DAY 31: GOOD FRIDAY, 18TH APRIL 2014, 12.36
PLAZA SAN MARTÍN, CÓRDOBA, ARGENTINA

STEVE

Cockroaches. Dozens of cockroaches. This was our welcome to Córdoba, as we arrived in the centre last night and checked into the nearest *residencial* (cheap hotel). We checked out again almost immediately, but by that time we were severely shaken and down 200 pesos (around £15).

We haven't fared much better this morning. We narrowly missed treading on a cockroach on our way to Plaza San Martín, a few blocks from our new, shabby-but-cockroach-free hotel. And then the wasps arrived. In swarms. And the pigeons. In packs.

Apparently wasps were introduced to Argentina some years ago to oust a plague of another bug – a grave error of judgement. In the cafe-cum-bakery on the edge of the plaza, there are dozens on every pile of pastries. We didn't buy any. On the plus side, we didn't see any cockroaches there, but this isn't to say there aren't any. As you can tell, our first impressions of Córdoba, Argentina's second city, have not been favourable.

Córdoba is more than 600km northeast of Mendoza. Our chances of getting here in one day seemed slim yesterday lunchtime, as we scoffed some *empanadas* and reflected on why no-one was stopping to pick us up at a service station 100km outside Mendoza.

We had been waiting there for an hour and a half. In that time, just one person had stopped to ask where we were going, but he was heading for Mendoza. A few others pointed in various directions by way of apology or excuse, but nothing more.

The day had started in a decidedly positive fashion. We waited for no more than 20 minutes on the eastern edge of the city before Matías, a 28-year-old wine trader, pulled over. During our short journey together – he was on his way to the next town, San Martín – we were told that Mendoza, home to 950 *bodegas* (vineyards) is in fact one of five international wine capitals (alongside Bordeaux, California, somewhere in South Africa and … he couldn't remember the fifth). It is also the nearest city to the tallest mountain in the Americas, Aconcagua. We had passed this giant peak on our way across the border but failed to appreciate its significance.

Aconcagua was in our sights as we waited for our second ride, at the start of the slip-road from San Martín to the dual carriageway running east – Ruta 7, the road to Buenos Aires, or in our case, Córdoba.

Again, we didn't have to wait long. Fabio, 40, a sweet-hearted country bumpkin, was our latest hero. We travelled in his white van for 30 minutes, until he dropped us at the service station, handing us two jars of Mendozan marmalade and a bottle of fizzy grapefruit juice as parting gifts.

Five minutes later, Fabio returned with his two daughters, Rebecca, 17, and Valentina, eight, who greeted us with kisses and handed us some homemade rolls to accompany our jam.

We were humbled by their kindness and clung to its memory as the minutes ticked by.

"The problem here is that people just don't seem to have any compassion!" I remarked, after no more than half an hour without a ride.

Matías had told us that people in Córdoba were much friendlier than those in Mendoza. A policeman at the petrol pumps seconded the view. An hour later, it was official. People in Mendoza were horrible, heartless folk who cared only for themselves.

And then Pablo, 36, arrived. *He* was from Córdoba. And *he* would be happy to take us there. "Naturally," I thought.

It transpired that our curly haired chauffeur was on a non-stop, 36-hour round trip from Salta, in the north, to Mendoza. (He said himself that he was "*loco*".) Pablo, you see, is in the transportation business and had just purchased his fourth lorry. After starting work as a lorry driver in Córdoba at the age of 18, Pablo moved to Salta 10 years ago to be with his partner, María, 33, who hails from the region and is an English teacher. Much of what we learnt about Pablo came when he handed over his telephone so we could talk to her.

Pablo's crazy 36-hour trip, which had started at 9pm on Wednesday, was fuelled by a combination of willpower and coca. Coca is the leaf from which cocaine is formed, and chewing it provides an energy boost not dissimilar to that of caffeine, or *mate*. Apparently it's completely legal and the staple diet of all lorry drivers in the north. I tried a bit. Jo did not.

Passing into the Córdoba region was like being transported instantly into another world. Gone were the vineyards and entirely flat plains around Mendoza. In their place was a carpet of green giving way to rolling hills.

It was 8pm when we arrived in Córdoba, by which time Pablo was a firm friend and had invited us to visit his home in Salta. We would have journeyed with him all the way that evening were it not for the fact that his three sisters were waiting in Córdoba for him to pick them up. They would be spending the Easter weekend together.

Pablo's driving was as "*loco*" as you might expect of a man who conceived such ridiculous journeys and hadn't slept for a few days, so it came as little surprise when he was pulled over at one of the frequent police checkpoints. Pablo had been spotted overtaking a row of vehicles on a blind corner.

We felt sorry for our friend. A 10-minute stop-go penalty and a hefty fine (1,290 pesos) was the last thing he needed. Furthermore, it didn't help his state of mind, nor his driving.

After a few more hair-raising overtakes, I told Pablo about our secret weapon: Jo's voice. One song was enough to calm him down.

"Joanna has a beautiful voice," he told María over the phone. (He spent most of the journey passing vehicles at 160km/hr with one hand on the steering wheel, the other on his phone.) "I feel much better now."

We were glad. Twenty minutes and a dozen songs later, we arrived in Córdoba and wandered into the nearest *residencial*.

DAY 35: TUESDAY 22ND APRIL 2014, 11.38
Café Bernasconi, San Miguel de Tucumán, Tucumán, Argentina

STEVE

It's raining outside as we adjust to our new surroundings. A day's worth of hitching has brought us 550km north of Córdoba, and it feels different here. Our latest Pablo, who drove us most of the way, said that it would: the climate is tropical, people seem friendlier and the majority are darker in skin tone, reflecting native roots from before the time of the Spanish conquistadors.

Despite what people told us about the friendliness of people in Córdoba, we were never truly won over. Perhaps it was the cockroaches. But no, our disquiet ran deeper. A few more streetlights would have helped matters. And fewer pictures of women posing in lingerie – they were everywhere. The men in Córdoba seemed to possess particularly wandering eyes, but who could blame them? I can't remember visiting a place in which the objectification of women was so blatant.

The region of Córdoba, we learned, suffers from a drug epidemic. Prostitution is also rife. On Sunday, Easter Day, we met the pastor from a church in Río Tercero, south of Córdoba city, who outlined the scale of the problem. The majority of his congregation, said 34-year-old Marcelo Nieva, are ex-addicts and prostitutes. He said his church is coming under increasing pressure for interfering with the trade from an apparently corrupt local police force. The church has been raided several times and windows smashed. The pastor's life has also been threatened, as have the lives of his wife and one-month-old daughter.

Our time in Córdoba was not all bad. Taking advantage of the thriving tango scene, we enjoyed a lesson on Friday night, followed by a dance in the plaza (with dozens of significantly more proficient couples) the next eve. We were also glad to pass the Easter weekend in the city; visits to the cathedral and a lively pentecostal church helped lift the gloom.

But our third driver out of Córdoba yesterday provided us with another reminder of the region's troubles – and we met him only because of the rain.

For some time, Jo and I had disputed whether the grey clouds overhead were rain clouds, as we waited in a non-descript village 50km or so north of Córdoba. Jo thought they were; I disagreed. And then the heavens opened. Suddenly, and with great gusto.

Seeking shelter under the roof of an abandoned petrol station, we were busy changing into our waterproof layers when a man approached.

"*Adónde van?* [Where are you going?]" he asked.

"*Norte!* [North!]" I responded.

The man, who had driven his car under the shelter to protect the cargo in the trailer, apologised, saying that he was going only 30km, to the city of Jesús María.

He seemed surprised when our faces lit up and we asked enthusiastically to join him for the ride. Thirty kilometres felt like a significant distance after two hours of standing in the same place.

After 10 minutes, there was little sign that the rain would stop, so the man, who went by the name of Jorge and was 38, decided it was time to go. We chucked our bags into his trailer, secured their waterproof covers and piled blankets over Jorge's cargo – half a dozen bags of cement mix.

One kilometre later, Jorge groaned, acknowledging that he had underestimated the ferocity of the downpour. His cement would be worthless now.

Yet something deeper was troubling our new friend, who had shaggy hair and sunken eyes.

We had been going through our usual staples of conversation, and this inevitably included questions about family life. Jorge told us that he has three sons, but that the eldest two, aged 20 and 18, are neither working, nor studying.

"They don't do anything," he said.

When we asked why, Jorge told us, with tears in his eyes, that their mother – his ex – is an alcoholic and his two sons drug addicts.

And then we arrived at a petrol station on the edge of Jesús María and it was time for us to part. We wished Jorge well and told him we hoped his cargo would be dry and that we would pray for his sons. And then he left.

This is so often the pattern of our relationships. The beginnings of a friendship are forged, hearts are opened, and then we part, unlikely to see each other again.

Our hearts were troubled as we wandered out into the rain, which had calmed a little, and prepared for a new relationship to begin.

Jo

Pablo, a 38-year-old on his way to Tucumán, picked us up just before the bulging clouds burst again. For the first hour of the journey we drove parallel to the storm; one bolt of lightning struck unnervingly close to the car, at which point Pablo casually revealed that a tornado could come and swallow the car at any moment.

Eventually we passed away from the clouds, and for the rest of our six hours together discussed philosophies and musical tastes as we traversed miles of nothingness, punctuated by salt flats. Pablo told us about his conflicting desires – freedom, on the one hand, and his family on the other – and confessed that his passion for music, travelling and women (announced in the plural) might one day jeopardise his relationship with his wife and three children. This led to a lengthy discussion between Steve and Pablo about the meaning of "freedom", followed by that of the existence of God.

All the while, nature continued its light show in the distance and I, for my part, was transfixed by the flashing sky for much of the final stretch until we reached our destination.

DAY 36: WEDNESDAY 23RD APRIL 2014, 17.35
ROADSIDE, SANTA LUCIA, TUCUMÁN, ARGENTINA

STEVE

This is soul-destroying. We have been waiting for more than three hours now and there is only another hour and a half of light. If, as seems increasingly likely, we fail to secure a ride in that time, not only will we have to spend the night here, in this dreary village (it's not really so bad, but over time we have grown to hate it); it will also mark my longest ever wait for a ride. Four and a half hours may not seem like such a long time (I'm sure other hitchers have known longer waits), but it's still quite a drag.

To add to our sense of despair, we hardly made any distance today before we arrived here, in Santa Lucia. I don't think we can be more than 50km from Tucumán, which seems ridiculous given that we've been on the road for more than six hours and in that time have travelled in four different vehicles.

Until we arrived in this godforsaken place, we had been doing rather well. It was a late start, but at 11am Pablo transported us to a village on the edge of Tucumán. Three rides and three hours later, we had arrived in the village of Santa Lucia and I was raving about our surroundings.

The tropical scenery makes it feel like we have arrived in Latin America proper. Pablo told us that there are three types of landscape in the north of Argentina, which are also present across Bolivia and Peru: *jungla* (jungle), *bosque* (woodland) and *puna* (arid highlands). Our current surroundings definitely qualify as *jungla*. And to add to the vista, there are mountains behind us, in the direction we wish to travel. Pablo told us that the route from Tucumán to Salta and on to Bolivia is one of the most beautiful parts of Argentina. Hopefully we'll be seeing it for ourselves soon enough, but it's out of our hands.

DAY 36 (CONTINUED): 20.37
SANTA LUCIA POLICE STATION, SANTA LUCIA, TUCUMÁN, ARGENTINA

JO

Well, we are to spend the night in a police station.

I am tempted to employ artistic licence and to talk about being incarcerated in a grotty cell, but in reality the three officers are very amicable and didn't hesitate for a moment to usher us in when we said we were looking for a place to stay. I'm feeling off-colour for the first time and my heart sank when a passerby informed us that there were no hostels, but the strong arm of the law has steered us towards a couple of mattresses – saggy but sufficient.

By the three-hour mark, it had become all too apparent that a lift was not to be as forthcoming as we have come to expect. We simply couldn't work out why, and it seemed that nothing was going to improve our prospects significantly enough for us to move position. The frustration was debilitating. We decided that we would give up at 6.30pm, and as that hour approached I felt relief creeping in – it meant that the endless hopes-raised-hopes-dashed cycle of watching vehicles approach and then pass would soon end.

I used the intervening time as wisely as I could by developing a solution for the agony of the hitchhiker's waiting game.

My eventual idea was thus: when a driver dropped us off, there would be some kind of sign – a large, luminous, inflatable arrow hovering in the sky, for example – indicating whether or not this was to be our resting place for the night. If yes, fine; we would hang up our hitching boots for the day. If not, we would continue to hitchhike as normal. Additionally, as cars drove past, an arrow would indicate whether or not that driver was going to pick us up. We'd still have to be present at the side of the road to secure a ride, but it would be a far more relaxing affair.

The plan was flawless, apart from the small matter of it being unachievable.

DAY 37: THURSDAY 24TH APRIL 2014, 20.07
HOSTAL LA MORADA, CAFAYATE, SALTA, ARGENTINA

JO

Our accommodation in the police station was neither clean nor quiet, but it mattered not. We were grateful for the officers' kindness, which even extended to a simple breakfast provided as their 24-hour shift drew to an end. We bade them farewell and were presently striding past the spot where we had stood for so many hours the previous afternoon, buoyed to be making progress at last, albeit on foot.

Steeling my heart against the thought that Argentinians are bad people (which would have been totally unfair, not to mention forgetful of our usual success) was a hard ask. It had been a night of broken sleep, battling mosquitoes and sweat, which made it even more difficult to be gracious as cars hurtled past.

In the end, though, the fight was short-lived. We saw a 4x4 pull over ahead and the passengers begin to arrange their belongings to accommodate us. Our spirits soared. Thank you! Thank you! Would it be OK if I just took a quick nap?

DAY 38: FRIDAY 25TH APRIL 2014, 10.40
EL ZORRITO, CAFAYATE, SALTA, ARGENTINA

STEVE

All is well with the world today. If you had asked us how we were doing at 5pm yesterday, we would have offered a rather different diagnosis. Such is the nature of our journey.

Today, not only do you find us well-rested and showered, we are also in a state of blissful peace, reflecting on that oh-so-special feeling of knowing that our next journey is already taken care of.

The three reasons for this change in mindset arrived at ten past five yesterday afternoon, as we stood by the road in Amaicha del Valle, discussing our options. We had been waiting in the same spot for two and a half hours and it felt highly likely that, for the second day in a row, we would soon have to call it quits on the outskirts of a random village and find a place to spend the night.

But then along came Sergio, 44, María, 40, and their charming four-year-old daughter Julieta, and the world changed. Two hours later, we had arrived in Cafayate, home to some of Argentina's finest vineyards, and checked into the same hostel as our new friends and saviours.

Those two hours were the perfect tonic for what had been a gruelling two days on the road. And then this morning came and the world became even brighter, as Sergio and María invited us to join them today on a tour of the local vineyards and tomorrow to journey with them to Salta, three hours farther north.

Not only does their offer, which of course we accepted, help us on our way. It also provides us with a feeling of unparalleled peace, safe in the knowledge that, for the next few days at least, there will be no more waiting by the roadside.

In the end, yesterday proved to be a thoroughly successful day, the only blot on the copybook being the hours between 14.30 and 17.00, when a stream of passersby either pointed in various directions or plain ignored us. We even received our first middle-finger gesture from a boy no older than 14.

But our preceeding five-hour ride with Jorge, 53, and son-in-law Facundo, 26, more than made up for the lonesome hours that were to follow. Two of the nicest men you could hope to meet, they took us out for coffee, then lunch, and told us all about the local region.

The road was steep and winding and we travelled slowly, stopping every so often to discuss the latest sight. We saw llamas, thousands of cactuses, and mountains galore. We were taken to the highest spot on the road, around 3,000m, and learned about the cactus thieves, who, at night, strip bark from the base of cactuses to sell to tourists. This action not only taints the beauty of the bizarre plants; it causes them to die.

"It's terribly sad," lamented Jorge.

After lunch, our sweet friends asked other diners at the restaurant in Amaicha del Valle if they were heading to Cafayate.

"Not today!" one man chirped. He seemed to find it very amusing.

The rest remained silent.

With a sigh, Jorge apologised and told us we should ask people at the nearby petrol station.

This we did for a while. I even returned to the restaurant to talk to a Swiss couple who I suspected might be heading our way. Indeed they were, but they told me they "never pick up hitchhikers". I found this rather hard to compute and pleaded with them for a few minutes, telling them that we were not just any old hitchhikers, but were in fact "special", and not at all dirty or dangerous. It was of no use. I even asked if they would like to take down the details of our blog to see if they might in time change their minds about hitchhikers. They declined.

Wearily, I trudged back to Jo at the petrol pumps and we decided we couldn't bear to approach another soul. Instead, off we trotted to stand at the start of the road to Cafayate.

Then 5pm came and the world changed.

DAY 42: TUESDAY 29TH APRIL 2014, 19.17
EL CAFECITO DE TUKUTA, TILCARA, JUJUY, ARGENTINA

STEVE

The world seems even brighter today. You join us in Tilcara, midway through our incredibly scenic tour of this swathe of Argentina, courtesy *still* of our new favourite trio, Sergio, María and Julieta. So far we have seen mountains, hot springs, salt flats, vineyards, forests, multicoloured hills, and fields upon fields of cactuses. We're running out of superlatives.

Five days have passed since our friends from Buenos Aires first laid eyes on us. I've never known a ride like it. Other than a day apart in Salta on Sunday (during which time Jo and I philosophised over how long they would be able to bear us), we have been together almost every hour of each day. And, mercifully, they are yet to tire of us. We will continue on with them tomorrow to Humahuaca, then Iruya, La Quiaca and on into Bolivia. By that time, our friendship will have lasted for more than a week. And what an intense way to begin a relationship!

But we like to think of ourselves as amiable sorts and we've certainly become very fond of our Argentinian friends, who deserve further introduction.

María, if you didn't know her, might intimidate you, with her lean face, spiky short black hair and fiesty temperament. But she is lovely. I mean, you have to be seriously nice to pick up a couple of bedraggled hitchhikers and allow them to travel with you for the duration of your holiday, next to your precious four-year-old.

Sergio has a smile uncannily similar to that of Javier Bardem, the Spanish actor renowned for his disquieting performances as a range of psychopathic villains. Again, this could be a rather disconcerting trait were it not for Sergio's gentleness, which shines through.

And then there's Julieta. Ah, Julieta. We love her. I think it would be impossible to dislike her, such is her charm. This beautiful creature, with her bright blonde hair and colourful trousers, has lit up our journey.

Needless to say, we are feeling very blessed. We haven't had to hitch a ride since Thursday, and won't have to do so for another few days at least. It has given us a welcome rest from the demands of the road, and especially from the challenges of last week. If all goes as planned, we won't need to hitch another ride this side of Bolivia.

Jo

We have settled into a routine with our new Argentinian family. Each morning we assemble five travellers' worth of luggage, and over the course of several minutes gradually squash and squeeze both people and packages into the awaiting car. Sergio and María sit up front, leaving us kids to occupy the back seats.

By way of bonding with our surrogate little sister, last weekend I created a simple yet effective game. It was called "I am a monster" and revolved around the modest premise of sticking out my arms in a zombie-like fashion and emitting a roar. Each time I did this, Juli galloped away, screaming delightedly.

As the screams became ever closer to ultrasonic, I decided to change tack.

"I'm not a monster, I'm an angel!" I declared. Cleverly, I adapted the Spanish word for angel to ensure I was not presenting myself as male.

At this, Sergio and María laughed, and I was pleased that they were so supportive of my efforts to instil calm. That was until Sergio provided clarification.

"I'm not sure this was quite what you meant," he said with a grin, "but do you realise that you're saying, 'I'm not a monster, I'm Angela'?"

… No wonder Juli looked confused.

5. BOWLER HATS AND DOUBLE PLAITS

DAY 45: FRIDAY 2ND MAY 2014, 19.26
RESTAURANT ROMELIN 2, VILLAZÓN, POTOSÍ, BOLIVIA

STEVE

The world has changed again, but this time the transition is more dramatic. Not only have we parted company with our dear friends Sergio, María and Julieta. We have also left fair Argentina and, in doing so, have arrived on what seems an entirely different planet. The contrast between Bolivia and Argentina is stark, although not in terms of landscape. Unlike our travels between Chile and Argentina, that remains unchanged – no 17km border crossings over mountains here.

Villazón, the border town shaping our first impressions of Bolivia, is but a stone's throw from La Quiaca, Argentina. But despite the proximity and unchanged *tierra*, the two countries are worlds apart.

Bolivia is very obviously poor. The streets are dirty and the pavements riddled with potholes. Even more obvious is the change from fashionable Argentina, with inhabitants who wouldn't look out of place in Europe, to a country that seems, at first glance, very much to belong to the Third World.

The contrast was softened slightly by our time in Salta and Jujuy, Argentina's relatively poor and undeveloped northern provinces, but a flourishing tourist trade counterbalanced the relative poverty there. Not so in Bolivia.

English pounds go further here. Upon purchasing a map of Bolivia, we pulled out a 100 boliviano (£10) note and were met with the response: "Oh, this is very rich!"

The moment has stuck in our minds. Not only did it make us feel awkward, as we received 97 bolivianos in change; it also added to the sense that here, unlike in Chile and Argentina, we really do stick out. Unfortunately, this seems only likely to increase as we attempt to journey north tomorrow. We were told by the young lady in the tourist office that the concept of hitchhiking simply does not exist here and that hitchhiking and getting a taxi are one and the same.

If true, it would not be the first time I have hitched in such a place. It is the same in Iran, Pakistan, Bangladesh and even in some parts of eastern Europe, but I have always managed to find a way to travel without paying for the privilege.

"No money" became something of a catchphrase for Will and me on our journey east – the simplest way of explaining our methods in languages we hadn't mastered. We are unlikely to need to resort to this, due to our relative proficiency at Spanish, but the underlying challenge may be similar.

As a result I find myself questioning the importance of sticking to our number one rule: never pay for transport. It tends to be the case that in poorer countries, the practice that we Westerners would call "hitchhiking" is replaced by the simple understanding that, if there is space in your vehicle, you will give someone a ride and receive a monetary contribution for the service. Herein lies our quandary: deciding not to pay for something that other, poorer people pay for, seems unjust and against the spirit of our adventure.

But at the same time, it is my dream to arrive in Alaska having made it the whole way with drivers already travelling in our direction. That is the essence of hitchhiking – that we shouldn't need to pay because we are only partaking in another person's journey. The opposite is true of buses and taxis, which exist only because of the passengers.

It isn't about the money. It's about everything else – the journey, the conversations, the people we meet. To pay someone to take you with them is a transaction. In a taxi or a bus, the life story of the driver is rarely a major concern. Conversely, hitchhiking is all about enjoying little snippets of the lives of other, ordinary people. These little windows into people's souls comprise the very reason for the adventure. To learn. To know. And to be known.

I dearly hope that hitchhiking here will prove to be as joyous and as life-enhancing as it was in Chile and Argentina. We have some wonderful memories of our time there. And none more so than of our week with Sergio, María and little Julieta.

María cried when we parted this afternoon, at the border. Jo too. Ten days is a long time to spend with someone, whatever the stage of your relationship. We grew to love them and they adopted us as their own. That is hitchhiking. That is what we long to experience here in Bolivia.

JO

I miss Argentina.

I will be straight: we have been in Bolivia for only about five hours. It would probably be unfair to judge it on the small border town where we're staying. However, the abrupt change from the colourful peaks and impressive contours of northern Argentina to the drab, run-down feel of this place means our departure from Argentina is a painful one, all the more so because we have bid adieu to our dear adoptive family.

How are we going to cope without Juli's bright innocence, Sergio and María's constant supply of *mate* and our collective tuneless squawking of popular classical songs? The strange circumstance that had thrown us together led us to forge a unique bond – although we were not without cultural differences.

"We think we'll take one of the blankets from the other beds tonight for an extra layer," Steve said over dinner one evening, in reference to the colder temperatures experienced the night before.

"Oh yes, we did that last night," María replied cheerily.

"And did you keep your heater on all night?" I asked.

The couple exchanged glances.

"Of course!" Sergio responded, as if it was the most obvious action in the world.

"… Ah," Steve and I uttered in unison. We hadn't even considered it.

There was much guffawing, and Sergio asserted, "That is *too* English! You must release it!"

DAY 46: SATURDAY 3RD MAY 2014, 23.19
LA TAPERA RESTAURANT, TUPIZA, POTOSÍ, BOLIVIA

STEVE

They said it couldn't be done, but we achieved the impossible this morning and hitched a ride in Bolivia. The fact that the couple who gave us a ride were from Argentina hasn't dampened our spirits, but as we have decided to remain here in Tupiza, a small city surrounded by mountains, for the weekend, our first hitch with Bolivians will have to wait.

Well, actually, at least one of our drivers this morning was born here in Bolivia, so maybe that counts. David and his wife, Maura, transported us from Villazón, and, though their accents were difficult to understand, we did grasp the essential detail: Maura's sister had been rushed to hospital in Tupiza, after a bad accident; the teary couple had driven through the night from their home in Tucumán, at top speed, to be by her side.

In comparison, our desire to hitch to Alaska paled into insignificance. Much of our journey was spent in silence and we were left to wonder at the compassion of this couple, who, in their moment of need, had taken pity on two wandering nomads. At one point, a policeman pulled us over for speeding, but even he was taken aback by their plight and allowed the couple to continue, unchecked.

After gathering our senses beside a sign that read "*EMERGENCIA*", we made our way back to the main road and recommenced hitching efforts. In the hour that followed, we were passed by dozens of taxis, a handful of trucks and a few cars, but each of the three drivers to pull over repeated the same phrase: "*Aquí, no más* [Here, no farther]". We decided to call it a day.

... A drunken Bolivian just came over to give me a hug and a kiss in this restaurant, on the edge of the city, in which we have taken refuge from the sun. We will return to the city centre soon and use the rest of today and tomorrow to attempt to acclimatise.

DAY 47: SUNDAY 4TH MAY 2014, 13.43
HOTEL MITRU, TUPIZA, POTOSÍ, BOLIVIA

Jo

To get to know the real Bolivia, I think we're going to have to look further than Tupiza, for here it is the tourist who reigns supreme.

Take our accommodation. In Hotel Mitru (the best hotel in town but still cheaper than any in Chile or Argentina) we are surrounded by Western faces. At breakfast, it felt as though we were foreigners at a conference: not a Bolivian in sight, except for the staff. Last night, searching for a place to eat, we chanced upon a pleasant-looking cafe (with real coffee), only to be joined by three other European couples. No Bolivians.

It feels particularly awkward because of the inevitable impression on the locals. The restaurants are mediocre but overpriced, in effect excluding anyone but foreigners. Hordes of tourists stare ignorantly at the mounds of unusual fruits, poking bits here and there before moving on to gawp at something else. We seem so comparatively rich, every one of us.

We're not sure how to resolve this situation. Maybe we will have to resort to even cheaper hotels, or to camping (although the nights are cold). Or maybe we will have to hope that because we are hitchhiking, we will taste true Bolivian culture and hospitality – not a sanitised, Western imitation.

This said, last night we managed to catch a glimpse of real life, and as it happens, it wasn't exactly what we had expected.

We had arrived on the day of two local events: the launch of a car rally, and a catwalk competition for the "Miss Potosí" contest. In the afternoon we watched a stage being constructed outside the church and as evening approached, there was a buzz of excitement.

The first event lasted interminably, with the MC rattling on and on, interspersed with the excessive revving of engines as drivers were introduced to the crowd. When that had finally wrapped up, everyone trooped over to the stage to watch a dozen teenage beauties attempt elegance and style in their matching bikinis and impossible shoes. Was there any greater embodiment of "boys and their toys" versus "girls love makeup"?

Usually I would have been tempted to moan about how skinny the girls were, but on this occasion pity overrode all other emotions. It might be a sign of progressiveness that the girls have broken free of the bowler hats and double plaits of the traditionally clothed older women, but to me it didn't feel particularly enlightened to have a throng of men gawping while the girls struggled to remain upright in their stilettos.

We left before the winner was announced, so, alas, we'll never know who strutted away with the chance "to become Miss Bolivia!"

DAY 48: MONDAY 5TH MAY 2014, 18.56
INÉS' STREETSIDE RESTAURANT, POTOSÍ, BOLIVIA

STEVE

We are steadily acclimitising to our surroundings here in high-altitude Bolivia. The city of Potosí, where we arrived after a full day on the road, is allegedly the highest "of its size" (whatever that means) anywhere in the world. At over 4,000m above sea level, it's difficult to breathe. We're having to walk very slowly. Apparently coca leaves help.

Today has been exactly the kind of day we needed to encourage us that hitchhiking might not be so hard here after all.

We were up early, and by 10am had wandered to the very edge of town, the junction separating the routes to Potosí and the salt flats of Uyuni. Here in Bolivia, an hour ahead of Argentina, we're going to have to get used to early starts to avoid hiking during the hottest part of the day.

The junction seemed like the perfect position to hitch a ride. Not only was it the place at which the road to Potosí officially began; it also happened to be the location of a police checkpoint, forcing all vehicles to stop. But having waited for an hour without success (only buses and taxis had shown any interest), we decided to act.

A jeep was waiting at the checkpoint and I wandered over to enquire where the trio inside were headed and whether they might have room for us. They seemed uncertain about the prospect, but were unable to argue that they didn't have space.

"But we're only going 20km," Aldo, the driver, added.

This didn't matter to us, and, 20 minutes later, as we were dropped at a toll, or *tranca*, we were sure we had made the right decision.

This feeling was enhanced by the helpfulness of the three officers in charge. After 10 minutes, a yellow truck approached and I signalled that this was precisely the kind of vehicle we were after. As the driver chatted with the policemen, I went over to enquire whether there was space in his truck. The driver nodded and our faces lit up.

For the next five hours we attempted, with limited success, to find comfortable seating arrangements in the empty open-air trailer, gazing all the while at the rugged scenery. After our long ride with Berty, 36, we have a much clearer view of *puna*. Throughout the journey we were surrounded by arid, mountainous terrain. In the *puna*, the only two types of vegetation that seem able to survive on the dusty ground are windswept bushes and lime-green cactuses.

Our joy at reaching Potosí has been added to this evening by the friendliness of its inhabitants. In the market, an old lady handed us two free bananas, for no obvious reason. And here at Inés's streetside joint on *Calle Bolívar*, we have been made to feel very welcome.

Jo

A common pitfall for the newcomer to a foreign language is to assume that misunderstanding is failing. As a perfectionist, it grieves me when I cannot comprehend what is being said, so I have gradually developed an arsenal of delaying, bluffing and diversionary tactics to avoid detection. None of these actually fool the native speaker, but, well, they make me feel better.

When someone asks me a question incomprehensibly quickly in Spanish with a broad grin on his face, I assume the answer must be "yes", and respond as such enthusiastically. If his expression gives nothing away and it is too late to pretend I haven't heard him, I look at Steve in order to defer responsibility. When I am sitting in the back of a car and Steve is ploughing gallantly through hours of conversation, I opt in or out of contributing according to my confidence in discussing the current topic. Often, this leads to drivers observing that I am the better Spanish speaker. This is not necessarily fair.

In Tupiza, I conveyed to a waitress that we had attended the second day of the car rally and that I had photos to show for it. Neither happened to be the case, but I was too busy enjoying the smiles produced by my words to be aware of what I had communicated. It was down to Steve to wade in and perform the necessary backtracking, apologising that we didn't have our camera with us at that moment and that we would return at another time to show her the pictures. It was all a bit unfortunate, and we can never again return to that cafe.

DAY 50: WEDNESDAY 7TH MAY 2014, 10.57
FRIDOLIN CAFÉ, LA PAZ, BOLIVIA

STEVE

Simon and Garfunkel's *Mrs. Robinson* is blasting out of the speakers in this cafe in central La Paz, as we take stock following another successful (and exhausting) day on the road.

We began the hike out of Potosí, a sizeable city formerly renowned as

'The End of the World', Ushuaia, Tierra del Fuego, Argentina

Patagonia, the windiest place on earth

Mate

Marta and Flor

Patagonia

Forest fire

Lago Chacabuco

Gauchito Gil

Competition

Solo como guanaco macho

A long wait in Santa Lucia, Argentina

Sergio, María and Julieta

the crown jewel in the Spanish empire ("as rich as Potosí" is apparently still a common phrase), at 8.30am and didn't arrive in La Paz until 10pm. And in that time, we were almost continually making progress towards our 540km goal. There were barely any intervals between our three rides, but the road was long and traffic steadily increased as we neared Bolivia's unofficial capital, where the government is based.

By the time we arrived, our heads were throbbing. Not only was it a full day of conversing in Spanish; we also had Bolivia's *Altiplano* (high plains) to contend with. La Paz is the highest seat of government in the world, almost 4,000 metres above sea level. Even so, La Paz sits in a basin below the neighbouring city of El Alto. The views, as we descended, were spectacular.

The sights along the road, as we returned sooner than expected to that irrepressible mountain range, the Andes, were equally awe-inspiring. Sun-scorched yellow shrubs replaced the greenery of the day before, as we arrived on the vast flats of the *Altiplano.*

Hitchhiking here in Bolivia is certainly different, but, for now at least, it hasn't been hard. We have yet to secure a ride without first approaching the driver (generally speaking at a toll or police checkpoint), but equally we have yet to be refused when doing so.

This was epitomised by our first ride yesterday, which came completely by chance. We had been walking for more than 40 minutes in our attempts to reach the beginning of the main road from Potosí to Oruro, when, for the third time that morning, we approached a local to ask for guidance.

"Is this the road to Oruro?" I asked a young man standing outside a garage beside a red Toyota Corolla.

"*Sí, todo recto* [Yes, straight on]," came the reply.

"Ah, OK. And is there a place nearby where we can wait for a ride with a truck or a car? We don't want a bus," I said, attempting to explain our goal in the simplest way possible. (*Hacer dedo*, the Argentinian and Chilean verb for hitchhiking, doesn't seem to work here.)

"Yes, not far," replied the gentleman. "… Or you could just come with me and my brother."

"Oh, right. Thanks," I said, somewhat unenthusiastically, considering the likelihood that he would want money for the privilege. "But we can't pay for transport. We just travel with *amigos*."

"No, don't worry," he replied, seeming surprised by how awkward I was making the transaction. "You can come with us … As long as you don't mind waiting for us to get a new tyre and some flowers."

We said that we didn't.

Twenty minutes later, with new tyre secured and flowers in hand, off we set, with our new friend Juan, 25, and his brother Enrique, 35, towards Oruro. They were on their way to visit a *santo* (saint, or holy site) in a village halfway there and left us at a toll.

Within half an hour, we were on our way again, with Jimi, 30, and his 18-year-old girlfriend Sofia. They had been a couple for just three weeks, Jimi told us, and were now travelling back to his home in Uyuni, south of Oruro.

Theirs was a strange relationship. Sofia, who was strikingly attractive, hardly uttered a word during our two hours together and seemed anxious. Jimi was equally on edge, although part of this may have related to his inability to drive. The road to the town of Challapata, where he dropped us, was mountainous and dotted with jaywalking llamas, necessitating great concentration.

Such concerns didn't seem to affect our long-haired friend, who looked like a Bolivian Johnny Depp. We were relieved when we arrived, unscathed, at the toll outside Challapata, where Jimi handed us a stick of sugar cane and may have mentioned something about posting him a present when we got home.

Jimi spoke very quickly and had a tendency to slur his words, which made him almost impossible to understand. At one point, I thought I caught him saying that the journey cost 10 bolivianos (around £1). I told him we didn't pay for transport and hoped he wouldn't mind. He didn't seem to. Perhaps all this talk of sending him a present when we got home was somehow related.

There was nothing complicated about our final ride yesterday, with Santos, a 35-year-old car salesman on his way home to La Paz after two weeks in the north of Argentina.

Once more, the hitch was achieved after a brief discussion at a toll. It went something like this:

Smile.

Wave.

Approach.

Window wound down.

"Do you have space for my wife and me?"

Look over shoulder.

"*Si.*"

"Great!"

Bags in.

And then, seven hours later, arrive in the centre of La Paz, heads thumping, and check into the nearest hotel.

6. THE ROAD TO BRAZIL

DAY 53: SATURDAY 10TH MAY 2014, 14.46
DAVID AND JENN'S HOUSE, COCHABAMBA, BOLIVIA

STEVE

For the next two months, we are to embark upon a minor detour, as we turn our attention to the small matter of the World Cup in Brazil.

It is for this reason that yesterday, given the opportunity to head west to Lake Titicaca and on to the Pan-American Highway running north through Peru, we instead went in the opposite direction. In one month and two days, the World Cup kicks off and we want to be there.

Our determination to head east was met with an early test when our first driver, 22-year-old Pablo, who rescued us from a petrol station in La Paz, asked if we'd like to go with him to Copacabana beach on the shores of Lake Titicaca.

As usual, my instinct was to say yes, but Jo was unflinching. One look and her intentions were clear: No, we are heading in the opposite direction, like we discussed!

Jo

I had anticipated that hitchhiking out of La Paz would feel akin to climbing up the side of a greased bowl. Our descent into the city (during which time we were passed by a presidential motorcade carrying the Bolivian premier, Evo Morales) was lengthy, and now we were to attempt to leave; somehow, the need to travel up, as well as away, made this goal seem even more challenging.

Well, no sooner had we pitched up at a petrol station and filtered out the minibuses and taxis, than we located Pablo. Away we went, spiralling out of the city.

In El Alto, walking was the fastest form of transport. We weaved our way through the queues of cars, coating our lungs and nostrils with fumes as we went. Our airways suffered further as we waited by some traffic lights, static victims of the belching pollution. It was there that we were reminded how atypical a sight hitchhiking is in Bolivia: three times Steve was mistaken for a beggar as he approached car windows. The image of drivers reaching for their loose change caused some embarrassment; we needed help, yes, but not of that kind!

Finally we were away. As we nestled between sacks of runner beans and attempted to respond to the oscillating temperatures – blistering heat as we crawled through the endless roadworks away from El Alto, a shiver-inducing chill when traversing the hills – our drivers basically ignored us. We had sandwiches with us and had earlier received a bag of biscuits from a generous passerby, so our food supplies were sufficient; it was our bladders that suffered most. Around four hours into the journey and with no offer of a toilet stop forthcoming, I settled into an awkward equilibrium of needing and not needing to go to the toilet, and remained that way until blessed relief was granted a further six hours later.

STEVE

We were shivering and deyhdrated by the time we were deposited by the side of the road in Cochabamba, where we were picked up by David, a former colleague of Jo's at the UK-based charity, Tearfund. We were also left scratching our heads as to what exactly had transpired. Since leaving Ushuaia, we had not known a ride quite like it; we didn't even learn the names of our drivers.

At one stage, having driven through Cochabamba for more than an hour, we wondered whether we had been forgotten, or worse, were in the process of being adbucted. But no, eventually, on surely the very far edge of the city, the truck pulled over and one of our drivers opened the hatch and said, simply: "*Hemos llegado* [We have arrived]."

Somewhat relieved, we threw our bags out of the trailer, climbed down and waved our would-be abductors goodbye.

After recovering from the experience, we were left wondering again about our ambitions on this adventure.

"What was the difference between that ride and just getting on a bus?" I asked.

"Not a lot," said Jo.

That morning, as the hours passed in El Alto, we had been offered a number of rides in taxis, buses and trucks – all for money. We had rejected each one, but as we travelled alone in the back of the truck, it was impossible to claim that our reason for hitchhiking on this occasion had been to get to know our drivers.

Still, I am glad that no money changed hands. Surely, that would have completely changed the parameters. OK, so we didn't speak to them, but at least we undertook the journey as equals: no contract, no money exchanged; just a shake of the hands and a friendly goodbye. It wasn't perfect, but we kept our integrity. I think …

DAY 56: TUESDAY 13TH MAY 2014, 16.19
DAVID AND JENN'S HOUSE, COCHABAMBA, BOLIVIA

STEVE

We went to visit a Tearfund project today. Through our hitchhiking endeavours, we are hoping to raise money for the charity, which works in developing countries around the world.

Bolivia is certainly a country in need. The rich-poor divide is stark, so although many of the city centres are well developed, farther out it remains poor.

Today, David took us to see a project in Cochabamba's red-light district, where Tearfund helps to provide a safe place for local children often left alone in the daytime by parents out at work.

Sexual abuse of women and young girls is one of the problems we have heard about here, in what seems a particularly patriarchal culture. Alcoholism is also rife. In many of the restaurants on Paseo El Prado, the city's main street, Bolivians stockpile empty beer bottles as a sign of their drinking prowess.

Tomorrow we hope to continue our progress eastward, first to Santa Cruz and then on to Brazil. David tells us Santa Cruz is Bolivia's richest city and – no coincidence, I'm sure – the heart of its drugs trade. Supposedly, shops purporting to sell wedding dresses here in Bolivia are often fronts for the distribution of cocaine. Wedding dresses, we are told, are advertised at lofty prices, allowing large sums of money to pass through without suspicion. We have also been told to watch out for stray pairs of shoes hanging from telegraph wires – apparently another secret signal for drug dealers across South America.

Another characteristic of the Bolivian landscape is the presence of beggars, many of them very old. On the short walk home from the city centre yesterday, we must have passed half a dozen. Life expectancy here is below 70, but each beggar has the appearance of someone 20 years older, presumably the effect of a tough life. Not since Mendoza have we seen so many beggars, but there the majority were immigrants; here in Bolivia, they are locals. It seems a far cry from a state pension.

Jo

All this time spent in the back of trucks has put paid to our usual probing interviews about the country through which we're travelling. To regain some ground, we have been keenly exploring David's insights into life in Bolivia, and the utmost priority was finding an answer to the burning question: why on earth do the women of the Quechua and Aymara tribes (two of the largest indigenous groups in Bolivia) wear bowler hats?

Legend has it that in the 1920s, a shipment of hats arrived from Europe for men working as railway engineers in Bolivia. The hats were too small, so they were peddled to the local women, who adopted the style as their own. They serve no practical purpose whatsoever, and yet this fashion has persisted for almost 100 years.

Arguably more important to our overall perception of Bolivia was hearing about the inequalities that pervade here, in a country where development projects are plentiful and a city which is said to host the most missionaries per capita in the world.

In churches, there are persistent problems around the status of women, and widespread adultery. If a wife leaves her husband because he has been unfaithful, it is often she who is chastised; male church leaders are rarely dethroned following infidelity.

We also heard that the penal system is one of the worst in the world, with a purported 86% of prisoners still awaiting trial. If prosecution does take place, time spent in prison pending sentencing doesn't count, even if it has been several years. Children are put in prison alongside their parents and can end up spending their entire childhood behind bars.

David told us of a 10-year-old girl who was raped in prison and became pregnant.

"We used to visit her in prison and bring her colouring pencils, and she would sit and play while her baby was sat next to her," he said. "When we told Bolivians about it they would say, 'Oh well, that kind of thing happens all the time'."

DAY 57: WEDNESDAY 14TH MAY 2014, 11.49
TRUCK STOP, SACABA, COCHABAMBA, BOLIVIA

STEVE

So here we are again, waiting beside a truck in the expectation that we will soon be travelling in its trailer, this time on the road to Santa Cruz. And not for the first time here in Bolivia, the old question of *dinero* has raised its ugly head.

Fortunately, at least from our perspective, we appear to have chanced upon a suitably gracious driver in the form of 22-year-old Diego. Having been informed by a dozen other truckers here that to travel by "*camión*" (truck) you need to pay, we were glad to find him.

But now, as we sit beside his truck, soon to embark upon a 500km journey together, we are contemplating afresh the ethics of our adventure.

"*Nuestra aventura es así!* [Our adventure is like this!]" I declared, proudly, to the first group of truckers who told us we must pay. "We are going throughout America without paying!"

They didn't seem impressed. And why should they? Everyone here pays. Even now, it seems we are to travel with a couple of stout Bolivian ladies, hair in plaits and dressed in the local garb (bowler hats and colourful skirts), and we presume they will be paying. So why shouldn't we?

Jo and I discussed the matter and decided henceforth to focus on petrol stations and tolls. Hanging around in truck stops for a free ride just doesn't cut it.

I'm glad to say that this morning hasn't all been like this. We did begin our day in a petrol station on the edge of Cochabamba and eventually secured a ride in a car, with a Seventh-day Adventist named Andrea. She called us moments ago to check we were OK and to say that she is going to call her sister to ask whether she might be able to show us around Santa Cruz.

Creating new friendships with people like Andrea brings meaning to our adventure. The question this morning is whether waiting by the side of a truck for a ride (free or otherwise) in the trailer is really the same thing. Does it still count as hitchhiking? I just don't know.

DAY 58: THURSDAY 15TH MAY 2014, 15.39
CAFÉ REPÚBLICA, SANTA CRUZ, BOLIVIA

STEVE

Now that was much more like it. Exhausting, but exhilarating and exactly what we signed up for.

In the end we travelled in the back of Diego's truck, with three of his *amigos*, for a whopping 14 hours. We didn't arrive in Santa Cruz until 3am, whereupon we were advised to sleep on the wooden tables of an open-air market until the traders arrived.

And if that wasn't enough to feed my hunger for adventure, then came the miraculous bit. In what is Bolivia's largest city, we somehow found ourselves just five minutes' walk from the old church of our friend Margoth in Argentina. She had given us the name and address of Pastor Marcos Caballero, so off we trotted, not sure what to expect but hoping for a warm reception.

It was 7am by the time we located Iglesia Buen Samaritano and the welcome we received was better than we could have hoped for. Marcos and his wife vacated their own room to give us a chance to catch up on some slumber. For the next four hours, we were dead to the world, allowing our bodies to recover from our longest day yet.

When we awoke, lunch was awaiting us, and we were told we could relax and remain for as long as we liked. Their room was now ours. "What *buenos samaritanos*," we thought.

So in the end, I needn't have worried. The journey with Diego was perfect. Tiring, but perfect. We stopped only once, for dinner (and a welcome chance to use the loo) and we ate together, as friends.

After dinner, back under the shelter of the tarpaulin-covered trailer, we slept – or tried to sleep – as the truck rattled on for another seven hours.

There was some excitement during the journey, as we stopped three times at police checkpoints, and were urged by Diego's three *amigos* to attempt to hide ourselves among the bags. Once it worked. Twice it didn't.

The first time we were discovered, our faces displaying the terror of uncovered illegal immigrants or drug smugglers, we watched money change hands. The second time, the situation seemed more serious. Perhaps the policeman refused the bribe. Whatever happened, Jo and I were left alone in the trailer for around half an hour as Diego and friends discussed matters outside. In this time, I wondered what would happen if it transpired that the dozens of bags around us contained cocaine.

I'm not sure how the matter was resolved, but eventually our friends returned and we continued our journey.

Diego appeared distressed when, at 3am, he opened the door of the trailer and told us we'd arrived.

"It wasn't my fault," we heard him say, as he and his friends exchanged some cash. Perhaps they had had to pay a fine. Or a bribe. I guess we'll never know.

But one thing we know for sure: this was a true hitchhike and all that passed has put my concerns to bed.

Jo

Travelling is valuable for many reasons: cultural immersion, language learning, character development. Our bodies, however, are gradually breaking.

Our bladders are contorted due to a lack of toileting opportunities. Our hearts are weakened by excessive thumping when at high altitudes. Our spines are curving from repeated abuse – heavy bags, slouching and crouching in trucks, attempting sleep in unusual locations. Our lungs are fogging up with fumes and dust. Our teeth are rotting and our cholesterol is spiking because of our questionable diets. It is highly feasible that we'll look 10 years older by the end of this adventure – or experiment, perhaps I should say.

My soul is also a little bruised after yesterday's mammoth haul from Cochabamba to Santa Cruz. Spaced a little more evenly, our lengthy ride, run-ins with Customs officers, arrival in the small hours and sleeping atop a market stall might have been manageable, but all at once? Marcos's wife said I was a brave woman, but maybe she would have reassessed had she known that I'd cried about seven times since arriving at their house.

There are two contenders for the most peculiar moment of the journey: lying stock-still in the bright glare of a Customs official's torchlight, knowing we had been discovered but not moving a muscle anyway; or catching an hour's kip in a market place, others dotted around us doing the same. The market was already bustling at 3am with sellers preparing for a working day that would begin in three hours and finish after maybe 13 more. What a different life!

As for feeling like a fugitive, it wasn't very pleasant at the time, but it would have felt worse had our back-of-the-truck companions not been the ones initiating the hiding. When we saw one of them bribing the guard with the swift transfer of a 100 Boliviano note, I wondered what Steve and I would have done had we been on our own and unaware of the fault, let alone this solution. However, it gradually dawned on us that the problem was related to cargo rather than people. When we were stopped a second time, our companions left the truck to discuss whatever was needed, and our presence was not required, nor was any action on our part.

I'm off trucks for the time being, though.

DAY 59: FRIDAY 16TH MAY 2014, 21.45
RESIDENCIAL CRISTO DE LA CONCORDIA, SAN JOSÉ DE CHIQUITOS, CHIQUITANIA, SANTA CRUZ, BOLIVIA

STEVE

You find us in San José de Chiquitos, one of a number of Jesuit-influenced towns in the region. There is a quite magnificent church here, harking back to the 18th Century.

Our 250km journey from Santa Cruz was long but enjoyable. We are in a particularly attractive part of the world, characterised by green plains, thick forests and enough birds to make an ornithologist blush.

And today, for the first time since our very first ride in Bolivia, we hitched a lift (two, in fact) by simply standing by the side of the road with thumbs outstretched. We had been somewhat fearful about finding ourselves on an empty stretch of road, away from the comfort of service stations or tolls, but it appears our fears were unfounded.

The day started in typical fashion. Having trekked to the eastern edge of the city, we approached an eatery to double-check we were heading in the right direction and to ask whether anyone inside was driving east. Two young men said that they were and, a few moments later, we were on our way in the back of their car.

Pleasantries were exchanged (our drivers were Bruho, 32, and Wilber, 24) and then, at the first set of traffic lights, we stopped and in climbed a young man our drivers didn't seem to know. His name was Freddy and he told us he was on his way to San Julián, which also happened to be where our drivers were going.

"Some coincidence!" I thought. But then a dreadful realisation dawned on me. The proof was right there, perched on Bruho's dashboard: a sign that read "SAN JULIAN". This could mean only one thing: Bruho was a taxi driver.

Summoning up courage, I asked Bruho what he did for a living, just to make sure.

"Er, I drive taxis," he said, with a hint of surprise.

Wasn't it obvious?

And then the panic set in. For the next half an hour – the duration of our time together – I attempted to make light of Bruho's comments and to clarify once and for all that we were in fact *hitchhiking* and not currently travelling in a taxi.

"We *never* pay for transport," I emphasised, as Bruho and Wilber looked quizzically at each other. "Never!"

When, eventually, Bruho pulled over at a junction separating the roads east and north, I took a deep breath and prepared for the big moment when he would declare how much we owed him.

But it never came.

All we received were warm handshakes, big smiles and best wishes for our journey. All that fretting had been for nothing.

Perhaps, then, it should have come as little surprise to us when, after waiting for no more than half an hour, worrying all the while at the prospect of hitching in such an isolated setting, a truck pulled over and two coca-chewing chaps offered us a ride in the back.

When this process was repeated a second time, we wondered why we had worried so much in the first place.

Jo

Steve and I have unwittingly checked ourselves into a *residencial*. Since the "Cockroaches of Córdoba" incident, the mere act of walking past a *residencial* has been accompanied by a silent scream and a strong urge to flee. This place, however, was not obviously labelled, so we were duped. Mercifully there have been no creepy-crawlies yet.

Last night we experienced our first tropical storm, rain thudding down fiercely for hours on end. We had been planning to set off early this morning, but there was no sense in leaving before the torrent had eased. The rain exhausted itself just as we finished a bowl of porridge prepared for us by Pastor Marcos's mother-in-law. This wonderful lady had charmed us with the twinkle in her eye, although it took this delicious breakfast to coax us into fully forgiving her for yesterday's jibe: "You are so brave! ... Because your Spanish is really not that good."

As if we had somehow planned it, our journey through Bolivia has been topped and tailed with fashion shows. Tomorrow is "Miss Santa Cruz", hosted in the plaza here in San José, and there was already a hubbub of anticipation as we wandered around tonight. Naturally, it is deeply disappointing that we will be moving on before the show is in full swing.

DAY 60: SATURDAY 17TH MAY 2014, 15.00
JUAN'S HOUSE, SANTIAGO DE CHIQUITOS, CHIQUITANIA, SANTA CRUZ, BOLIVIA

STEVE

A pair of toucans just took flight from the tree in front of where I sit, here in the garden of Juan, a gentlemanly 82-year-old whose home we shall inhabit for the next two nights.

Aiming for the Brazilian border this morning, we didn't expect to end up in the sleepy town of Santiago de Chiquitos, but we're very glad that we did. And it's all thanks to José María ...

DAY 60 (CONTINUED): 21.30
JUAN'S HOUSE, SANTIAGO DE CHIQUITOS, CHIQUITANIA, SANTA CRUZ, BOLIVIA

STEVE

No sooner had I written those words than in walked the man himself to take us on another excursion in the back of his flash pick-up truck. We must have ridden over 200km with him today and each kilometre was taken at breakneck speed. From our perch on the rim of the vehicle, we watched with a mixture of horror and amusement as his two young sons, Rafael (five) and Nicolás (three), sporting matching bowl haircuts, practised somersaults and took it in turns to ride on the driver's knee. Also in the car were José María's 18-year-old apprentice, Gerardo, and mother, Kitty. Neither seemed at all phased by the goings-on, nor by José María's tendency to look at anything but the road.

During our journey to Santiago de Chiquitos, and then a return trip to some hot springs, we were twice inches from crashing into a ditch, once survived a tailspin and narrowly missed a head-on collision with an errant cow. Only the last of these caused even the faintest murmur from José María's other passengers. The man himself never flinched.

Taking to the road today at 9am, we had it in mind to reach the border by sundown. But then, just half an hour later, along came José María, slamming on the brakes and reversing back to collect us, and our plans changed entirely.

"You should come to Santiago with us," he said. "It's beautiful."

And so we did.

As we neared the town, we were busy congratulating ourselves on our achievement and the likelihood that we'd soon be invited to stay with them, when José María pulled over by the plaza and told us we had arrived.

"*Suerte!* [Good luck!]" he said, and signalled that we should remove our bags from the back of his car.

"*Si, suerte!*" echoed his mother and the apprentice. And just like that, off they went towards José María's holiday home, without us.

"… Right," I said to Jo, as we stood there, windswept and slightly stunned. "I didn't see that coming."

"Yes, not quite what we'd hoped for …" Jo replied.

As we adjusted to our new surroundings, and to being suddenly alone again, along came Juan, who asked us if we had anywhere to stay the night and, hearing that we didn't, invited us back to his homestay.

After checking in, we found a restaurant on the plaza, where we attempted to process all that had passed. And then José María and family arrived, and it was as if we had stepped back in time. We were soon the best of friends (as we had thought we had been all along) and José María invited us to join them at some nearby hot springs.

Roll on a couple of hours and it was déjà vu. After narrowly missing that cow on our speedy return to the town, we arrived at the plaza, José María slammed on the brakes, and once more, ever so abruptly, our friendship ceased.

Jo

This afternoon we went swimming in a river the temperature of bathwater. A *whole river* of thermal water! How marvellous! I think we should have these in England.

José María's driving was excessively fast for both my liking and my complexion: it cannot be beneficial to blast one's skin with winds of such velocity. What's more, we had a clear view of his sons clambering at will over the car seats. One of them knocked José María's arm, causing a mini swerve.

"It's not you I don't trust!" I wanted to say to our driver. "It's other people!"

Since leaving Santa Cruz, Steve and I have been baffled by a mysterious matter. At various points on the journey – a dingy roadside restaurant yesterday, a petrol station today – we have come across some European-looking folk, conspicuous in their matching outfits (blue dungarees for the men, plain dresses for the women) and seeming, frankly, quite odd. Earlier we greeted a man of this description at the *residencial* in San José; his response was a blank stare.

We had thought these people might be Jesuits, considering their historical influence in this particular area, but when we brought up the subject with José María to see if he could shed any light on our observations, he explained that Jesuit descendants looked different from the original settlers and wouldn't be easily identifiable.

I tried a different approach to see if it would prompt him, drawing a sketch on a napkin and focusing my profound skills on reproducing the expressionless faces of the people we've seen. Astonishingly, my picture provoked a response.

"Ah, Mennonites!"

The Mennonites, José María told us, are a community of conservative Christians formed in Germany at the time of Martin Luther, the Protestant reformer. In the late 1700s, certain Mennonites fled Europe due to persecution and settled in Canada. A quest for land caused a migration to Paraguay, but a drought forced the Mennonites to seek fresh pastures. They headed north through the jungle to Bolivia, where those who survived the long trek settled.

According to José María, the Bolivian Mennonites are among the most traditional and conservative of all the Mennonites in South America. They dwell in closed communities and tend not to mix with local people.

I wished I could hear a Mennonite's point of view. Why are the communities so closed? Do they feel Bolivian? And are they really as miserable as they look?

DAY 61: SUNDAY 18TH MAY 2014, 20.32
JUAN'S HOUSE, SANTIAGO DE CHIQUITOS, CHIQUITANIA, SANTA CRUZ, BOLIVIA

STEVE

This afternoon we encountered an American couple who have for decades been an integral part of the local community here in Santiago de Chiquitos. Milton, a heavily bearded man now in his seventies, first came to the area as a Quaker seeking alternative service during the Vietnam War. After wedding Katherine 20 years ago, the couple, originally from Indiana, moved here to start a family (they now have five children) and to do their bit for the upkeep of the town. Milton, who was for a long while the head of the local school, is still the president of the company that supplies clean water to the town's 1,000 inhabitants. The couple even offer cheap rooms to backpackers and feature in several guidebooks.

We met Katherine and her eldest daughter, Ramona, 18, on our visit to the Evangelical church on the plaza. Invited home after the service, we were treated to lunch and a myriad of interesting tales about Santiago and Bolivia as a whole, including its relationship with the coca plant. Milton said that although the country is way behind Peru and Colombia in terms of production, more than 70% of its coca leaves are used to make cocaine. Meanwhile, the habit of chewing coca leaves – ubiquitous today – apparently didn't exist when he first arrived.

Evo Morales, the President, also happens to be the head of the conglomerate of coca companies, which may go some way to explaining why many think him corrupt. It may also explain why the industry continues to flourish.

Evo certainly divides opinion. A speaker of the Quechan dialect, he is popular with the majority of his fellow native Bolivians, but is thought by most white Bolivians to be in the mould of Hugo Chávez and intent on curtailing Western influence in the country.

We have seen many more white Bolivians in the east of the country, but nothing like the number of Spanish descendants we saw in Argentina. From their skin tone alone, it appears the majority of Bolivians are of native descent. In Argentina, we were told that the reason most Argentinians are fair-skinned is because of the systematic ethnic cleansing of natives by the conquistadors across the continent. Perhaps the Bolivians escaped relatively unscathed.

It struck me as surprising, although no bad thing, that several people in Bolivia and Argentina told us that no enmity exists between races. I will be interested to hear whether this holds true in other South American countries, where the conquistadors are still a relatively recent and certainly influential part of the continent's history.

DAY 62: MONDAY 19TH MAY 2014, 12.29
EL MERCADO, EL CARMEN, CHIQUITANIA, SANTA CRUZ, BOLIVIA

STEVE

This is the life.

We find ourselves in the wonderful position of having already achieved our day's ambition. Although we are yet to arrive at the border with Brazil, our passage there has been secured. Within the next two hours, Florencio, a 21-year-old truck driver with a missing digit, will return with his 18-year-old "*muchacho*" (assistant), Ervin, to take us the remaining 100km.

We travelled with the two young men – both native Bolivians for whom Spanish is a second language – for three hours this morning. It hasn't been our quickest ride (we stopped in most towns between Santiago and El Carmen for our drivers to unload the bottled drinks in the back of the truck) but that doesn't matter to us.

"*Tenemos tiempo* [We have time]," I reassured Florencio when he asked us whether we minded all the stops. "Until December!" I added.

Over the past few weeks, December has become our self-imposed deadline. We have three family celebrations to return for and have also been informed that parts of Alaska are shrouded in total darkness by the end of November. It would be a shame to travel all that way and not see anything.

Six months to go, then. We have much ground to cover and for the moment we're travelling in the wrong direction, but once the World Cup has run its course, the plan is to return to the Pan-American Highway in Peru (thereby missing out on Venezuela), with four months still in hand.

We hope this will be sufficient. We wouldn't want to rush the last stretch. Given how far we've travelled these past two months, I'm quietly confident that four months will prove ample, but right now Alaska seems some way off. Today our sights are set only on Brazil. Providing Florencio keeps his word and returns to collect us, there is every chance we will be there tonight.

Jo

A bit of drama in the market toilets just now.

Having paid the 8p entrance fee, I entered a cubicle and shut the door – so far, so normal – only to discover that there was no handle on my side of the door, and as such, no means by which to exit. Oh.

Surveying the scene, I decided that the best option was to use the panels of the six-foot door to elevate myself up and over the frame in an army obstacle-course fashion. I began to do this, relatively successfully (even if I do say so myself), when a lady suddenly appeared, departing from a cubicle farther along the row. She stared at me curiously.

A rather odd exchange followed as, breathlessly, I requested that she opened my door and she duly obliged, no words uttered. Her role fulfilled, she disappeared again. Rescued! And only a bruised big toe worse off.

DAY 62 (CONTINUED): 21.49
HOTEL BOLIVIA, ARROYO CONCEPCION, BOLIVIA

STEVE

So things didn't quite go to plan. Two and a half hours passed, and there was still no sign of Florencio and his *muchacho*, so we decided to take matters into our own hands. Enough waiting.

Not knowing if something had prevented our friends from returning, or whether they were simply running late, we took up our bags and began the hike to the edge of town. This way, we figured, either our friends would soon pass by, or we could continue our progress with someone else. Either way, it was better than sitting still, as hope, and light, faded.

It was 3pm when we recommenced hitching towards Brazil. By 6pm, we had arrived, courtesy of a further three rides. We never saw Florencio again.

Now we sit in a hotel in Arroyo Concepción, just minutes from the border. Having arrived after dark, we decided to pass the night here and cross into Brazil tomorrow, feeling fresh.

During our 17 days in Bolivia, we have covered a lot of ground. For us, the country was a slow burner. Our first moments provided us with a greater culture shock than we anticipated; hitchhiking, in the main, proved more difficult than we had expected; and although the people were generally friendly, it wasn't until our last four days here that we truly began to take the country to heart.

Those four days provided us with precisely the kind of experience we had hoped for. Hitchhiking proved more than possible. Easy, in fact. Almost every driver stopped at least to enquire where we were going, or to say they weren't going very far or didn't have space in their vehicle. We were also treated to that wonderful sensation of spending quality time with one of our drivers – José María.

And then there was the beauty of the landscape. On our journey today, we saw the beginnings of the Pantanal, a giant wetland that reaches deep into Brazil. Ever since Santa Cruz we have been wowed by *jungla* and the sight of countless species of tropical birds. So much have we enjoyed the past four days that we have discussed whether our perceptions of Bolivia as a whole might have been very different had we entered from the east.

7. THE INVISIBLE MAFIA

DAY 63: TUESDAY 20TH MAY 2014, 14.31
RESTAURANTE BATIDÃO, CORUMBÁ, BRAZIL

Jo

BRAZIL yeah, yeah, yeahhhhh!

This has been our shortest hitching day to date: we have travelled only seven kilometres between our Bolivian hotel and the nearest city on this side of the border. We could have walked it, but considering the skin-melting heat, we were thankful for our first – and extremely easy – hitch in Brazil, achieved as we strolled away from immigration. This was only shortly after being told by the lady in the tourist office that hitchhiking is illegal and dangerous. I think I'm just about used to such warnings now.

We don't yet know the exchange rate, so I'm currently scrabbling around with vague mathematical logic to try to make sense of the world: if coffee costs this much and lunch related to our hotel bill in this way, then £1 is … nope, no idea.

I have just allowed myself a moment's distraction to analyse the Brazilian soap drama playing on the television screen. Yes, just the same as all the rest. At any moment now the heated argument between this incomprehensibly beautiful couple will turn into a passionate kiss … right about … there we go.

STEVE

On first impressions at least, Brazilians appear friendlier than any race I've ever encountered. More than Chileans and Argentinians. Perhaps even more than Iranians and Afghans.

Take our first drivers here, Marcos, 42, and his brother-in-law, Paulo, 55. Only the second people to pass us on the road from the border, they didn't think twice about stopping.

Twenty minutes later, we had arrived at a *pousada* (basic hotel) and they had secured us a cheap room. They then took a further half an hour from their working day (it seemed as though the concept of time didn't really exist for them) to show us a map of the region, Mato Grosso do Sul, and to tell us the best places to visit.

As if this wasn't enough, Marcos then told us that he would happily drive us tomorrow to a police checkpoint on the outskirts of the city, where we would stand a better chance of securing a ride. Or, he said, if we wanted to wait another day, he could take us a farther 200km to the town of Miranda, or even all the way to his home in the state of São Paulo.

Our first experience of Brazilian hospitality was overwhelming, but not overbearing; it felt like the most natural thing in the world.

DAY 63 (CONTINUED): 15.16
DOLCE CAFÉ, CORUMBÁ, MATO GROSSO DO SUL, BRAZIL

STEVE

We have been forced to move location, although the way it transpired felt wonderfully Brazilian ... if I can say that after less than four hours here.

It was approaching 3pm and the lady in charge of the restaurant was clearing tables and chairs. I hadn't noticed, but Jo suggested we should leave.

"Ah, don't worry," I said. "If she needs us to go, she'll tell us."

But the clock passed 3pm and the lady still hadn't been able to bring herself to throw us out, so we decided to give her a helping hand.

"*Hola ... Cerrado?* [Hello ... Closed?]" I asked, in Spanish.

She nodded, mournfully, and fetched the bill.

What a wonderful place! OK, so we've only been here a very short time, but our first impressions are singularly positive.

And the language barrier, although present, is not proving as great as we imagined. Portuguese, to these untrained ears, sounds like Spanish spoken with a Dutch accent ... or by a drunkard. A friendly drunkard, mind.

Take for example the command "Use both hands", which I encountered moments ago when reaching for the paper towels in the bathroom.

In Spanish, this would be "*Con las dos manos*".

In Portuguese, it's "*Com as duas mãos*".

Similar, I'm sure you'll agree, and if spoken with a slur almost the very same.

The peculiar yet lovable accent only adds to our joy at being here. No-one seems to mind that we can't speak a word of Portuguese, nor do they appear annoyed when we shout Spanish words at them, incredibly slowly. They just smile and slur Spanish-sounding words back at us. For now at least, we seem able to understand each other, at least sufficiently well. Given that we've only just arrived, we feel we're doing OK. Perhaps after a few beers, we'd do even better.

DAY 64: WEDNESDAY 21ST MAY 2014, 18.32
HOTEL POUSADA CALLIANDRA, BONITO, MATO GROSSO DO SUL, BRAZIL

STEVE

Well, this is new. Tonight, for the very first time, we are sharing a hotel room with one of our drivers. It wouldn't have been our first choice, but we can hardly complain. The driver in question, 76-year-old Benedito, has taken us all the way from the outskirts of Corumbá, where Marcos dropped us, to Bonito, a popular tourist town recommended by José María back in Santiago de Chiquitos. And Benedito wasn't even planning on going here. He came for us. *And* he's paying.

The morning started with the return of the finger-pointers, and they returned with a vengeance. For an hour after Marcos had waved us goodbye, apologising in advance if *carona* (the Brazilian word for "hitchhiking") proved difficult, we received nothing but friendly smiles, waves and signals in all kinds of directions, including straight on (always the most confusing).

It had only been half an hour, but Jo was close to breaking point.

"I thought it was supposed to be easy here!" she complained.

I had certainly expected it to be.

But then our knight in shining armour arrived and all was well.

At first, we had asked only for a 100km ride east to a place called Buraco das Piranhas, which we had been told was the heart of the Pantanal. But when we arrived and before us lay only a scattering of huts and a police checkpoint, we reconsidered.

In the end we settled on José María's recommendation and said we wished to go to Bonito.

Benedito nodded and told us he would take us to Miranda, the next major town. But when we arrived there, the old man had a change of heart and said something about going to Bonito together.

After another few hours on the road, and some erratic driving ... Ah, speak of the devil! I'd better be off.

Jo

Despite two whole months of successful hitchhiking in South America, it took only half an hour's wait this morning before I began to tiptoe back to my former ways. I was feeling rattled by the "*PROIBIDO CARONA*" (hitchhiking prohibited) signs on the windscreens of several trucks, and the weight of rejection mounted as the minutes passed. Also, if I didn't count our success with Marcos and Paulo (which I should have), this was our first attempt at hitching in Brazil; the lack of accomplishment was making the prospect of the next two months feel very bleak.

"No-one's even acknowledged us!" I wailed, which was entirely untrue.

Thank goodness for Benedito, the second driver in two days who went specifically out of his way on our behalf.

I confess that despite this act of kindness, my capacity for gratitude was sorely challenged by Benedito's utterly terrible driving. Normally I'd suggest we're safer with local drivers than, say, in buses or with me at the wheel in a foreign country, but in this case it was definitely not true. Benedito was blind to lane markings, treated slowing down at corners as contemptible and reacted to the umpteen speed cameras in the same way every time:

What's this? A speed camera? Never seen one of those before. And I'm travelling significantly faster than the speed limit? Better SLAM ON THE BRAKES then.

In the end I chose to stare fixedly out of the window, rather than keep a running tally of how many errors were being made.

The majestic scenery softened the effect of the jolting drive. The road from Corumbá to Miranda skirted alongside the waterlogged fields of the Pantanal, and the wetland teemed with all kinds of wildlife. We saw crocodiles, toucans, parrots, salmon, a tortoise, and two rather more exotic types of road kill: a jaguar and an anteater.

We soon forgave Benedito for his questionable road skills. Over ice cream this evening, we were discussing how few of the fruit flavours Steve and I had ever heard of when Benedito's expression shifted, and he said how grateful he was to God for bringing us all together. Then he spoke of his late wife, who died in September.

"I miss her terribly," he said, the third time he had mentioned it. He wiped tears from his eyes and apologised for crying. "We did everything together."

It was a horribly sad moment. In the silence that hung, our Portuguese totally insufficient for speaking solace, I thought about the gaping hole that Benedito's wife had so evidently left. Maybe it was this fact that caused dear Benedito to take pity on us – for the company. Perhaps it was also the reason he seemed not to care where he ended up.

"I don't know where I'm going," he had said after picking us up. "I'm just driving."

DAY 66: FRIDAY 23RD MAY 2014, 15.46
HOTEL ALVORADA, NOVA ALVORADA DO SUL, MATO GROSSO DO SUL, BRAZIL

STEVE

It's official: Brazil is my new favourite country. (Sorry Iran.) The people here are simply wonderful. As in Iran, you can hear it just by the way people speak; their very voices are friendly.

Yesterday was a case in point. Having progressed from Bonito to the town of Sidrolândia by sundown, thanks to two lifts with truckers (Wagner, 33, and Fabio, 27), we sought refuge from the rain in a service-station café. And then the fun began.

For some reason our presence attracted great attention. (I don't think they see many *gringos* in this part of Brazil; we have yet to see any others.) Within minutes, a lady had been fetched who knew some English. Her name was Zañir, a middle-aged woman with fair skin and a delightfully unassuming manner. Before long we were hopping into her car on our way to Hotel Piana, the cheapest place in town. Zañir had called ahead, and insisted on driving us there.

On our arrival we were greeted by two ladies sipping coffee in the lobby. One, it transpired, was the owner; the other was passing through on her way back to São Paulo.

"It's a shame you aren't going to São Paulo," said the latter, introducing herself as Mih and handing us both a cup of coffee, "or you could have come with me."

Our eyes lit up and we hurriedly pulled out a map. We have been told by many people we must not miss Iguaçu Falls, so we have made it our next target. We were therefore delighted to discover that the road from Sidrolândia to São Paulo runs in that direction for the first 170km.

And then things got even better as Zañir, who had lingered throughout, asked whether we would like to go back to hers for some homemade pizza. All of a sudden, having done very little, we had been found a cheap hotel, free food for the night and a ride for the morrow.

What's more, everything has gone exactly as planned. We had a lovely time with Zañir and her husband Amir, who is of Italian descent (hence the pizza). Then this morning, bright and early, Mih, a 30-year-old Brazilian Buddhist who works in "popcorn quality control" (you couldn't make it up), knocked on our door and told us it was time to go. Nova Alvorada do Sul was our destination for the day. It was too wet, she decided, to go any farther.

So here we are, in this rather drab commercial town, taking some time to refresh. Tomorrow will be our sixth straight day on the road.

JO

After a day with Mih, I have three new words rooted securely in my Portuguese vocabulary. There was no escaping Mih's most favoured adjectives. "*Perigoso, muito perigoso* [Dangerous, very dangerous]," she would comment about any and every location in Brazil, "*e muito caro!* [so expensive!] … *e FRIO!* [SO cold!]"

This said, Mih's bubbly disposition was not dampened by her outlook, and she remained remarkably cheerful about being Brazilian.

The oppressive heat of our first couple of days in Brazil has given way to rain. The downpours are apparently uncharacteristic for this time of year, but for the sake of our demeanours and t-shirts – both of which have been sagging to new, sweaty lows – this reprieve has been granted none too soon. The weather must be beneficial for the land, too; we have left the Pantanal behind now and entered an agriculture region, rolling past acres of crops and grazing cattle.

At one point on our journey yesterday, we climbed a steep hill, whereupon we were distracted by a stomach-churning sight: a lorry cab lay far below one of the bends in the road, separated from its cargo and crumpled almost beyond recognition. As we drew closer, we could see another mangled cab nearby, and the railing at the side of the road was flattened. Our driver at the time, Fabio, told us this happens about once a month, a terrible statistic considering the slim chance of survival.

DAY 68: SUNDAY 25TH MAY 2014, 09.52
SANTA MARIA HOTEL, CASCAVEL, PARANÁ, BRAZIL

STEVE

There is a palpable sense of fear in Brazil, as the World Cup edges ever closer. The country seems divided about the event. Of the seven drivers we have had here, three have expressed discontent, saying that the government should focus on health, education and alleviating poverty, rather than waste huge sums on a month-long football competition. Rising crime rates and fears of a spike in the drugs trade have caused police to tighten security at weak points along Brazil's 16,000km-long border.

Yesterday we skirted close to the border with Paraguay, as we made our way south with 65-year-old Vicente, a Brazilian Catholic with Italian grandparents and 15 siblings. Vicente's views on the World Cup mirrored those of several others we have spoken to.

"I'm Brazilian, so I love football," he said. "But I don't think Brazil has the infrastructure to host a World Cup. It's good for FIFA and for foreigners like you, but not for us."

At lunchtime Vicente took us to meet one of his sisters, who told us we were very courageous for hitchhiking in Brazil and advised us to take extreme caution. The consensus here is that the country is dangerous – now more than ever – and that we should be on our guard.

Mih must have used the word "dangerous" more times in our 24 hours together than I have in my entire life. Zañir also warned us and said she would be "preoccupied" on account of us. And then last night, at a Lebanese restaurant here in the underwhelming city of Cascavel, our waiter told us of an increase in murders in the region, "even of foreigners".

All in all, we are feeling rather put upon. On the one hand, I have found the people here to be remarkably friendly; on the other, it seems they all live in fear.

"I'd like to live in the United States," Vicente told us as we passed into the lush state of Paraná, which is said to boast some of the richest soil in the world. "In the USA they have values, and people respect the law."

As the Champions League final was broadcast over the airways, I gazed out of the window, wondering how anyone could possibly wish to live elsewhere. In the rain, the reddy-brown soil looked especially fertile; everything else was green.

Paraná is said to be a very wealthy state, home to many of Brazil's agricultural exports. Vicente told us that Mato Grosso do Sul is also a chief exporter of cereal, livestock and sugar cane. At one stage, as we were surrounded by fields of sugar cane, Vicente said that everything before us belonged to one man, a certain wealthy American by the name of Bill Gates. (Apparently it has something to do with oil.)

Yet, despite the value of the land and the warmth of the people, disquiet rumbles beneath the surface. In Mato Grosso do Sul, we passed a great number of outdoor shacks, said to be home to Brazil's people "*sem terra*" (without land), whom the government provides with ramshackle huts and a daily allowance for food. Some of them, Vicente told us, find jobs. But the majority do not, and cannot. Mih told us to keep clear of them. Apparently they're dangerous too.

Jo

This morning we were greeted with heartfelt joy by the cleaner outside our room, as we headed downstairs for my favourite aspect of Brazilian food: breakfast. Café de manhã (literally "morning coffee") offers fresh juices, exotic fruits, muesli (sometimes of several varieties), bread, cheese, ham and often a toastie maker for grilling one's morning sandwich. What a delight! Oh, and how could I forget the cakes, of which there are usually at least two or three on display. Cake for breakfast? Well done, Brazil.

In my attempt to avoid developing the belly blubber sported by a worrying number of locals (we affectionately refer to it as the "Brazilian bulge"), I am trying to stick to the healthy options. With such extensive choices, it's no sacrifice.

Yesterday we enjoyed a luxury door-to-door hitching service. Vicente brought us all the way to this hotel, a journey of eight hours, from the ("dangerous") junction where Mih had dropped us. I could get used to that kind of hitchhiking.

Our early lunch with Vicente's family brought the number of meals shared with new acquaintances to an impressive five in five days. Of these people, only Zañir has spoken any English, but we have managed to get by; seemingly our odd hash of Spanish, French and newly discovered Portuguese is going to be sufficient. We hadn't fully grasped Spanish verb conjugation and our knowledge of Portuguese grammar is non-existent, but this doesn't appear to be a problem. Who needs tenses anyway?

DAY 69: MONDAY 26TH MAY 2014, 17.53
PARK FOZ PIZZARIA, FOZ DO IGUAÇU, PARANÁ, BRAZIL

STEVE

Still no sign of the Brazilian mafia, despite all the warnings. Only hospitality. Today, for the seventh day in a row, we were invited to share food with Brazilians. Last night, our invitation was the result of our presence at the Presbyterian Church in Cascavel. This afternoon, it came courtesy of Leonardo and Nyara, a young couple here in Foz do Iguaçu with whom we share a mutual friend. We were treated to *feijão* (literally "bean", made into a stew) at their home and are enjoying mates' rates at Nyara's father's B&B.

We've even received compliments on our Portuguese, which seems faintly ridiculous.

"Where did you learn?" asked our second driver this morning, 40-year-old Marcelo, who told us he had seven tickets to World Cup games and was on his third marriage. (He said he liked women and changed wives every five years. He didn't seem to be joking.)

Our journey here to Foz, 140km west of Cascavel, went relatively smoothly. After taking us half the distance to Foz, Marcelo left us at a service station, where the pump attendants treated us to two free cups of coffee and attempted to persuade us to accept a free ride on the next bus. We politely declined and went to wait by the side of the main road, where we were soon found by Luis, 63, a former hitchhiker who was on his way to Foz.

"Have you ever had a bad experience hitchhiking?" he asked, as the conversation moved swiftly to the topic of security.

"No, never," I assured him.

Luis said that he hadn't either and that he believed that good people, or those searching for a higher purpose in life, were somehow attracted to one another. I'd never thought of it quite like that before, but it seemed to make sense. In all my travels, I have never regretted accepting the offer of a ride. My conclusion has always been that only those wishing to help have any reason to pull over. The rest, whether by looking the other way, pointing a finger, or raising one, simply drive on by.

Jo

We have been informed by several drivers recently that our special interpretation of Portuguese carries an official title: "*Portuñol*" – as in *português* meets *español*. *Portuñol* is the unofficial language of the border towns linking Argentina, Brazil and Paraguay, but the term can be applied just as well to the language adopted by hapless foreigners attempting to use Spanish as the main foundation for getting by.

While it is excellent that we are managing to communicate, and gratifying that people keep complimenting us on our proficiency, in reality we are woeful novices; complicated yet essential vowel sounds, for example, are yet to feature in our speech. Recently, I learnt the words for grandmother and grandfather: *avó* and *avô*. Well, how on earth am I supposed to know the difference in pronunciation? I am told that one of the "o" sounds is like the "o" in "for" and the other like the "o" in "clock", but I have already forgotten which is which. It's a minefield.

DAY 74: SATURDAY 31ST MAY 2014, 12.47
CASA DA VELHA BRUXA, GRAMADO, RIO GRANDE DO SUL, BRAZIL

STEVE

Three and a half weeks ago, we were in La Paz. Since then, we have travelled approximately 4,000km in the wrong direction.

Our latest detour came as something of a shock. Leaving Foz on Thursday afternoon, we were taken out of the city by Nilton, Nyara's father, and left by a police checkpoint on the road east. Our plan was to return to Cascavel by nightfall and then awake early on Friday to continue eastward towards Curitiba, near the Atlantic coast.

All seemed to be going to script as, after a ride with a man named Ivanir to a petrol station within 50km of Cascavel, a car pulled over.

"*Onde vais?* [Where are you going?]" asked the driver.

"Cascavel," I responded.

"OK, come on," he said. "We're going 8km from there. We can leave you at the crossroads."

We needed no further encouragement and squeezed onto the back seats among a good deal of baggage, anticipating a straightforward end to the day. It was 4pm. There were two hours of light remaining and soon we would be just 8km from our target. Even if all went awry, we could always walk the final distance, or seek refuge in a hotel on the periphery of the city. Whatever happened, it seemed the hard work was over.

"So where are you guys going?" I asked.

"*Longe!* [Far!]" said the driver, a 30-year-old Seventh-day Adventist by the name of Elio.

"Porto Alegre," clarified his travelling companion, Fernando, 23, who wore a wide-brimmed pink cap. "It's 1,000km south."

Within a few moments, Porto Alegre had been located on our map, Elio told us the region of Rio Grande do Sul was the best bit of Brazil and that we really shouldn't miss it, and so we agreed that, OK, we wouldn't.

For the next 20 hours, aside from a four-hour break for a nap, Elio and I took it in turns to steer his white Renault Clio in a southwesterly direction. Elio told us the three regions we crossed – Paraná, Santa Catarina and Rio Grande do Sul – sustain the rest of the country.

We finished here in Gramado, a town with a distinctly Germanic feel, rather by default. In the end it transpired that Elio and Fernando hail from Sapiranga, a city a little north of Porto Alegre, and not from the state capital itself. After eating lunch with Elio and his wife, Luana, we got the feeling that our hosts were ready for us to move on. With four hours of sleep and 1,000km under our belts in the past 24 hours, we really didn't feel like going anywhere, but there were several hours of light remaining and Elio told us the "most beautiful place in Brazil" was just an hour's drive away.

So it was that at 2pm we found ourselves standing beside another service station, hitching … again.

The mood in the camp was not strong. Jo wore the expression of someone entirely devoid of optimism, while my reserves of unfounded energy and enthusiasm received their greatest test.

We prayed for a quick ride all the way to Gramado, or Canela – the other "most beautiful town" in this region – but we didn't really believe it would happen. So it felt nothing short of miraculous when, in a matter of minutes, Diego pulled up in his swish Toyota sports car and told us he was taking his "special friend" Ana Paula to Canela for the weekend.

After a bit of to-ing and fro-ing over where we might end the night, the loved-up couple left us in Gramado, which Diego, a fluent English speaker, told us was "much nicer". Having not yet seen Canela, we cannot comment, but it is certainly very plush here.

Jo

If I were feeling more delicate, my rational mind would be raging against the journey we undertook two days ago. We have returned to the same latitude as when we were in Córdoba – which we left six weeks ago. Alaska is actually getting farther away.

As it is, I'm adopting a go-with-the-flow attitude and rewarding myself with a creamy hot chocolate, which is warming my insides on this morosely wet Saturday. Until yesterday we'd never heard of Gramado, let alone appreciated that it is very popular with national tourists. This town couldn't be further from our preconceived idea of Brazil: the architecture is Alpine, as is the cuisine – fondue for dinner last night, chocolate shops galore – and it is extremely upmarket. It has also rained almost constantly since we arrived. Are we back in Europe?

We are definitely out-priced here: everything is expensive, *everyone* is expensive. We are staying at the cheapest hostel available and it is still our entire day's budget. However, it seems reasonable to loosen the purse strings in the name of recuperation after such a marathon journey.

My spine – and limbs in general – were the main losers during our 20-hour ride. Renault Clios are not known for their roominess, though eventually my cramped legs reached a settled level of numbness and ceased to be a bother. My heart underwent its own challenge, skipping a few beats when, as we were speeding down a curvy country road, the tyre of the truck in front exploded and smashed one of its rear lights. My brain quickly computed that the loud and sudden bang had not been emitted by our vehicle, but nevertheless, the sight of swirling debris and a swerving lorry caused a jolt of panic. Thankfully, the truck pulled over with apparent ease and we escaped unaffected.

My teeth also fared badly. An unpleasantly furry film coated them by the end of the journey, and they have had to undergo a period of dedicated scrubbing. I was already feeling self-conscious about the condition of my teeth, having observed a phenomenon in Brazil we haven't noticed elsewhere: brace-wearing is no longer the reserve of long-suffering teenagers, with adults taking to the treatment in their hordes. We presume this is the result of influence from the US, and in all probability comes with the reputation of us Brits having terrible teeth. Now, not only do we have the challenge of speaking Portuguese, but also speaking it without showing our wonky gnashers.

DAY 75: SUNDAY 1ST JUNE 2014, 21.36
GRAMADO HOSTEL, GRAMADO, RIO GRANDE DO SUL, BRAZIL

JO

The wonderful (and occasionally mind-bendingly boring) thing about the universal language of football is that there is always a new aspect to discuss – for hours on end, if one is so inclined. On this adventure, for example, there has been the pre-World Cup chat in Argentina, Chile and Bolivia; now we've reached the "We're here for the World Cup" stage; hereafter we will be able to reminisce about "When we went to the World Cup". Football ranks in the top three topics we discuss with our drivers, and I don't even like the sport.

Here in Brazil, our usual conversation starter is: "The World Cup in Brazil: good or bad?" It is generally a given that Brazilians love football, but ever since Brazil won the bid, there have been news stories of controversy relating to the *Copa*.

Our driver to Gramado, Diego, told us about the eye-watering cost of the stadiums.

"Labour in Brazil is cheap, and they're using the cheapest materials they can, so there's no way that all that money is really going on the stadiums," he said. "People are saying that 30 per cent of the budget has disappeared, and most people think it's been taken by politicians and the mafia."

Some have opined that if the Brazilian football team are crowned champions, all will be forgotten; others are not convinced. We will see soon enough.

DAY 76: MONDAY 2ND JUNE 2014, 18.34
PADARIA E CONFEITARIA DOIS IRMÃOS, CAMBARÁ DO SUL, SERRA GAÚCHA, RIO GRANDE DO SUL, BRAZIL

STEVE

Tonight we must pay tribute to the good people of Cambará do Sul – in particular to the Secretary of Tourism and a 61-year-old *gaúcho* (cowboy) called Renato, who combined forces to provide us with a free bed for the night. We didn't ask for it, nor do we consider ourselves deserving, but we are surely glad of it, especially after an expensive weekend in Gramado.

It's been a topsy-turvy kind of day. It started well, with a free tour of the Jolimont vineyard in Canela. All was bright and cheery at midday, as Jaime, the vineyard's transport man, took us to a petrol station in Canela and told us we were at the start of the road leading northeast towards the "BR" (motorway). An hour later, when the petrol-pump attendant approached us to tell us we were in a bad spot, we weren't feeling quite so cheery and wondered why he hadn't told us sooner.

After half an hour, we had located the edge of town but felt no closer to securing a ride out of it. Traffic was flowing freely past and despite our efforts to attract attention, it seemed we were invisible.

But at around 2pm, our fortunes changed. First along came Sergio, a cross-eyed 23-year-old, with his elderly father Anuncio. They took us to a toll a few kilometres out of the town (a few kilometres farther than they intended to drive) and told us we'd have better luck finding a ride there.

Indeed we did, as only the fourth passing car pulled over and we were invited to join Alessio, a smooth 32-year-old with slicked-back hair and sunglasses, and an appreciation for extremely loud trance music, on his way to work in the next town of São Francisco de Paula.

It was 3.30pm when Alessio left us underneath a sign that read "CAMBARA DO SUL 80".

After an hour came and went and the sun began to descend, Jo declared loudly: "I don't want to live here!"

I concurred, and went to ask the security guard at the adjacent cereal factory whether he knew of a better place to *carona*. But before I could reach him, I heard a yelp and spun around.

"He's stopped! He's stopped!" shouted Jo, and beckoned me to hurry back to discuss terms with the driver of a white 4x4, the aforementioned Renato, who was on his way back to his home in Cambará do Sul.

For the next 30 minutes, we sat back and enjoyed the ride, safe in the knowledge that our day's work was done. Pine trees were soon all around as we crossed into *gaúcho* country. The Tourism Secretary, a personal friend of Renato's, told us 90% of the people here are *gaúchos*, though we're still not exactly sure what it means. "Cowboy" doesn't quite seem to fit. Renato works on a farm, but drives a 4x4 and doesn't look very much like a cowboy should. Saying that, we have passed a few men wearing baggy trousers, cowboy boots and wide-brimmed hats, so evidently the traditional dress still exists.

Still, there is no disputing who our favourite cowboy of the moment is. Step forward one Renato Gaúcho.

Jo

"*Tá frio, frio, FRIO!*" as Mih would say: it was 6°C in this part of the Serra Gaúcha at 5pm and the temperature is dropping now that the sun has set. I was cold to the core when we arrived; despite the welcome and unbroken sunshine during the day, there was little warmth accompanying it. I am repressing the thought of the temperatures we'll experience as we approach Alaska: -20°C in November, we've heard.

Hitchhiking felt faintly embarrassing at points today. We didn't know exactly where we were in relation to the edge of Canela, and I thought we must look ridiculous, standing there trying to flag down drivers who could be going any which way. Once we had relocated to farther out, our confidence reasserted itself: in this new position, those who schmoozed past and didn't stop for us were simply bad people, as opposed to not heading in our direction in the first place. (I am mostly joking, although it was surprisingly difficult not to castigate each driver with a petulant shout of: "We're not the waving committee, you know! We need you to stop, not just smile!")

DAY 77: TUESDAY 3RD JUNE 2014, 14.42
ROADSIDE, PARQUE NACIONAL APARADOS DA SERRA, RIO GRANDE DO SUL, BRAZIL

Jo

Temperature update: last night, the thermometer read 3°C when we left the restaurant where we'd had dinner. Though we had warmed the cockles awhile, even the open fire wasn't as roaring as it needed to be to expunge the frosty bite in the air. Unhappily, it was no warmer in our bedroom when we returned, the bare brick walls insulating about as effectively as a pair of fishnet stockings. Any uninhabited mattress space remained frigidly cold, so that the slightest deviation from one's sleeping position sent a chill shooting around the body.

After thawing out this morning just enough for our limbs to function, Steve declared that his feet were cold – possibly the first time I have ever heard him say this. I have developed a blocked nose. Room, I shake my fist at thee!

Now (because nothing happens in normal measures) we have flitted to the opposite condition, a mere three hours since I was wearing two thermal vests, a t-shirt, a jumper, a thick jacket and was still chilly. The sun cuts a bold figure in the sky as we wait on this largely unfrequented strip of road, and we are employing our full armoury of sun-protection methods. Why hasn't anyone invented a way of bottling daytime heat for later release into the evening chill?

Our current wait – more than an hour so far – is much easier to endure than one of equal length beside a busy road or outside a petrol station. There has been no traffic at all in our direction; everyone turning out of the junction behind us has given us a cheery, apologetic wave before heading back to Cambará. That's just fine: it feels likely that as soon as someone is driving east we'll get a ride.

STEVE

Our decision to hitch 1,000km south is starting to feel rather silly. OK, so we have seen some wonderful sights and enjoyed witnessing the peculiar blend of German, Italian and *gaúcho* cultures here in Rio Grande do Sul, but hitchhiking is proving problematic.

For the past 70 minutes, Jo and I have sat here at the side of the road, next to the entrance to the Parque Nacional de Aparados da Serra (home to the Itaimbezinho Canyon), waiting in the vain hope that someone might be driving eastward. In that time, 10 cars have passed, but not one has been going our way.

The tranquil nature of our surroundings was enjoyable for the first 30 minutes or so, but now we long for the motorway. Curitiba, our next target, stands about as far away now as it was back in Foz, five days ago, but this time our chances of making it there in the next couple of days appear slim.

Maybe we should just relax and make the most of this southern section of Brazil, but it is hard to do so when a deadline looms. The World Cup is but nine days away and we have made plans to meet a friend in Rio for the big kick-off. Rio de Janeiro is probably only around 1,000km from here, which doesn't seem so far, but if the last hour is anything to go by, it may take us some time.

If it weren't for our current plight, the undoubted news story of the day would have been this morning's ride in the back of a trailer filled with straw and seven goats. Fortunately, our travelling companions began the bumpy 18km ride safely tethered to the other side of the trailer. Unfortunately, with around 3km to go, one of our hairy friends wriggled free from his noose and began to stumble in our direction.

"Ah!" shrieked Jo, alerting me to the fact and drawing her legs back to her chest.

"Oh dear," I replied, and asked whether I should fend off the creature with a nearby spade or attempt to re-attach its leash.

Jo suggested we simply bide our time and hope the movement of the vehicle proved enough of a deterrent. An awkward stand-off passed between us and the beast, but I'm glad to report that we escaped unscathed and leapt free from its reach as soon as the vehicle ground to a halt, much to the amusement of drivers Sergio and Antonio, a couple of undisputed *gaúchos*.

… Ooh, must dash, a car approaches …

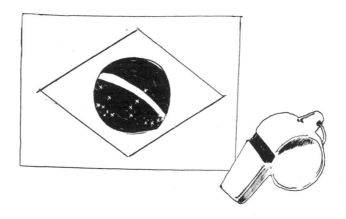

8. THE WAITING GAME

DAY 78: WEDNESDAY 4TH JUNE 2014, 23.33
HOTEL SUÍÇA FABER, BALNEÁRIO CAMBORIÚ, SANTA CATARINA, BRAZIL

STEVE

We hit rock bottom today. At around 5pm, Jo was in tears and I wasn't far off. By that stage, we had been waiting at a busy service station, or *posto*, on the main coastal motorway, the BR-101, for more than three and a half hours. In that time, hundreds of vehicles had passed, as we waited by the exit, and just three drivers had stopped to apologise that they could be of no help.

This was worse than our 70-minute wait yesterday. It was worse even than our four-and-a-half-hour wait back in Santa Lucia. At least in those locations we felt partly responsible for our failures, for attempting to hitchhike in the middle of nowhere. This afternoon our location was without defect; in hitchhiking terms, it doesn't get any better than a service station on a busy motorway, but this only made our failure harder to stomach. As driver upon driver passed without even a glance in our direction, our morale was given its sternest test since we left home, and it didn't hold up so well.

I was venting even more than usual about the dire ethical state of the locals, while Jo sobbed uncontrollably.

In defence of the people of Santa Catarina, the state where this travesty occurred and where we remain tonight, around 25% of drivers did at least acknowledge us, either with a finger-point or a friendly, if apologetic, smile. But for the rest, for that loathsome 75%, I can find no words. Even a look in our direction, a shrug, a feigned smile – anything! – would have lifted our spirits. But no, just grip the steering wheel and drive on past! Don't worry that we're standing here, burnt to a crisp and feeling more deflated by the minute! I take back what I said about Brazil being my favourite country. This would never have happened in Iran.

Our first driver today, a 68-year-old named Raymundo, and his friend Francisco, 32, told us Brazil is going through a "difficult moment". Our second driver, dope-smoking 32-year-old Wesley, who left us at that godforsaken *posto* near Criciúma, said that he thought the country was better off now than 30 years ago, at the time of the military dictatorship, and that it would be a good place to live in 50 years. I missed his exact reasoning, but I think it had something to do with oil and the USA.

Perhaps in 50 years, if I'm still around, I should return to find out if hitching is any easier. To my mind, hitchhiking is a barometer by which a great deal can be learnt about a place. Are the people friendly? Do they have compassion? Outside Criciúma yesterday, the answer to both of these questions was a resounding "no".

Yet there are always exceptions, and in this case our saviour was 50-year-old Atilano, a *caminhoneiro* (Portuguese for "trucker") on his way home to Itajaí, some 200km north of Criciúma and just three hours, he told us, from Curitiba.

We travelled with this dear man for four hours: the same length of time we had waited for him to arrive.

Atilano, a divorcé, seemed so lovely that you couldn't imagine him ever falling out with his wife. Perhaps it wasn't as straightforward as that. He told us he didn't like the idea that a woman could be considered a man's possession.

"If a woman wants to leave, I don't think you should stand in her way," he said.

Atilano said he couldn't blame his wife for walking out; he was away from home a great deal.

"I hate this life," he told us.

Atilano had moved from Rio Grande do Sul to Santa Catarina in search of a job that would allow him to spend more time at home.

He dropped us here, seven kilometres short of his town, at the popular beach resort of Balneário Camboriú. It feels that we have come full circle since leaving the beachfront in the city of Torres at 8.30 this morning.

We're very glad to be here. Yes, 200km is not a lot of ground in the grand scheme of things, but it's more than we managed on Monday and Tuesday and a darn sight better than the 50km or so we had achieved when we arrived, bright-eyed and bushy-tailed, at that dreaded *posto* just after lunchtime, dreaming of Curitiba.

Jo

What is it about Wednesdays?

It has been six weeks to the day since that crushing afternoon in Argentina that led to our stay in the police station – just enough time for the memory to be but floating and distant. Today, the emotional weight of such an experience came crashing down again, and we are both exhausted.

Until the three-hour mark, I felt I had coped really rather well. With the *posto* only a pebble's throw from the main road, and with the volume of traffic going in our direction, hope was still alive.

Eventually, though, I was worn down by the sheer number of sneering stares we received.

"Do you know your window isn't *that* tinted?" I wished to yell. "Yes, I know I look ridiculous in my country-bumpkin sun bonnet. I *have* to wear it because it is VERY HOT. Would you stare like that at your daughter? Have some compassion!"

This internal rant was not at all useful, but my energy levels were so sapped by the sun and the frustration of it all that it was difficult to channel my thoughts positively.

Just before the inevitable tears, I developed a new survival technique: the middle-distance gaze. Thanks to my sunglasses, my eyes weren't visible, and I discovered that my body could be facing the passing cars without once having to look whether a driver was acknowledging us or not. This was a useful self-preservation tool and helped my chin stay up for a little while longer.

It was the image of Steve bent over dejectedly as a car pulled away from him that pushed me over the edge. We both loathe approaching drivers to ask for a lift, feeling that it corners people rather than leaving them a choice, but the situation was sufficiently painful to justify extreme measures. Steve had dragged himself over to the cars at the petrol pumps and I was employing the middle-distance stare to lessen the will-they-won't-they tension, but there were no prizes for guessing the outcome of this particular case as the driver and his female passenger passed me with a regretful wave. Steve trudged back despondently and my resolve decided it had had enough.

While there is considerable relief when such a situation is finally over, there seeps in an even greater tiredness. The need to stand tall and persevere is replaced by a desperate desire to stare out of the window and become lost in thinking about nothing important. My wish was granted: while Atilano and Steve chatted away, I drifted off, awake but not really present.

DAY 79: THURSDAY 5TH JUNE 2014, 16.55
POSTO BEYOND ITAJAÍ, PARANÁ, BRAZIL

Jo

Sometimes, when one is in the midst of mental turmoil, the solution is not clear. Rest or activity? Company or solitude? Analysis or avoidance?

This is not one of those situations. I know precisely what is required to put a halt to this gnawing agony. All I'm looking for is a ride to Curitiba. Simple.

Our proximity to our desired destination has compounded the frustration of the past two days. Last week we covered an enormous swathe of southern Brazil, so there was no reason to anticipate that this week's ambition of a mere 700 kilometres would be difficult. Furthermore, Monday and Tuesday's slow progress was understandable as we were off the beaten track.

But since then, there has been a reasonable possibility that, at any moment, the next car to pull over might carry a driver going all the way to Curitiba. We've had countless lifts of that length so far. There really is no precedent for this crawling, crawling.

DAY 80: FRIDAY 6TH JUNE 2014, 10.55
DIRCEU'S APARTMENT, CENTRO HISTÓRICO, CURITIBA, PARANÁ, BRAZIL

STEVE

If Wednesday was difficult, yesterday took our troubles to a whole new level. By the time we arrived here in Curitiba at 10pm, having practically begged for our final two rides, we were emotionally and physically exhausted. The accumulation of disappointments over the past few days have left us almost completely devoid of energy.

So it was with great relief that we saw the smiling figure of Dirceu, 58, the father of our friend, Artur, waiting for us at a petrol station in Curitiba. It took our tally of petrol station visits yesterday to five in 10 hours, but that doesn't tell the half of it.

Each of the first four provided us with a different challenge, and we were not in the mood for a challenging day. When we arrived at the first, just outside Balneário Camboriú, thanks to a free ride in 50-year-old Arnaldo's taxi, we were hoping it would be our last. Curitiba was just over 200km away and we found ourselves, once more, waiting at a service station on the motorway running north. Surely someone must be heading our way.

But no, after 45 minutes it was clear that no-one was. This particular service station, it seemed, served only the local population.

"You should try the next *posto*, 10 kilometres up the road," the pump attendant told us. "You won't find a ride to Curitiba here."

This was the last thing we needed to hear. Wearily, we picked up our bags and wandered to the next entry ramp to the motorway, hoping it would provide us with more luck.

When, an hour later, we arrived at Posto Santa Rosa, thanks to a helping hand from Diego, 32, an Evangelical Christian, he told us we would be sure to find a ride all the way to Curitiba. The *posto* was teeming with vehicles; Diego said it was the most frequented in the area.

With new hope, we approached the nearest member of staff and enquired about our chances.

The response was as unexpected as it was unwelcome: "You won't find a ride to Curitiba here. You need to be on the other side of the road. There's a *posto* 10km away, in Itajaí. You should go there."

We said that we had already *been* there and that we had been assured by several sources that, despite this *posto* being on the wrong side of the motorway, it was so popular that we could find vehicles going in both directions.

He disagreed.

We took a moment to try to compose ourselves. We couldn't face going back to Itajaí, nor did we see any point in it. We were told that there was another, smaller *posto* 6km farther on, but we couldn't bear the thought of walking there.

Reaching in my pocket, I pulled out the business card Diego had just given us and dialled the number. He had told us to call if we needed anything and it definitely felt like we did.

Diego was back in a flash and apologised for dumping us in an unhelpful spot. Ten minutes later we were at our third *posto* of the day, less than 20km from where we had started.

We thanked Diego for the second time and he wished us luck.

"Don't worry," I assured him. "I'm sure we'll get a ride this time. We'll send you a message to let you know when we have … Less than 20 minutes, I bet!"

Three hours later, as the sun set over the mountains to the west, we were still there and, needless to say, we were not feeling at our best.

It might have been our obvious misery that led Talvas, a 58-year-old naval officer, to approach us.

"Where are you from?" he asked.

We told him.

"And you're trying to get to Curitiba?"

We nodded.

"Would you like a ride to Joinville? It's a little closer. You'll find it easier to get a ride from there."

We said that we most certainly would.

Then passed a rather awkward exchange involving the checking of our passports and Brazilian visas.

"*Carona* is dangerous here. You can never be too careful," Talvas told us, after we had entered his car, inspection passed. "If you were an Argentinian or Brazilian, I wouldn't pick you up … Don't you think it's dangerous?"

I said that I didn't.

"Don't you get scared?" he asked Jo.

She said that she didn't, but she later informed me that she shed a few silent tears at this point, such was the man's insistence that we shouldn't be doing what we were doing – certainly not in Brazil and categorically not any farther north than Curitiba.

Talvas also suggested that if we were bent on hitchhiking, we definitely shouldn't do it at night.

We said that we tried not to but that on this occasion the night had caught up with us.

"Why don't you stay in Joinville tonight and find a ride to Curitiba tomorrow?" he asked.

We thanked him for the suggestion but said we simply couldn't. Curitiba really wasn't very far away and it really, honestly, truly, shouldn't be so hard to get there. Please!

It was pitch black and the rain was pouring down as we arrived at our fourth *posto* of the day. It was 6pm and we were ready, or as ready as we could be, to give it one final push.

For the next two hours, I roamed around the petrol station and surrounding eateries in search of our next ride. With every rejection, my heart sank a little further. At intervals, I tried to reassure Jo, who was slumped on a bench looking after our bags, that we would soon find a ride. I'm not sure I really believed it.

At 8pm I spotted a young lady with a Joinville number plate and went over just to double-check she wasn't going farther north.

"*Que pena!* [What a shame!]" she said, that she could be of no help.

I told her that it was indeed a great shame.

And then – then – I saw it. A car had pulled up at the adjacent petrol pump and on its number plate was written "CURITIBA".

I could hardly contain my excitement as I hurried over to ask the young man behind the wheel if he was driving there. When he said that he was, I think I squealed. Goodness knows what the poor man must have been thinking. He looked less than convinced.

Not knowing what to do next and aware that I must seem like a loon, I waved madly at the lady in the next car to provide a character witness. I needed some time to compose myself.

A glowing reference was duly given, but the man still seemed unsure.

Not willing to let him escape, I blabbered something about us being really nice people and waved frantically in Jo's direction to signal for her to come. Quickly.

This she did. And then came the crucial moment.

"So ... Can we come?" I asked.

We held our breath.

And then he uttered that beautiful word, that word we had been longing to hear for the past eight hours: "Yes". And in that moment all our troubles passed away.

Jo

Steve just turned to me and said, "Can you imagine still being on the road now?"

"If you like," I said in response, "we could try to head back to Joinville today. Or how about São Paulo tomorrow? I think I'll be ready."

"Don't make me! Don't make me!" Steve replied. He was joking, but he couldn't hide the terror in his eyes. Lightweight.

DAY 82: SUNDAY 8TH JUNE 2014, 10.06
DIRCEU'S APARTMENT, CENTRO HISTÓRICO, CURITIBA, PARANÁ, BRAZIL

STEVE

Such was our trauma at the events of the past few days that we have taken the rest of the week off here in Curitiba, where dear Dirceu has made us feel very much at home.

Yet, as I reflect on all that passed, I can't help but think that we were at least partly to blame for our trials. If we had not been in such a rush to get here, which in hindsight seems unnecessary given how long we have stayed, things could have felt very different.

Take Thursday morning, for example. After a long sleep, we popped down to the beach in Balneário Camboriú to take stock before returning to the road. As we sat, three Brazilian retirees joined us and offered us some of their *chimarrão* (the *gaúcho* word for "*mate*"). One of them then mentioned that he was driving to Curitiba the next day and that we could join him if we wished. We thanked him for the offer but said we really must press on.

This played on my mind as we went back to our hotel to collect our bags. It was still on my mind as we headed out to the road just after midday. Surely in rejecting the man's offer, we had not only gone against one of our principal rules; we had also paved the way for the struggles of the day. Perhaps this will be a lesson for us henceforth.

Upon reflection, many more of the week's troubles related to our hurry to get to Curitiba. If only we had been prepared to go with the flow, we needn't have worried so much about when our next ride would come along. On paper, the week really wasn't so bad. In fact, our first two days were veritable success stories, even if the going was slow; our lack of forward progress owed much to our decisions to visit the vineyard in Canela and canyon near Cambará do Sul.

On Wednesday, aside from that four-hour wait, we couldn't complain. Thursday was certainly inauspicious, but, it is clear now that this owed much to our mindset. We were so desperate to reach Curitiba that we barely gave hitchhiking a try, at least not in the ordinary sense. In our first spot, we waited just half an hour. In the second, we were picked up before too long. The third, we were told, was a dreadful spot, so on to the fourth and fifth we went, but not once did we wait with our thumbs outstretched. Instead, we began the long and increasingly frustrating process of essentially begging for a ride. No wonder it was a bad day.

As we hit the road again tomorrow, I am determined we will not fall into the same trap. We must return to our rule of never refusing an offer, and accept whatever comes our way. In doing so, not only will our experience be a better one; we will also save ourselves a lot of undue stress.

DAY 83: MONDAY 9TH JUNE 2014, 16.23
POSTO 28, EMBU DAS ARTES, SÃO PAULO, BRAZIL

STEVE

Now this is much more like it. Here we sit in our fifth *posto* of the day and unless something disastrous occurs it is to be our last. On the fringes of the sprawling metropolis of São Paulo, we await the arrival of our latest friend-of-a-friend, who has offered to give us a ride into the centre. We would have walked the last bit, but we are glad we won't have to. Not only is it still rather far away (the city is huge); we've also been told time and again how dangerous São Paulo is. Even here, in what feels just like any other *posto*, our kind-hearted truck driver, Elson, 28, who brought us all the way here from the outskirts of Curitiba, told us we must be careful. "*Cuidado!* [Watch out!]" is a popular exclamation in Brazil.

The fact that this is our fifth *posto* today is misleading, because we were with the same driver in each one. In many ways, the day could not have gone much better. Dirceu took us to a *posto* on the outskirts of Curitiba, at the intersection with the main road from the south, and petitioned the man in charge of security to help us. (Perhaps this should be our new tactic.) I was dubious at first, as the man, who introduced himself as something that sounded like "Marteens", went about his business all too slowly in a *posto* not exactly teeming with trucks.

So dubious was I that, after watching him fail to convince the first three truckers, I thanked him for his help and went to wait at the exit.

We hadn't even time to lay our bags to rest before I was forced to ingest my latest dose of humble pie. The smiling figure of Marteens was approaching with a big thumbs-up. I met him halfway, where he informed me, as if it was the most normal thing in the world, that he'd found us a ride.

"Oh, *legal!* [Cool!]" I enthused. "To São Paulo?"

"Mmm, *não sei* [I don't know]," he replied. "*Provavelmente* [Probably]."

I chuckled. Of course he didn't know.

But sure enough, Elson was passing São Paulo on his way farther north and has brought us all the way here.

... Now, where is that friend of ours?

DAY 86: THURSDAY 12TH JUNE 2014, 07.15
CLODOALDO'S APARTMENT, ANDARAÍ, RIO DE JANEIRO, BRAZIL

STEVE

A gunshot just went off outside. At least I think that's what it was. There are three favelas on the hills in front of Clodoaldo's apartment here in Rio de Janeiro, so I guess I'm supposed to assume it related to them.

We survived São Paulo unscathed, despite the multiple warnings we received. Indeed, it wasn't until we arrived here in Rio last night that we saw our first favela. And then we saw a few more. It seems there are quite a few here, although we had expected as many in São Paulo and weren't aware of passing any.

The World Cup starts today and we are glad to be in Rio to soak up the atmosphere as Brazil kick off against Croatia at 5pm. Artur, whose mother Elsa and her boyfriend Clodoaldo are hosting us, plans to take us on a tour of the city.

The hospitality of Brazilians continues to amaze, as does their obsession with danger.

"You're very courageous," said our first driver, Enrique, yesterday morning, as he took us to a *posto* on the edge of São Paulo.

We thanked him, but said we didn't feel very courageous because we had yet to feel in any danger. (Perhaps we aren't trying hard enough.)

Enrique was the first of seven drivers yesterday and with each one we discussed the topic. Yet with each one we felt less in danger from and more enamoured with Brazilians. Gone were the trials of last week. This was a good old-fashioned day's hitchhiking, each driver adding his story to our tale.

… Another loud bang has just sounded outside, but maybe it wasn't gunfire after all. It could just as easily have been a firecracker. Brazilians get a day off to enjoy the start of the World Cup and it seems to me that you're much more likely to encounter a partying Brazilian than a dangerous one.

DAY 87: FRIDAY 13TH JUNE 2014, 21.20
CLODOALDO'S APARTMENT, ANDARAÍ, RIO DE JANEIRO, BRAZIL

Jo

This morning I was dreaming of home, when we were awoken by an almighty explosion.

"What was th-"
BANG!
"-at?"
"I don't -"
BANG! BANG!
"- know! A bo-"
BANG! BANG-BANG-BANG!
"-mb?"

What with Rio's reputation, and the anti-World Cup protest that took place not long after our recce to the centre yesterday afternoon, a bomb seemed a possible explanation. We sat still for a few moments as the deafening crashes continued, the noise exacerbated by echoes ricocheting around the valley.

Once we'd established that death was not imminent, we slid open our window to inspect the view. There was no burning wall of fire in the vicinity, which suggested that our guess was probably wide of the mark. Soon enough, coloured lights in the sky revealed the cause of the cacophony: fireworks. We didn't know what they were for, or why 6am was a good time to be setting them off, but it calmed our nerves enough for us to return to sleep when the assault finished 15 minutes later.

Assuming that we weren't the only ones disturbed by the goings-on, at breakfast we asked around for an explanation. Clodoaldo came to the rescue: June 13 is a day of celebration for Santo Antônio, the patron saint of marriage. Now, we've nothing against Saint Anthony per se, but at a church we visited in Curitiba the congregation sang a hymn to him, and now we've had cause to fear for our lives in apparent celebration of him. That's quite enough of Santo Antônio, thank you.

Though I had entered São Paulo and Rio with high hopes regarding our safety, today I finally felt I was sinking, unable to keep my head above all this talk of fear and danger. It is never-ending. The frequency of warnings was already high – every taxi driver in São Paulo, every driver we've hitched with, every host – but now we're in Rio, I'm finding that the intensity has increased. Artur is uneasy, having been mugged recently; it's understandable, but with every street on which we're told to be careful and every time he glances over his shoulder, I am more desperate to shrug it all away.

The difficulty is that, not having had any time on our own in Rio, we just don't know if we need to be so hyper-cautious. Is it really, as we've been told, bristling with malicious intent on every corner? Or can we behave as we would in, say, London (a city of around the same population), taking normal precautions but without being burdened by this blanket of unease?

Of course, London doesn't have favelas. They are everywhere in Rio, glittering at night on the hillsides yonder and stretching into every district we've passed in the daytime. Artur tells us favelas spring up illegally but that after a time the land legitimately belongs to the occupants. While the leaders of the drug cartels hold the power in the favelas, most of the inhabitants are normal people who simply cannot afford to live elsewhere. Rent on an average apartment is around 2,000 Rs (£500) per month before bills; a bus driver earns 1,800 Rs. Safe areas are rendered unaffordable.

The cartels look out for the residents in their favelas, paying for healthcare or covering bills. In the run-up to the World Cup, 200 of Rio's favelas (there are around 500 more) have been "pacified", meaning that the police have stormed in, overthrown the drug lords and installed their own lookouts. That's not paying the medical bills, though. It's a complex situation.

9. AN UNEXPECTED HITCH

DAY 90: MONDAY 16TH JUNE 2014, 16.11
ICARAÍ BEACH, NITERÓI, RIO DE JANEIRO, BRAZIL

STEVE

Now this was not supposed to happen.

You find us on a beach in Niterói, a city separated from Rio by a 13km bridge, attempting to work out a new plan of action. The old one didn't work out so well.

It all started on Friday afternoon, when we arrived (for the first time) at the federal police office in Rio's International Airport. It had been quite a trek just to get there, but all would have been worthwhile if we had achieved our visit's aim: two visa stamps providing us with an extra 30 days in Brazil.

Ever since receiving just 30 days upon arrival in Corumbá, we knew we would need to extend our stay somewhere along the line. We just didn't expect it to be so hard.

We left empty-handed on Friday (apparently the police don't work on Friday afternoons) but with the promise that all would be resolved if we returned on Monday morning.

But then Monday – today – arrived and we went back only to find ourselves in the hands of one of the most odious men I have ever had the misfortune to meet. The "Big Boss", as his colleagues referred to him, was altogether disagreeable from the moment he set eyes on us.

At first he disguised the fact that he spoke English. (It wasn't obvious why.) And it was all downhill from there.

"I'm sorry, I can't help you," he told us, when eventually he remembered his English. "You don't have the necessary documents. I'm surprised they gave you 30 days in the first place. I would have given you *one*!"

The document in question was a receipt proving purchase of a ticket out of the country, something that on our journey is of course impossible.

We had hoped to avoid this dilemma by printing a bank statement proving our worth and handing the man a letter from Jo's old employers, verifying our intentions. We had hoped these documents, plus a little compassion, might be enough to see us through. Unfortunately, compassion was in short supply. The man only apologised again, with zero sincerity, and shoved me out of the way to make space for his next victim.

By this time it was around midday and we were advised by the man's more sympathetic colleague to try our luck in Niterói.

"Sorry guys, he's really just a terrible man," said our young ally, as we left with Jo in tears and yours truly in a quiet rage.

"Don't worry darling," I said to Jo, as we headed for Niterói. "All will be well."

Well, I was wrong about that. Four hours later and it is clear that little is well. When eventually we arrived at the right office in Niterói, having been misdirected twice, we were told that the passport service for foreigners operates only on Wednesday mornings, and for a maximum of just 20 foreigners.

"And it's the *Copa*," said the lady behind the counter, "so you'd better make sure you get here really early!"

This news, which would have been difficult to stomach without our previous trials, took us to breaking point. Tears streamed from Jo's eyes and I struggled to summon the required strength to promise, once more, that all would be well.

Now we must decide whether to wait here for two days in the hope that we make the cut on Wednesday morning, or to hitch swiftly northward to Belo Horizonte, hoping there to find a friendlier federal police officer before our visas expire on Thursday. If those plans fail, I'm not sure what we'll do.

DAY 92: WEDNESDAY 18TH JUNE 2014, 08.25
NITERÓI FEDERAL POLICE OFFICE, NITERÓI, RJ, BRAZIL

Jo

I am in a state of complete agitation – it's a wonder I can write at all. My heart is running a sprint race, while my stomach has been left somewhere near the start line, and they don't seem likely to reconcile in the near future. I slept terribly last night, continually interrupted by lucid dreams of passport disasters.

For someone in such emotional flux, the passport office waiting system is a form of slow torture: arrive as early as possible (8am – we left Clodoaldo's just after 6am) to put one's name on a list; wait until 9.30am to be issued a ticket; wait until 10am for people to start being seen; wait as long as it takes for your turn. The office shuts at noon, though, so good luck!

According to all the lists we have been given, we now have all we need (and more) for that tiny little stamp that would mean we won't be thrown out of the country tomorrow. Saying that, we thought we'd be fine on Monday, and even more so yesterday, as we returned to the airport having paid the visa-extension fee and booked a bus ticket to prove our exit strategy (with no intention of using it, of course). We should have known that the office would shut early for the Brazil v Mexico game.

This is another situation in which our attitude has played a significant role: if we'd have viewed this running around as but a minor annoyance, I would not now be melting slowly from the tension. It hasn't helped that everything takes so long – it is two hours on various modes of public transport from Clodoaldo's to the airport, and another two hours from the airport to Niterói. There is no such thing as a quick fix when it comes to Brazilian bureaucracy.

Yesterday, as we tried to book our bus ticket, the unreliable Internet service at the airport became our latest enemy. Why are you being THIS SLOW? Is it deliberate? Who are you working for? We were advised to go to the main bus station in person instead, a suggestion we refused point-blank – it would have been another two-hour round trip from the airport.

Later, heading away after discovering the closure of the airport office (thwarted for *another* day!), we passed that bus station.

"To think," Steve said, "we would just be getting here, only to return to the airport to find it was a completely wasted journey."

I shuddered.

So now I am frozen in my chair, shackled by the suspense of it all. It will be a euphoric moment if the process is just a quick-stamp-and-we're-done once our turn comes around. Surely that isn't so much to ask?

DAY 93: THURSDAY 19TH JUNE 2014, 22.18
JORGE'S BAR, JORGE E CLAUDETTE'S HOLIDAY HOME, CORREAS, PETRÓPOLIS, RIO DE JANEIRO, BRAZIL

STEVE

Our visa troubles seem a lifetime ago now. In fact, they ended only yesterday, but with that a great weight lifted off our shoulders.

In the end, the process concluded in the kind of straightforward manner we had expected all along. No questions were asked about proof of onward travel; no bank statements were required. Just a smile, two stamps and an "on you go". I'm not sure which was greater: our love for the lady in charge at Niterói, or our hatred for the "Big Boss" at the airport. If he'd had his way, we'd be deported today. As it is, we have another 30 days to enjoy Brazil.

Today was another of those days when hitchhiking seems indisputably the best way to travel. It started with a ride out of the city, courtesy of Elsa and Clodoaldo. They insisted that the centre of Rio was no place to try *carona*, and we were only too glad to accept their offer of a ride.

We waited barely five minutes at our latest *posto* before our next ride, with Vinícius, 22, his father-in-law, Pedro, and their friend, Ronaldo – "Like the football player," said Pedro, as he handed us a Brazil flag to keep as a souvenir.

Given how difficult we had expected it to be to hitch out of Rio, we felt we were doing rather well. And that was before the arrival of Jorge, 82, a retired lawyer with a striking resemblance to Al Pacino, and his wife Claudette, 75, on their way to their holiday home in Correas.

It is blissfully quiet here, a far cry from the firecrackers of Rio, and we are thoroughly appreciating this unexpected treat.

Other than our troubles with the federal police, we enjoyed our stay in Rio. It was there that we watched the start of the World Cup and, despite the protests, it is clear that this nation truly loves football.

Brazil flags colour the streets, though we are told that there are usually considerably more of them. And when Brazil play, the bars are crowded and the cold beer flows freely.

So far the *Copa* appears to have been a success, although the protests rumble on. In São Paulo today rioters ransacked shops and clashed with police. Still, we are yet to witness any violence first-hand. Only kindness. Over and over again. Save for that dastardly fellow in the federal police.

Jo

"What have we done to deserve this?" Steve just asked me. It was a rhetorical question, because as usual the answer is "absolutely nothing".

We have been adopted by an octogenarian called Jorge, invited to join his family in their holiday home and put up in the cosy pool house. Jorge and Claudette cooked us a feast and insisted that we consider the house our own. All of this more than compensates for their decision to serve dinner at the very moment the England v Uruguay match began, forcing us to peer surreptitiously at the television screen from across the room. There wasn't much to see in the end, anyway.

So, our time in Rio is over, and we're lucky (apparently) to have made it out alive. If I am to have understood correctly the gestures accompanying the ceaseless warnings, we were to run a very sincere risk of being stabbed by some kind of sabre if we had walked out of the city on our intended route. It was just as well, then, that Clodoaldo and Elsa gave us a helping hand, and from then on the day went swimmingly: another enormous city exited successfully.

DAY 95: SATURDAY 21ST JUNE 2014, 21.26
HOTEL VITALY, CONTAGEM, MINAS GERAIS, BRAZIL

STEVE

The friendliness of the people here is quite extraordinary. Everywhere we go, we are treated like royalty, just for being foreigners. Sometimes it is slightly overwhelming.

Take today, our first day in Belo Horizonte, the state capital of Minas Gerais. Over the course of the day, we were approached around 10 times by a variety of curious strangers asking where we were from and whether we liked Brazil. On each occasion, the inquisitor seemed overjoyed to learn we were from England, and sympathised with our country's premature World Cup exit.

The incident with the police in Rio and the incessant talk of danger had threatened to cloud our judgement of the country, but we cannot ignore the kindness we continue to receive. Elsa just called to tell us that a friend of hers here in Belo Horizonte has agreed to host us. We had almost forgotten what a hotel looked like before we arrived here last night. For two weeks, from Curitiba to Correas, we had known nothing but Brazilian hospitality.

Our time in Correas ended as it had begun, in the back seats of Jorge and Claudette's car. After treating us to a fine breakfast, our new adoptive grandparents transported us back to the BR running north and left us in the nearest *posto*.

"I have great admiration for what you're doing," Jorge said as we parted.

Our next driver, a 40-year-old *caminhoneiro* named Adeílson, who brought us all the way to Belo Horizonte, offered a rather different perspective. His English was non-existent and his Portuguese almost incomprehensible, but the man was so expressive that it was easy to catch his drift. At first he asked if we were hippies. When we told him we weren't, and after learning about our plans to *carona* to Alaska, he pointed to his head and gestured that we might have a few screws loose.

Adeílson, with his swept-back jet-black hair and cowboy hat, was quite the character. For seven hours, we shared jokes and perspectives on life. Adeílson said he was "half Catholic, half Allan Kardec" (the Frenchman who founded Spritism, or Kardecism), but that he didn't really practise either.

Kardecism is popular here and we have met several adherents. Apparently the philosophy is based on the teachings of Jesus, to some extent, but has an added emphasis on communication with the spirit world. We are told Kardecists believe in communicating with the dead, but don't tend to practise it. That is left to followers of Umbanda, a religion that came to Brazil from Africa and incorporates many of Allan Kardec's teachings. One of our friends in Curitiba, who practises Umbanda, told us that Kardecism is a philosophy, while Umbanda is a religion, which uses mediums who actively seek to interact with spirits.

As in Argentina, Chile and Bolivia, we have found that religion, or spirituality, is part of life here. "*Vai com Deus*" (Go with God), "*Meu Deus!*" (Oh my God!) and "*Se Deus quiser*" (God-willing) are common phrases. The question of whether God exists seems irrelevant here; perhaps more relevant would be *which* god exists.

Jo

It occurred to me earlier that my fluency in the language of football is about on a par with my fluency in Portuguese. I get so far and think I'm doing rather well, and then something exposes me for the pretender I am.

This was displayed most recently when Steve was verbally processing the various options allowing England to qualify for the next round of the World Cup, despite a second defeat on Tuesday. If Italy did one thing and Uruguay did something else and Costa Rica were either really good or really bad, then, in one way or another, it would be significant for our boys. I got lost somewhere in the midst of it all.

When we stopped for a snack break with Adeílson yesterday, we heard that Italy had lost their match against Costa Rica. This was the one eventuality that would lead to the England team packing their bags, I'd got that much. Once again, football will not be coming home to our shores. Steve keeps sighing forlornly.

The World Cup is proving advantageous for our hitchhiking – no-one looks surprised to see us. The addition of a Brazil flag, now my left-hand accompaniment to my right-hand thumbing, is proving popular. Several passersby in central Belo Horizonte this afternoon deliberately approached us to say how pleased they were to see so many tourists (and that we should watch our bags, obviously).

DAY 97: MONDAY 23RD JUNE 2014, 12.31
OLGA'S HOUSE, CORAÇÃO EUCARÍSTICO, BELO HORIZONTE, MINAS GERAIS, BRAZIL

STEVE

I've been forced to re-evaluate some things over the past few days. It would seem that I could be accused of having had blinkers on for the past month. Perhaps it's time they came off.

As you know, we've heard a multitude of stories relating to violence and danger here in Brazil, and while we are yet to experience anything first-hand, it would be churlish to disregard them. The latest came this morning over breakfast with our new hosts, Elsa's friend Olga and her 27-year-old son Bruno.

I had just made a comment about how grateful we were that they hadn't burdened us with further tales of woe, when Bruno forced me to reconsider.

"You know, Brazil really is a dangerous place," he said. "I haven't ever been robbed, but I can tell you many stories. Everyone here in Brazil has a friend or family member who has been mugged."

Bruno proceeded to tell us a few tales (most involving guns) of muggings and car hijackings in the streets surrounding their apartment here in the Coração Eucarístico neighbourhood of Belo Horizonte. And this neighbourhood, he said, is no more dangerous than any other. Wherever we went, we would hear the same thing.

About this, we had to agree. It has been the same wherever we have been. From Mih to Talvas, Artur to Clodoaldo, we have been told to watch our backs.

It has been easy for me to shrug off these warnings, having heard similar horror stories around the world, but perhaps it is time I admitted that there must be a foundation to them. Whether or not Jo and I make it through the country unscathed, it is quite apparent that the vast majority of Brazilians live with an element of fear.

"We feel imprisoned by the bad people, and they are free to walk around the streets," Bruno said. "This is why all our houses have barbed wire fences and security cameras."

So where does this leave us, as we consider our plan to hitch westward in the coming days? Are we to change our mindset? Should we allow ourselves to feel scared? Or should we go on, as if we were none the wiser, and hope for the best? Is that naive? Is it misplaced optimism? Or justified faith?

The dangers here are now clear, but equally we know we can rely on the goodness of the vast majority of people here. Given we have made it so very far in the past five weeks, without mishap, I'm tempted to continue on as before, praying that someone overhead will lead us safely on to the border, and beyond.

DAY 99: WEDNESDAY 25TH JUNE 2014, 17.47
OLGA'S HOUSE, CORAÇÃO EUCARÍSTICO, BELO HORIZONTE, MINAS GERAIS, BRAZIL

Jo

Steve is sick. Some germ or other has struck lucky in his internal system and is throwing a party at both ends of his body. It was all very sudden – everything was totally fine until 6 o'clock this morning when Steve checked in for an emergency appointment in the bathroom and remained there for about an hour. Since then he has been mainly horizontal on the bed, apart from a few repeat visits to use the facilities.

We don't know what has brought this on, and I am showing no symptoms; it leaves me to be the designated bucket cleaner, which isn't a perk. Olga and Bruno are entirely unfazed by the situation and have urged us to stay for as long as we need. Depending on how Steve progresses, we might not do any hitchhiking this week, which would feel very odd.

Yesterday we went to a live World Cup match – England v Costa Rica – in Belo Horizonte's Mineirão Stadium. It was fun, if not exciting; the result was a 0-0 draw, but it didn't make a difference to England's future in the *Copa* anyway. We wondered what the reaction of the core England fans to our left would be, as the Brazilians in the crowd started shouting, "HEY! *ELIMINADO!*" (equivalent to "See you later, losers!"), but as English footy supporters aren't renowned for their proficiency in foreign languages, they simply cheered rowdily in response.

We've also finally had our first proper taste of Brazil's dance culture. Bruno invited us to a barbecue with his friends, all of whom like to play music, or to dance, or both. We were introduced to *forró*, a genre of dance from north-eastern Brazil, and the music and singing went on for hours. This happened again on Monday night after the Brazil v Cameroon game, when the same group socialised together in the middle of a street, grooving until about 1am. That's just what happens here.

DAY 102: SATURDAY 28TH JUNE 2014, 20.00
PAULINHO'S POUSADA, CAMPO REDONDO, NR. IBICOARA, CHAPADA DIAMANTINA, BAHIA, BRAZIL

STEVE

Oh dear, we've gone the wrong way again! Aiming for Brasília in the central state of Goiás, and slightly closer to the border with Peru in the west, we find ourselves in Bahia, the southernmost state of Brazil's famed northeast, and some 1,000km east of Brasília.

"Bahia is Brazil's soul," enthused Daniel, 33, who drove us here yesterday. "This is Brazil! Not São Paulo. Not Belo Horizonte. Not Brasília. *This* is Brazil – the real Brazil – and I love it!"

Daniel, a sound engineer, and his best friend, 26-year-old radio DJ Sandra, picked us up from the service station where Olga left us yesterday morning. We remain with them tonight.

This couple of dope-smoking hippies are on a 20-day vacation in the place they see as their homeland.

"My homeland is not my queen, my government, my city, or my football team; it is not samba or Carnival. It is the land, the birds and the trees. It is Bahia," said Daniel, who wore a purple t-shirt sporting a giant picture of the Hindu elephant goddess, Ganesha, on front and back.

Sandra, who has a tattoo of the outline of Brazil on her right shoulder and looks like a young Helena Bonham Carter, spoke of Bahia in the same glowing terms.

We learnt a great deal from this enlightened pair on our more than 1,000km journey together. And yes, we are now farther from Brasília than when we started out yesterday morning. But, not for the first time, we were told we really mustn't miss this part of Brazil, so we haven't.

For 10 hours yesterday and another three today, we travelled in the back of Daniel's blue VW, wedged between our bags, staring ahead through the windscreen past Daniel's lucky mascot (a little black plastic cow) as the world whizzed by. For the bulk of the journey, the car was a hotbox of marijuana fumes. My head is still spinning. Even now, the familiar haze floats into our room from the kitchen next door, in the extremely hippie-fied *pousada* in which we rest.

Daniel's lucky cow deserves slightly more introduction, for it provides some insight into his philosophy.

"My cow is my 'open way'," Daniel told us yesterday, raising his outermost two fingers to make the sign of a bull. (He seemed to be suggesting that the road was open to him and his cow, and that nothing could stop them.) "For more than seven years and 10,000km, I have travelled in this way."

It reminded me of something our friend Pablo from Tucumán had said.

"I just do *this*," Pablo said, licking the tip of his index finger and raising it to feel which way the wind was blowing. Pablo told us that he had done that very thing before electing to pick us up. *Should I or shouldn't I stop? Finger up ... Yes!*

Daniel's philosophy seems similar. It is certainly spiritual.

Our Bohemian friends told us they practise no religion but have "a lot of faith". In nature. In people. And in the spiritual realm.

Here in Bahia, everyone seems to be "spiritual". Daniel and Sandra are very much at home. This week it is the turn of Saint John to be remembered with a festival here in Brazil, and nowhere is he celebrated more than in Bahia. There are green, yellow, white and blue flags everywhere, and they're not for the *Copa*. They're all for St. John, apparently one of the most important saints here, who is believed to possess the capacity to bless the land.

We poor Protestants are struggling to understand this take on Christianity, but the spirituality goes much deeper than Catholic saints.

Bahia, Daniel told us, is also home to Brazil's African community – the largest outside Africa – and it was they who founded Candomblé, a religion which shares similarities with Umbanda and Kardecism, and named its gods after Catholic saints. The blending of religions in South America continues to amaze.

Daniel and Sandra told us that Bahia is the heartbeat of Brazil and possesses a "unique energy". That heartbeat was certainly thumping today at around 3.30pm, as Brazil conquered Chile on penalties to reach the quarter-finals. We watched the end of the game at a party with some of Daniel and Sandra's fellow Bohemians, two of whom are hosting us tonight.

Tomorrow, we are to undertake a two-day hike to a nearby waterfall. It is very beautiful here – mountainous and green. Easy to see why people like it.

DAY 103: SUNDAY 29TH JUNE 2014, 15.17
PAULINHO'S POUSADA, CAMPO REDONDO, NR. IBICOARA, CHAPADA DIAMANTINA, BAHIA, BRAZIL

STEVE

The waterfall hike didn't pan out – apparently it's too cloudy – but we have enjoyed a sleepy Sunday here in the tranquil settlement of Campo Redondo, 20km from the nearest town of Ibicoara. In fact, there are so many waterfalls around here that we did manage to visit one, just a short walk away. That was impressive enough.

Indeed, everything is quite impressive here in the national park of Chapada Diamantina, famed for its flat-top mountains, waterfalls and diamond mines. Gold in Minas (which means "mines"), diamonds in Bahia; this was once a very rich part of the world, although we are told that much of that wealth has since found its way overseas, not least to Britain.

Yet it is Brazil's spiritual wealth that is on my mind again today, and in particular a religious movement I had never heard of before, named Santo Daime. This movement, which like many others here borrows elements of Christianity, translates literally as "Saint Give Me" and is known for its use of an hallucinogenic tea that is believed to tap into a seldom-used part of the brain to produce chemical reactions that can take the user deep into the spiritual realm.

Daniel refers to his experience of the tea, deep inside the Amazon rainforest where the religion began, as one of the defining moments of his life. Such was its impact that he has thoroughly recommended that we try it for ourselves if we come across it as we journey west.

Daniel said the tea stimulates the chemicals in the brain released only at moments of intense emotion, such as near-death experiences. He said that when he drank it, his brain slowed and he was able to see every aspect of his life in great detail. I suppose I can see the attraction of that, but I am satisfied to wait until the end to experience it.

Tomorrow we will return to the road to Brasília. We are slightly in the middle of nowhere, so it may take us some time, but we hope it won't be too long, as we have just three weeks now until our second lot of 30 days expires, and more than 4,000km to cover before we reach the border with Peru.

DAY 103 (CONTINUED): 23.10

JO

This evening, as we were strolling around Ibicoara, a group of smartly dressed adults and children invited us to join them at their Baptist church.

"Ah, Baptists," I thought. "I know their ways."

I was wrong.

These particular adherents of the denomination evidently hailed from a school of teaching promoting that the louder you shout, the better God will hear you. We were a little taken aback as several demure-looking women gave short testimonies from the front and, one by one, ended up shrieking passionately.

"Nothing to worry about," I thought. "It's just a different style. It'll be fine."

This was before the preacher began, however, whereupon my eardrums imploded and I developed a possibly permanent hearing defect. (This was my concern at the time. I have since made a full recovery.)

He looked so normal. He can't have been older than 20, with black-rimmed glasses and a mouth full of braces. Within seconds of beginning the sermon, however, he was screaming. I don't think he could have been any louder. There was a vein throbbing on the side of his head, and I had to adopt the favoured middle-distance stare for fear I would at some point witness his head exploding.

It might have been bearable without amplification, but the addition of a cranked-up microphone made the noise intolerable. I have no idea what the chap spoke about, either, because it was impossible to listen. Every time I tried, within moments I had reverted to a silent but desperate protest: "WHY ARE YOU SHOUTING AT ME?"

We bid a retreat before the service was fully over, hoping that no-one would intercept us to ask why. We wouldn't have been able to hear them, anyway.

10. A CAMINHONEIRO'S LIFE

DAY 104: MONDAY 30TH JUNE 2014, 18.10
ALBERTO'S TRUCK, EN ROUTE TO LUÍS EDUARDO MAGALHÃES, BAHIA, BRAZIL

STEVE

As if hitchhiking the length of the Americas wasn't challenging enough, Jo and I are now attempting to add almost the entire breadth of South America – not the most logical path to Alaska. I blame the Amazon rainforest. If it wasn't for that small cluster of trees, we could take a more diagonal approach.

As it is, even after crossing the border with Peru, we'll still have some way to go to reach the Pan-American Highway on the Pacific coast.

Upon reflection, perhaps it is unfair to blame the Amazon. After all, we were once relatively close to Peru. Since La Paz, we have been travelling farther and farther away.

Well, no longer! Now, in the cabin of Alberto's truck – our fifth and final ride of the day – we are steadily undoing all of the kilometres of the past two months. I'm not sure how many kilometres we will have travelled today, when eventually Alberto deposits us in Luís Eduardo Magalhães, but it will have been a lot. Perhaps 900. Perhaps even 1,000. Not a bad start.

DAY 104 (CONTINUED): 23.54
POUSADA LIMA, LUÍS EDUARDO MAGALHÃES, BAHIA, BRAZIL

JO

In contrast with the 800km in 10 hours that sped by with Daniel and Sandra, the journey with Alberto dragged on endlessly. It might have been because my spine was grumbling about my forced-upright position, or that five hours of the ride took place in darkness, or that we were almost the slowest vehicle on the road.

Alberto provided excellent distraction, however. His appearance was the opposite extreme to our other truck drivers – he was really quite thin, a diminutive figure. At first he came across as somewhat quiet and surly, but before long he had emitted a wicked chuckle and we knew we were going to get on well.

Amongst other things, we talked about the wildlife that could be found in the local area, which included an impressive list of snakes.

"*Não tem cobras na Inglaterra* [There aren't any cobras in England]," I said. Our unprecedentedly in-depth conversation about reptiles had already taught me that while "*cobra*" means "snake", it also means "cobra", but I couldn't be sure exactly how to distinguish between the two.

"*Não tem cobras? Não tem cobras?*" Alberto spluttered in response, plainly flabbergasted by this revelation.

Our discussion progressed to other topics, but apparently the impact lingered, for later I heard Alberto muttering under his breath, "*Não tem cobras!*"

It seems quite feasible he will have nodded off to sleep whispering the same.

DAY 106: WEDNESDAY 2ND JULY 2014, 11.23
DÉSIRÉE AND FRANCOIS' APARTMENT, ASA SUL, BRASÍLIA, DISTRICT FEDERAL, BRAZIL

STEVE

The plan is working. Yesterday we added another 500 kilometres to our journey west by reaching Brasília, Brazil's modern capital, designed (in the shape of an aeroplane!) by the nation's favourite architect, Oscar Niemeyer. And if the last few days are anything to go by, we should have no trouble reaching the frontier with Peru before our visas expire in 17 days.

There are still more than 3,000km to cover, but that doesn't seem so bad when you consider that we have crossed 2,500km – even if not always in the right direction – over the past five days. My only concern is talk of the road being prone to flooding and closure, but there's little we can do about that.

On Monday, we must have waited cumulatively for less than half an hour for our five rides, which ended in our 10-hour journey in Alberto's truck, and yesterday we had to wait for just 10 minutes for our one and only ride in Anderson's white Toyota Hilux.

Anderson, a 28-year-old *fazenda* (farm) worker, was on his way to his native state of Paraná in the south and seemed in a hurry to get there. It took us just four hours to cover the 520km to Brasília, on a single-track road with a not insignificant sprinkling of traffic. We were deposited under a bridge named after another Brazilian racing driver, Ayrton Senna, and it was there that Désirée, 32, our latest friend-of-a-friend, found us, and brought us back to her apartment in Asa Sul, the south wing of Oscar's aeroplane.

DAY 108: FRIDAY 4TH JULY 2014, 07.43
BENCH, JBS MEAT FACTORY, GOIÂNIA, GOIÁS, BRAZIL

JO

As our heads begin to clear following a simple breakfast of plain bread rolls and tongue-numbingly sweet black coffee, Steve and I have had a moment of enlightenment about how ridiculous our life is.

We have just spent a night sleeping in the back of a truck usually occupied by raw meat; both dinner and breakfast were consumed within the perimeters of a meat factory; along with our driver, José, we are almost the only people in the vicinity not kitted out from head to toe in matching white overalls, wellies and hard hats. A whole herd of these workers just shuffled out for a break and the man relaxing on the adjacent bench has blood stains on his boots. This is not within the usual confines of normal.

The stench from the meat factory grows increasingly pungent. I suppose the workers become acclimatised. My innocent nostrils, however, are protesting.

The temperature was high and the empty blue sky appeared fierce and unforgiving as we wended our way yesterday towards our target of Cuiabá, about 1,000 kilometres from Brasília. We passed several patches of land on fire, the cracking earth vulnerable to the smallest spark; apparently this sight is common, and often the fires are just left to burn.

My favourite moment, if I had to put my finger on it, was procuring one lift while still in motion in the previous one.

A crinkly-eyed *caminhoneiro* called Reinaldo had picked us up outside a backwater *posto* and used his truckers' radio to see if he could communicate with any other drivers going our way. No-one responded, so instead, as we approached his stopping point, he slowed down to drive parallel to a huge lorry carrying a tractor.

"Where are you going?" he yelled over the noise of the traffic.

"Goiânia," the driver mouthed back.

"Can you take these two?"

"Sure!"

And that was that.

STEVE

I doubt many other travellers have found themselves inside the compound of the JBS meat factory in Goiânia, waiting for fresh produce to be loaded into the back of a truck. But this is the life we are leading, a *caminhoneiro's* life.

Our night in the back of José's truck was accompanied by the unwelcome scent of meat. I guess it could have been worse. José joked before locking us into the trailer that he could set the temperature to -18°C if we liked. My mind flicked to horror movies, and that was before we arrived here and saw all the blood-speckled factory workers. It's like something from *A Clockwork Orange*.

Fortunately, our new friend is as harmless as he is kind, a big friendly giant with a gappy smile, who looks like the truckers of Eastern Europe (he has Polish blood) and is currently coming to the end of a three-month stint on the road. José told us that, since splitting with his wife seven years ago, he has gone from one three-month journey to the next. He tells us that he likes the lifestyle, but we can't help but feel sorry for him. Our friend, at 40 years of age, says he loves children (he has nine nieces and nephews), but it seems unlikely he will meet anyone with whom to start a family of his own in his current line of work. His story, like so many of the *caminhoneiros* we have met, seems a sad, lonely one.

José was our ninth driver of a long day yesterday, as we began our journey west from Brasília. Goiânia, where you find us, is less than 200km from Brazil's capital. Nine rides seems an awful lot for so short a stretch.

... Oh, what's this? A lady dressed in white has just joined us on our bench and is playing rap music through the speakers on her phone. Lovely. Thanks for sharing.

... Oh good, she's gone.

Once José's truck is fully loaded and ready, we will depart on the road to Campo Grande, back in Mato Grosso do Sul. José has agreed to take us until our routes diverge (300km or so), after which we will seek an alternative ride to take us the remaining distance to Cuiabá.

This has been a record-breaking week. Counting the 1,000km we travelled last weekend, we will have covered around 3,000km in just eight days.

DAY 109: SATURDAY 5TH JULY 2014, 19.43
HOTEL TALISMÃ, RONDONÓPOLIS, MATO GROSSO, BRAZIL

JO

Our night in José's truck was broken periodically by feelings of cold and discomfort, such that yesterday I daydreamed of a wonderfully clean, white-sheet-bedecked, perfect-sleep-inducing bed. This, alas, was not forthcoming. When we arrived at the *posto* that was to be our farewell point with José, it was already 8.30pm. As it was too late to hitch any farther, and with no hotel nearby, we were forced to resort to our tent.

The prospect of a second night's terrible sleep did not fill me with glee. The last time we camped was nearly four months ago, and we haven't risked it since. Begrudgingly, I assisted setting up camp in a corner of the car park, and then consoled myself with a warm shower, using the *posto* facilities. Slowly, reluctantly, I returned to our little blue home.

I slept wonderfully.

STEVE

We're back in tropical-bird territory: Mato Grosso to be exact – the state directly north of where we entered Brazil almost two months ago. No toucans were spotted as we arrived here, but a handful of colourful macaws more than sufficed as a welcome gift.

The last three days have been a slog. We remain short of Cuiabá by 200km, although our progress this past week has been steady. In two weeks our visas will expire and we are still 2,500km short of the border with Peru: quite some way.

This is a large country; that is very apparent. During the 2,000-plus kilometres we covered this week, when we weren't passing staggering metropolises, we were crossing huge expanses of unpopulated land, as far as the eye could see. The horizons seem to extend further here. There is so much space, and it appears that it is being put to good use: corn, maize, cotton, cassava, beans, sugar cane … and hundreds of white cows. Brazil is quite the agricultural giant.

Talking of giants, we had a ride today with one of the tallest women I have ever met. At 192cm, Luanne, 22, dwarfs her truck-driving husband, João, who is 14 years her superior. This couple, like many of our *caminhoneiro* friends, spend most of their lives on the road. Today they were returning home here to Rondonópolis after a week-long trip to Goiás. Sometimes, they told us, they go away for up to a month.

Still, not a patch on José.

DAY 111: MONDAY 7TH JULY 2014, 20.47
HOTEL TREVO, VÁRZEA GRANDE, CUIABÁ, MATO GROSSO, BRAZIL

JO

All right, no need to panic. We may have been forced to move hotel rooms due to an amassing congress of creepy crawlies, and now we may be only half a step across the corridor from the previous one, but there's no reason to suppose that said creatures might *actually* creep and crawl. Is there?

Rondonópolis, we have heard, is Brazil's second-hottest city. Hitchhiking away from such a city was never going to be pleasant – no use complaining. Still, when we learned at 9am that the temperature was already 30°C, it did feel a bit daunting.

Following an early breakfast, we departed from our hotel just before 8.30am; within 15 minutes, trickles of perspiration were sliding down my back. At 10am we elected to move locations, at which point cleanliness wholly surrendered itself to the inevitable effects of such activity. By the time we ended up at the *posto* where we finally found a ride, both of us were coated in a layer of sticky dust, patches of red earth clinging to the most sweat-drenched areas of our t-shirts.

Steve's transformation was particularly startling. Having worn flip-flops to counteract the heat, his feet were now almost entirely camouflaged against the ground beneath them and his clothes looked like he'd been tobogganing on sand dunes. Even now, a shower and a thorough foot wash later, souvenir streaks of dirt remain. Maybe this is what people mean when they talk of being at one with nature, and we should celebrate it.

DAY 113: WEDNESDAY 9TH JULY 2014, 06.43
HOTEL TREVO, VÁRZEA GRANDE, CUIABÁ, MATO GROSSO, BRAZIL

STEVE

Brazil crashed out of the World Cup yesterday. A crushing 7-1 defeat to Germany in the semi-finals ensured there will be no dream World Cup win on home turf for the five-time champs. The humiliating loss brought tears to the eyes of players and fans alike. The pressure on the players had been immense since the big kick-off in São Paulo almost one month ago. One could argue that Brazil's marketing wagon didn't help matters. The banner on the team bus particularly comes to mind: "Brace yourselves, [World Cup] number six is coming!"

Many of the Brazilians we have spoken to have said the political fortunes of the current President, Dilma Rousseff, were aligned to the fortunes of the national team. This year's elections, they said, would be a formality if the team won.

Some of our friends predicted riots if they failed to win. Some, like Daniel in Bahia, said the World Cup has been good for Brazil simply because it has brought the nation's problems with money and corruption to light.

"I hope we lose, so people continue to fight," he told us.

I suppose only time will tell whether the World Cup has benefited the country. It will certainly leave an impact, and now that Brazil has exited the competition, perhaps the time has come for that impact to be felt.

In some ways it feels like a pity we won't be around to see it. Jo and I are ourselves heading firmly for the exit door, hoping today to hitch a ride north-west towards Porto Velho, and onwards to Rio Branco and the border with Peru.

Jo

Steve and I have almost stopped noticing the number of hugely overweight Brazilians who waddle along the streets around us. It's a sad realisation that, along with the continuing trend of adults with braces, it's probably the most unifying trait we've observed. It's not surprising that the *caminhoneiros* are usually large, such is their lifestyle, but the problem goes beyond that.

It doesn't, however, seem to deter many women from wearing impressively skin-tight tops and short-is-the-word shorts, accompanied by skyscraper heels. No wonder they're waddling – they should get some credit for being able to move at all in such shoes.

Walking is not the norm here, though, which might be part of the problem. It is a common occurrence that when we're in a city and stop to ask for directions, we're pointed towards a bus stop, as happened in Cuiabá yesterday.

"Do you know a good place to watch the game?" we asked a passerby.

"Yes … but … well, it's very far from here. You can take a bus from over there."

"Oh, OK. How long would it take to walk, roughly?"

"Oh, about 15 minutes. *Bem longe!* [Far. Really, really far!]"

We walked.

DAY 114: THURSDAY 10TH JULY 2014, 13.53
RAYMUNDO AND DELMA'S HOUSE, COMMUNIDADE SÃO JORGE, MATO GROSSO, BRAZIL

STEVE

Never refusing an offer can wreak havoc with one's schedule. Here we are attempting to reach the border with Peru, yet once more we find ourselves side-tracked.

This time it is the fault of the latest Brazilian family to have taken us into their home. Raymundo, 57, and his wife Dilma, 56, picked us up at 9am from just across the road from our hotel, and quickly invited us to join them for the night in the tranquil community of São Jorge, a settlement of around 60 homes that you won't find on most maps.

Raymundo's 84-year-old mother is currently singing spiritual songs from a chair on the other side of the patio, as Jo and I relax in a couple of hammocks. The day is still young, but our work ended some hours ago. We have been here since 10am and in that time have been well fed, shown some of the sights (fields of white cows, a neighbour's house and the local well) and even gone fishing at a nearby fresh-water lake. Raymundo caught a fish, which we consumed. We contributed nothing. Indeed, once more it feels we have done little to deserve this latest showing of kindness.

"My family won't believe it when I tell them we had an English couple at our home!" Raymundo told us. "They will think me very important."

Perhaps that's it, then. Just by being English, we have earned ourselves a free bed for the night and a day off in the countryside, with nothing but the sound of singing birds and Raymundo's sweet old mum.

DAY 117: SUNDAY 13TH JULY 2014, 09.09
HOTEL ECOS CONFORT, PORTO VELHO, RONDÔNIA, BRAZIL

JO

Some drivers we spend several hours with; some even more than a day; and then there are some who intersect with our journey only briefly. Brito was one such driver: he picked us up from the *posto* where Raymundo left us and took us to the federal police stop only a couple of kilometres away.

Our drive together was short, but Brito fully capitalised on the time, seizing the opportunity to castigate us for not having children yet, thereby denying God's blessing upon our lives.

"In the Catholic wedding service," he informed us, "we're asked if we'll accept all the children God gives us. We answer 'yes'."

"It's OK!" I wanted to plead. "We do want children! Like, maybe a hundred?"

I thought this might have placated him, but, unfortunately, in the eight minutes of our acquaintance, I was unable to get a word in. There was certainly no time to discuss that, in Britain, we are considered rather young to be married at all, let alone to begin producing offspring.

Brito had moved on. Before we parted, he made sure to add that we should be careful about Colombia, informing us matter-of-factly that all Colombians are communists and related to Hugo Chávez – or words to that effect.

STEVE

My body clock is all over the place. Nine o'clock may seem a normal kind of time to be up, but it doesn't feel very normal today.

This time yesterday we were walking into the centre of Porto Velho, having caught just a couple of hours' sleep in our tent at a *posto* on the edge of town. The previous day – Friday – seemed to go on forever. Indeed, after just two hours' kip it didn't feel like a new day on Saturday when we began our hike into the city.

To add to our confusion, we had travelled over 1,000km on Friday, a journey that comprised three rides in 23 hours. The third of these was by far the longest and began at the federal police checkpoint where Brito left us.

We were still questioning why Colombians might be related to a Venezuelan dictator when an officer approached. Introducing himself as Adeílson, the officer informed us that *carona* would be very difficult for us and told us to sit down for a while and enjoy some coffee while he considered the matter.

The half-hour or so we spent there seemed endless, as vehicle after vehicle passed on the other side of the road, while we sat, unable to thumb a ride. Eventually Adeílson decided it would be best if he asked drivers on our behalf. We agreed that this sounded like a good plan, but our adviser didn't quite understand our urgency, and enquired only of truck drivers and only every so often.

"This is a difficult time to be asking for a ride to Porto Velho," he told us, after approaching one *caminhoneiro*. "Trucks don't go there until later."

This surprised us. It was still early in the day and Porto Velho was a long way away. Surely it would make sense to leave as early as possible. We told him we didn't necessarily need to find a ride all the way to Porto Velho – anywhere would do. Adeílson considered this for a moment, told us not to worry (our expressions must have betrayed us) and assured us he would find us a ride. We weren't convinced, but could do little else but wait.

Then three trucks approached and our helper was stirred back into action, calling the first to a halt. We crossed our fingers as he conversed with the driver.

Thumbs up; he'd done it. We were told the trucker wasn't going to Porto Velho, but that he could take us some of the way.

"Phew," we thought. Anything to get us moving again.

What we didn't see coming was, well, anything that followed. The first surprise was the character in the driver's seat, 46-year-old Fernando, complete with *caminhoneiro* cap and beer (or fizzy drink) belly. This man was possibly the most talkative that I have ever encountered and chatted at length and in great detail about anything and everything from the moment we entered his cab until the moment we departed, at 4 o'clock the next morning. This was the second surprise – our driver's destination – and it took us several hours to work it out.

For quite some time, we assumed we were to be dropped halfway, in the town of Vilhena.

"I'm not going to Porto Velho on this journey," we felt sure we had heard Fernando say.

And then we thought he had asked us what we were going to do in Vilhena. Would we stay in a hotel, for example? We told him we weren't actually planning to do anything in Vilhena and would probably just search for another ride, to Porto Velho.

Fernando had nodded, but then Vilhena came and went and on we travelled. By the time the sun went down, we had arrived in the town of Pimenta Bueno and understood for the first time that, in fact, our friend was planning to drive to Porto Velho on this very journey, but that he would not arrive there until the morrow.

We spent some time searching for a hotel in Pimenta Bueno and discussing where and at what time we might meet the next day, but then Fernando noticed that the cooler on his trailer was malfunctioning and, for the sake of the tomatoes inside, it was decided it would be better if we carried on to Porto Velho at that very moment.

Thus, the next 10 hours looked rather different than they might have, but much like the 10 hours before. Fernando talked at us incessantly until we were released at a posto on the edge of Porto Velho.

(Oh, and yes, we saw more parrots, a toucan and the carcasses of lots more exotic species, including huge tapirs and an armadillo, which had sadly met their end on the road.)

All in all, it has been an exhausting few days. Thank the Lord for Sunday, our day off and a very welcome and deserved rest.

Jo

If you are looking for an experience that will get the blood racing, try sitting in the cab of a truck when one of its tyres bursts. Terrifying. We had been with Fernando for almost three hours when this occurred: a sudden "BANG", and then nothing. There were no obvious consequences, the other 15 wheels seeming to compensate sufficiently, so we continued at a slightly reduced speed to the next *posto*, 10 minutes away. My blood pressure had just about recovered by then.

For a double thrill, allow a further three hours or so of normality to pass, and then send a beautiful, exotic bird to slam, breast-first, into the passenger side of the windscreen. Not only will this ensure brief delusions of terror that the sky is falling in, but also there will be the accompanying wrench of sadness that a delightful red and green macaw has prematurely met its end.

Up until the point that we stopped to mend the tyre, our journey with Fernando had been unremarkable. Steve sat next to him in the cab and I was positioned by the window; most of the conversation was between the boys, with Fernando's Portuguese generally easy to follow.

"He's quite chatty, isn't he?" Steve commented at lunchtime. "It's a bit tiring!"

Little did we know what was to come.

About an hour into the next stint of our 1,000-kilometre day, it became clear to me that there must be hidden cameras in the cab, and that in the future viewers would be watching us on some sort of Candid Camera show. Their giggles would become guffaws as the clips showed us after 20 minutes, 90 minutes, three hours, four hours … always with the same set-up: Steve looking drained, me vacant, and Fernando talking. Always talking. Talking, talking, talking.

It was unbelievable. At first I wondered whether he was just relishing having people to converse with, considering that usually he must experience hours and hours of solitude. However, this wasn't being talked *with*, it was being talked *at*. When Steve had already been bullied into silence for a while, I began to time how long it was before he was required to make an affirmative sound. Ten minutes passed before Steve uttered a mere "hmm". Fernando paused briefly to take a breath, and then launched into his next anecdote.

My brain couldn't cope with the sheer volume of words per minute, and I drifted off into my own world for lengthy periods. The views provided enough distraction to keep my mind happily engaged, with vast horizons of agricultural plains followed by patches of hilly forests, and pink-flowered *ipê* trees galore. When I focused back in on the diatribe, I was doubtful I had understood correctly: at one point, Fernando seemed to be telling Steve that his ex-wife had tried to kill him.

"What was he showing you earlier?" I asked Steve when we stopped for a toilet (and talking) break.

"I have no idea," he replied. "It was accompanied by a stabbing gesture, but all I could see was his nipple."

The day and the road wound on, and we swung between being impressed that Fernando had so much to say and being desperate for him to stop. Briefly tiring of his own voice, Fernando rifled through his CD collection to provide us with a new torture: every track of the CD he selected was scratched, and yet we sampled each one just in case, twice round.

The only logical explanation for this farce was that surely, soon, thousands of people would be gleaning cruel enjoyment from our discomfort. There was no other satisfactory explanation.

DAY 119: TUESDAY 15TH JULY 2014, 09.02
MERCADO VELHO, RIO BRANCO, ACRE, BRAZIL

STEVE

For the first time since leaving La Paz more than two months ago, we can now say we are closer to our final destination. After we have navigated the Peruvian border and dipped down slightly to Cusco, we will journey westward to the Pacific coast and then onwards in only one direction: north.

Yesterday, on reaching Rio Branco in Brazil's westernmost state of Acre, we passed the 20,000km mark since leaving Ushuaia. Given that Peru is only around 6,000km from where we started, it is clearer than ever that our route has been anything but linear. Still, we know that once we hit the Pan-American Highway, we will need only to travel the same distance in the next four months as we have in the last four, and, providing we go in a straight line, our target will have been achieved.

We are now just over 300km shy of the Peruvian border and are rewarding ourselves for recent progress with a day off. Four days for 300km should prove straightforward enough. If all goes to plan, we will arrive with time to spare and together breathe a sigh of relief. No more clashes with the federal police of Brazil for us, thank you very much!

The journey yesterday was particularly picturesque, as we skirted along the bottom of the great Amazon rainforest. On a road that is closed by flooding for two months of the year (April and May, we were reliably informed by one of our drivers), we crossed several rivers whose waters had breached the neighbouring fields. For 200km, we were surrounded by tropical trees and vast rivers, above which fluttered hundreds of yellow butterflies. We are sad to miss out on the Amazon proper farther north, but yesterday's journey rivalled our passage through the Pantanal for sheer stunning scenery, the like of which we had never before seen.

From a hitchhiking standpoint, it was also blissfully pain-free. Aside from a one-hour wait for our third ride in the town of Jaci Paraná, we spent hardly any time waiting, which was just as well given the temperature. In this part of Brazil, there is no winter; only hot and wet, or hot and dry. From a practical perspective (not least the road being open), we are glad to have arrived in the dry season, but the heat and humidity are overwhelming.

Our fourth ride, which I spent clinging on to the back of a trailer, was my favourite, but it was our sixth and penultimate ride that proved the most insightful. We travelled with Wolmer, a 40-year-old *caminhoneiro* of German descent from Santa Catarina, for five hours, during which time he taught us a great deal, especially about his fellow truckers. One thing, in particular, sticks in the mind.

"More than 50 per cent of truckers use cocaine to stay awake at night," Wolmer told us. "Maybe even 80 per cent."

Wolmer said that he had never tried cocaine, but that it was common practice among *caminhoneiros* and easily accessible, particularly in Acre, which borders Bolivia, Peru and Colombia.

"Don't truckers have problems with the police?" I asked.

"No," he replied. "The police are very corrupt. A 50-real note is all they need."

We had heard similar stories before, both about the police and about *caminhoneiros*, but we had never assumed the problems could be so pervasive. Was Wolmer exaggerating? Whom, we wondered, of all the *caminhoneiros* we had travelled with, used cocaine? Did they do so while we were with them?

"Where did you hear those statistics?" I asked.

"Oh, nowhere," he replied. "But I've driven to every state of Brazil and seen it for myself. It's everywhere."

Jo

With so few clothes in our possession, the weekly use of a hotel laundry service is essential. As the temperature rises, the need is even more pressing: Steve turns into a Neanderthal every time we travel, and it isn't pleasant to don our bedraggled rags for more than a couple of days in a row.

Yesterday we set out in clean outfits, yet within two hours had reverted to disgraceful exhibits; 60% humidity is a killer for the unsullied veneer. As we stood with the sun pounding heavily on our delicate bodies, I realised that my biological composition had shifted to 80% sweat, 20% human. Had we not been picked up, I believe I might eventually have melted onto the dust-covered tarmac beneath me.

As well as hearing about corrupt cops and coke-head *caminhoneiros* during our ride with Wolmer, we learned about the problem of prostitution in Brazil. At the time of the World Cup there were reports of an increase in the trade, but the industry was already strong – there are motels everywhere here, with flashy neon signs and outrageous names, where prostitution seems to exist free from restriction.

Since Cuiabá, we've passed three ladies-who-were-actually-men standing on street corners, dressed more immaculately and glamorously than I ever am. I didn't know how to broach this particular aspect with Wolmer, but I wanted to ask: do the men who pick up ladyboys already know they're men? If not, what happens when they find out?

To add to my confusion about this strange world, Steve and I had a very awkward exchange with a man on our way into Rio Branco.

We were on the final traipse from *posto* to hotel when we saw a car pull up ahead of us, and decided to enquire directions of the driver. Steve approached and waved through the tinted passenger window, stepping back to wait for the window to lower. It didn't. Steve waved again and still the window stayed firmly shut. The car moved forwards fractionally as if the driver was going to make off.

"I don't think he wants to talk to us," I said, but, just as Steve shrugged and turned away, the window opened. There in the passenger seat, next to a twentysomething-year-old man, sat a striking bleach-blonde ladyboy.

Steve went through the motions of asking where to go, while I looked away to disguise my discomfort. The driver had been reluctant to open the window because he had just solicited a male prostitute ... was this too wild an assumption?

The interaction grew stranger. Steve and I continued to trudge on, gaining a fresh layer of perspiration, when a car stopped next to us. It was the very same man – without his passenger.

"I'll give you a lift to the centre – I'm going that way," he volunteered, altogether more amenable now.

So we got in, and discovered that his name was Romero, and that he was a nice enough chap. And I tried to allow for other explanations for what we had witnessed, as I looked across at the baby seat beside me.

DAY 119 (CONTINUED): 22.19
HOTEL LOUREIRO, RIO BRANCO, ACRE, BRAZIL

Jo

Now that we're one day, maybe two, from leaving Brazil, we're starting to look ahead and are pleased to be moving on. It's not that we've completely fallen out of love with the country, but we have moved on from the heady days of romance when we first arrived.

Steve and I have decided that Brazil is a country of opposites. There's its reputation for beautiful women, and then there's the abundance of grossly fat people. It's a country abounding in exotic fruits of all shapes and flavours, and yet it is impossible to escape food and drink laden with sugar. The people here are so open, generous and warm-hearted, and yet many carry suspicion and fear about the rest of their kinsmen. Living and travelling alongside these tensions is exhausting after a while.

11. PERU'S DIRTY SECRET

DAY 121: THURSDAY 17TH JULY 2014, 06.52
UNNAMED BREAKFAST BAR, IÑAPARI, MADRE DE DIOS, PERU

STEVE

We crossed over the Brazilian border late yesterday afternoon and checked into the nearest hotel on the Peruvian side. Well, I say "Peruvian side". We have yet to pass through Peruvian passport control, but other than that it certainly feels like we're in another country.

Everything is different again. We have just downed a plate of chicken and rice – the only breakfast on offer – and are slowly making our way through a cup of Nescafé. It reminds me of something we were told back in Bolivia: "Nescafé *no es café*! [It just isn't coffee!]" Yet somehow here in Peru, a nation known for its coffee exports, we are suffering instant goods from Switzerland. As in Brazil, where we had to endure already-sweetened (and *seriously* sweetened) coffee, it seems here too we may struggle to find a good brew.

Other than that, I must say the transition has been fairly painless. The taxis here are more prevalent and pestering than in Brazil and the people certainly look different with their round Incan faces, but this is no Villazón. As border towns go, Iñapari is decidedly peaceful and clean. No-one has bothered us, apart from the taxi drivers, and everyone we have spoken to has been very

123

welcoming. Perhaps our greatest challenge here will be remembering our long-lost Spanish. Two months of nothing but Portuguese has left us in the unexpected position of speaking better Portuguese than Spanish.

If our second driver yesterday, Ivan, 42, was right, one pleasant change will be significantly less talk of danger. Ivan, who drove us for more than 200 of the 340km to the border, spoke at length about the dangers in Brazil, but he had nothing but positive things to say of Peru. We hope the same will be true of the natives here.

Brazil continued to teach us things right until the moment we departed. On our final day there, we were told – twice – that we weren't hitchhiking in the right manner. After two months in Brazil, this came as quite a shock.

"You know, in Brazil, we don't do *carona* like *this*," Ivan told us, stretching out his thumb.

Apparently the Brazilian way to hitchhike is more of a motional gesture – a shaking of the thumb in the direction you wish to travel.

We might have shrugged off Ivan's tardy advice if he hadn't been the second person to tell us the same thing that day. Our first driver, Alfonso, a 50-year-old judge on his way to work with his eight-year-old son in tow, told us the reason he had hesitated before stopping was because at first he hadn't understood what we were after.

"I've seen people hitchhike like that in films," he told us, "but here that is just a way of saying 'How's it going?'."

Who knows how different our hitching experience in Brazil would have been if only we were told these things on our first day, instead of the last.

Alfonso also taught us more about Brazil's drug problems – "It has destroyed us," he said – and that it is in fact wrong to think of Brazil as just one country.

"Brazil has three countries within it," he said. "Coastal, interior and Amazon. And each one is completely different. Coastal is fiestas and football; interior is industry, and Amazon is another world entirely."

I suppose that during our stay in Brazil we had a small taste of each, but spent much more time in the interior. It feels strange to have left Brazil, a land that taught us so much. I am glad to report that we both left the country in one piece and didn't ever even feel in any particularly danger. Whether this was down to luck, or something else, I don't know, but if we ever return to Brazil, we will do so without fear.

So on to Peru. In a few minutes, we will hike to passport control on the far edge of Iñapari and see if we can hitch a ride south to the first major town, Puerto Maldonado. From there, Cusco and Machu Picchu will be in our sights.

I don't feel quite ready for this new challenge – not just because of our flailing Spanish, but also because of generally feeling rather exhausted after four months on the road – but the show must go on.

Jo

Our official immigration status is at present unclear. Last night, discovering that we'd casually strolled into Peru by accident, we returned to the Brazilian checkpoint and received our exit stamps. Back in Peru, we were advised by an official that, as we were to sleep in the town between the two immigration huts, we should come back another time for our entry stamps. This led to our spending the night in Peru without our passports registering the fact. Does this make us illegal immigrants?

In addition to this confusion, we have also discovered that (contrary to our earlier belief) the clocks have not changed – we were misinformed by a Brazilian driver – and our breakfast included potatoes and peas. It is a perplexing time.

Our final day in Brazil was successful – and possibly the sweatiest of my life. I found myself having to blink defensively to prevent streams of perspiration inhibiting my vision. We knew the five-kilometre walk to the edge of Rio Branco would leave us in a sticky state and wore Monday's dirty t-shirts to allow for this, but by the end of the day the fresh ones were in an equally sorry condition. Steve informed me that I had a collection of bark on my back by the time we reached Peru, goodness knows where from. Par for the course, I suppose.

DAY 122: FRIDAY 18TH JULY 2014, 10.45
PLAZA DE ARMAS, CENTRO HISTÓRICO, CUSCO, PERU

STEVE

Our first day on the road in Peru really couldn't have gone any better. We didn't know what to expect as we arrived at Peruvian Customs around 8am yesterday. We certainly didn't expect to find a ride all the way to Cusco, some 700km southwest, but that is what happened, thanks to a Brazilian couple off on their own adventure.

Daniel, 23, and Diane, 24, left their home in Cuiabá on Tuesday to set off on a round trip to Ushuaia. Their car, advertising their route, was parked at the border as we arrived, and we soon introduced ourselves, enquiring if we might join them on the next leg of their journey south. Daniel seemed slightly unsure, but unable to think of a reason to refuse, so, passports stamped, off we set towards Cusco.

The road was long and there were few other vehicles. If it hadn't been for our Brazilian friends, it is likely our journey would have proved much more challenging. As it was, we were able to sit back and enjoy the view. The road, as Ivan had told us, was in very good condition, but we wondered whether he had been misguided in informing us that there was little poverty in Peru. For the first few hundred kilometres, we saw only wooden shacks. Life was clearly very simple, and poor.

Indeed, other than for the city of Puerto Maldonado, which we passed at lunchtime, it wasn't until the final stretch to Cusco that we began to see a shift from shacks to brick houses.

It is easy to see why this city, the former Inca capital, is flooded with tourists. Tuscan-brown roofs provide an eye-catching vista that stretches from the centre into the surrounding hills.

It feels strange to have arrived here without once conversing with a Peruvian, aside from transactional exchanges, but that is what happens when you journey with fellow foreigners. For the next few days, we will rest easy as just another pair of tourists, before setting out again to discover what hitchhiking in Peru, and Peruvians in general, are really like.

Jo

Yesterday prompted fresh consideration of whether the conditions we're putting our bodies through might be detrimental in the long-term. During the course of the day we went from wondering how we could possibly be sweating so much at 7am, to getting our winter coats out, putting thermals on, and sleeping under several blankets. Furthermore, we reached an altitude of around 5,000 metres, having started near sea-level, before eventually descending to the 3,300 metres where Cusco sits. I have only a mild headache to remind me of the error of my ways, but concern remains that one day my actions will come back to haunt me.

We were all ready to put our Spanish brains back in gear – Steve had even been practising his rolled "r"s – when Diane and Daniel came along and granted us one final push at Portuguese. We congratulated ourselves later that, aside from grammar, our grasp of the language is really quite impressive (in our own humble opinion). We understood almost everything that was said on the 14-hour journey and were ourselves mainly understood, we think. Now, though, it's time to close the lid on Portuguese. If only I could stop saying "*obrigada*".

DAY 125: MONDAY 21ST JULY 2014, 11.54
PLAZA DE ARMAS, CENTRO HISTÓRICO, CUSCO, PERU

STEVE

The road has taken its toll on us. Jo is still tucked up in bed, as we take another day here in Cusco to recover our strength. We have enjoyed our time in this charming city, although we have also been struck by the stark inequality. As in Bolivia, there are a great number of beggars – the majority of them very old – and it is discomforting to see so much money spent on the local attractions, while these poor old folk spend their last days on the streets, grasping buckets in the hope of some loose change.

Then there are the street sellers, many of whom are also beyond retirement age. All day, every day, they roam the city centre, seeking tourists who will buy their little trinkets. Perhaps it is a good way of making money, but the work looks exhausting. It reminds me of begging for rides while hitchhiking in Brazil, but here they have to do it every day. No wonder many of them look dejected.

Yesterday afternoon, as we sat upon a bench in our favourite plaza here, Plaza de Armas, we were approached by a 75-year-old man carrying his wares in a giant sack.

As usual, we pursed our lips and apologised.

"We don't have the space," I protested, as the man showed us a hand-carved pumpkin shell.

But, this time, he persisted. Goodness knows how many rejections he had had from the swarms of tourists that day.

"Please sir, it is my work," he said.

I looked at Jo, who nodded.

Twenty-three Peruvian soles (about £5) later, we had ourselves a hand-carved pumpkin shell with the artist's signature scrawled on the bottom. His name was Dacio, and he seemed like a lovely old man: the sort who'd make the perfect grandfather; the sort, we felt, who at 75 should be resting in his armchair at home, not roaming the streets, essentially begging.

Here, as in Brazil, we have also passed several poor people rummaging through the bins on the streets, in search of some food or something to sell. We passed one man crawling on the floor, using bits of cotton as pads for his hands and knees, because, we presumed, he was unable to walk. We passed a blind old beggar, probably in his seventies, playing a tune on a mouth organ while shaking with what appeared to be a case of Parkinson's. And we watched, pained, as another old man shuffled slowly forward, with a bucket around his neck and a walking stick in his hand, while tourists passed without a second glance.

Beautiful and rich the city may be, but there is great poverty too.

DAY 126: TUESDAY 22ND JULY 2014, 14.26
PLAZA DE ARMAS, URCOS, CUSCO, PERU

STEVE

I sit in another Plaza de Armas, while Jo rests in another hotel. Our progress today was not monumental, but at least some was made.

Three hours ago, as we waited on the edge of Cusco following a gruelling trek out of the centre, it seemed hitchhiking in Peru might be a real challenge. That may yet prove the case, but a ride with Jesús, 28, and his mother, Paula, to the town of Urcos, around 50km from Cusco, has lifted our spirits, if not Jo's sickness.

Until Jesús saved us, the morning had entailed a lot of walking and a multitude of quizzical looks, as we attempted to explain our intentions to various drivers. It seems that, as in Bolivia, hitchhiking isn't very common in Peru. Consequently, we found ourselves begging in a number of petrol stations for a ride anywhere out of the city – anything to curtail our seemingly endless walk along Avenida de la Cultura, which runs all the way from the centre to the perimeter, a distance of more than 10km. With Jo's ill health, we felt in need of assistance, and eventually we found some in the form of Victor, a sweet 23-year-old, who agreed to take us a few kilometres in his truck. During our short journey with this young man, our first Peruvian driver, we received an invitation to spend the evening with him, his wife and one-year-old son, if we failed to make any further progress, and learned that Victor had never ventured out of the region of Cusco. His world, like many of the people we have met, is a small one.

... A man on the bench next to me just told me he is going to Arequipa – our next destination – tomorrow in a *camión* (truck). Naturally, I asked whether there might be space for Jo and me. Unfortunately, it seems there isn't, but I've taken his number just in case. That would be a stroke of luck, and just the kind of pick-me-up we need.

DAY 128: THURSDAY 24TH JULY 2014, 11.01
RESTAURANTE TANTA, AREQUIPA, PERU

JO

Leaving Cusco on Monday, Steve went to ask a duo of old men in their dusty Toyota whether we could travel a few kilometres with them. After establishing that we didn't want a bus, the two chaps giggled with a mixture of delight and disgust at our request, before driving off with no word of farewell.

It was a moment in which I could have been tempted to feel rather glum about hitchhiking in Peru, but, as I am a hardened hitchhiker now, I let the experience pass me by.

Shortly after, a second incident occurred that might also have been interpreted as an inauspicious sign. As we continued our uninspiring plod through the outskirts of Cusco, I looked up to see a pigeon in flight, spraying bullets of moist poo as it went. Before I could utter more than a gasp, Steve became the victim of this fetid airstrike, his bare arm and newly cleaned only pair of trousers suffering the principal impact.

In situations like this, one can choose between a sink or swim attitude, and I knew which I would have elected. Steve is more inclined to be positive, however, and a few wet wipes later all was forgotten.

Our trudge continued, and to keep my spirits raised, I turned my mind to one of our primary pastimes of late: compiling a list of favourite badly-translated t-shirt slogans. Our eyes were opened on our first day in South America, when we saw a girl wearing a top declaring: "F*** YOU, WORLD". The English was fine, but we did wonder if she actually knew what it meant. Since then, accuracy has slumped. "Best afternoon than ever" was a highlight in Brazil, presumably a mistranslation of "better late than never". Here in Peru, I have spotted "Here are fun!"

Maybe Steve and I should tap into this lucrative foreign-language t-shirt market. There would be no need to improve our Spanish, clearly.

STEVE

I hate deadlines. We've been in Peru for just one week and already we're panicking about making it out on time. Twenty-five days is our visa allocation on this occasion, leaving us just over two weeks to cover more than 2,000km to the Ecuadorian border in the north.

Now you might argue that we have made life unnecessarily difficult for ourselves, once again, by choosing to hitch here to Arequipa, directly south of Cusco (yes, completely the opposite direction from Alaska), but we have friends here and they invited us, so what were we to do?

Tammy and Chris, the latter of whom is another former colleague of Jo's, have fallen for this city in the south of Peru and we can already see why. Surrounded by three volcanoes and with a host of buildings constructed from crumbling volcanic rock, Arequipa is striking.

It feels somewhat fraught too. Tammy tells us that, should the Misti volcano erupt, it would take just 15 seconds for lava to cover the city.

"No point running," she said. "You may as well just sit back and enjoy the show."

Strangely, no-one else seems worried by the prospect.

Our journey here yesterday proved delightfully straightforward – just what the doctor ordered. Alex, a 37-year-old *camionero*, brought us all the way from the outskirts of Urcos to Arequipa, and, unlike those truck rides in Bolivia, we spent the nine-hour journey alongside our driver in his cabin. Together we covered more than 600km, passing out of the green province of Cusco into Puno and on to Arequipa. Winding our way through the Andean mountain range once more, we were struck by the dryness of the terrain (everything was yellow) and the mountains of litter on the roadside.

"PLEASE PROTECT THE BEAUTY OF THE COUNTRYSIDE," read one sign, under which was strewn another heap of man's thoughtless waste. It was the greatest display of rubbish we had seen anywhere on our journey so far. Alex agreed that it was very sad. We were glad when, unlike some of the truckers before him, he threw the many plastic bottles of Powerade he consumed on the floor of the truck, rather than out of the window.

DAY 131: SUNDAY 27TH JULY 2014, 11.18
JUGUERIA POCHITA, CHALA, AREQUIPA, PERU

STEVE

No more faffing. It's time for business. Four weeks ago, we were in Bahia, near Brazil's Atlantic coast. Now, more than 6,000km later, we sit beside the Pan-American Highway with a view of Peru's Pacific coastline and the road that is to take us all the way to our final destination.

It's been quite a few weeks. Quite a few months, in fact, but no more wiggling for us. From here, it's north, north, north.

Yesterday, we rejoined the Pan-American Highway for the first time since leaving Tierra del Fuego, as Arequipa's three grand volcanoes gradually faded out of sight on the desert road. I'd never before seen coastline and desert at the same time, but this was the view that met us as we arrived in Camaná, the next major town from Arequipa, and stopped for lunch with our main driver of the day, Fernando, or "Fernandito" (little Fernando), as he introduced himself. As in Bolivia and Brazil, they have a great fondness for the diminutive here – just add "ito" or "ita" to everything, and you'll get on fine.

We travelled with Fernandito all the way from the outskirts of Arequipa to this, his hometown, the rather underwhelming Chala. There were some worrying moments in our journey together, not least when he answered my question about his profession with the word "*transportista*" (little transport man). Our fears were further aroused after lunch when our driver, a 48-year-old with a healthy stomach and a round Incan face hidden under a black cap, took on two more passengers in the unmistakable manner of a Peruvian taxi driver.

"Cha-la! Cha-la!" he yelled out of the window, thrusting his finger forward.

For the first half of our journey, there had been none of this, but our lunchtime stop in Camaná seemed to have awoken the taxi-man inside. Had this been the reason he picked us up? If so, surely he would ask us for money. Had we implicitly agreed to pay by accepting the ride?

Jo

On our journey, it was impossible to ignore the piles of sun-bleached, sand-filled plastic bottles and other unsightly rubbish blemishing the increasingly arid habitat. The striking sand dunes were strewn with innumerable items of waste; farther along, where the terrain became flatter, the effect of time and the wind meant that each object was evenly spaced from the next, giving the impression of a plantation of refuse. It was such a jarring sight, and I felt both disheartened and frustrated that Peru is so spoiled.

The tainted landscape marred the excitement of reaching the Pan-American Highway, as did our decreasing confidence in Fernandito's driving.

"I left for Arequipa at midnight last night and arrived at 6am this morning. This is the return trip," Fernandito said over a bowl of chicken soup at lunchtime.

"No time for any sleep?" Steve asked.

"No," Fernandito confirmed, his small eyes suddenly appearing tired.

"I thought I'd caught him dropping off a few times," Steve said to me later, while Fernandito ran an errand. He'd noticed Fernandito using various sleep-avoidance tactics – opening the window wider, playing the music louder, initiating conversation more frequently: classic signs of a driver trying to fight fatigue.

Maybe this caused me to be more attentive to Fernandito's behaviour, for, once back on the road, I began to notice little lapses of concentration – slight drifts into the other lane, sloppy decision-making. My concern was heightened when we reached the ocean road, beautiful but unarguably treacherous in places.

"What are we doing," I wondered, "placing our trust in a man who has admitted he's too exhausted to drive, on a road where the slightest deviation would probably be fatal?"

We'd seen a lorry earlier in the day that had ploughed into a sandbank, presumably after the driver's own momentary lapse. Thankfully the truck had driven into the sandy verge, as opposed to falling off the sheer slope the other side. When we passed the scene, the driver was standing away from his crumpled vehicle, looking indifferent; perhaps he was too in shock to appreciate how close he had come to death.

This memory came to mind as I raged inwardly at Fernandito's irresponsibility and my own lack of assertiveness, unable to find it in myself to suggest to Steve that we should no longer be in the car.

"My friend died here," Fernandito piped up, pointing at a small shrine on the cliff edge we were passing, and making the sign of the cross on his chest.

I was just about ready to jump out while the car was still in motion, but Steve, equally aware of our driver's precariousness, took his own, more practical, form of evasive action.

"I can drive if you like," he suggested innocently, as if the idea had just come to him.

"Oh. Yes, OK then," said Fernandito.

Steve took over and Fernandito instantly fell asleep beside him, as I gazed out over the darkening sea, finally able to relax.

STEVE

It was a struggle to wake Fernandito when, an hour and a half later, we arrived in Chala. We held our breath as we removed our bags and shook hands, hoping desperately he wouldn't ask us for any money.

I don't know whether it was tiredness, confusion or the fact I'd driven the last 150km, but he left without asking us for anything and only wished us luck on our travels.

Did I catch a disappointed look on his face as we parted without passing over any cash? I can't be sure, but we were certainly very relieved, not only to have escaped without payment, but also still in one piece.

DAY 132: MONDAY 28TH JULY 2014, 20.20
HOTEL LEO, CHILCA, LIMA, PERU

JO

Chala was a lacklustre location for our brief weekend stop. It smelled faintly of urine everywhere (less faintly in some places) and litter encroached upon the beach, deserted but for a washed-up sea lion.

We visited a bakery on Saturday evening to cheer ourselves up, and the waitress struck up a conversation.

"What's the money called in England?" she asked.

"Ah, it's unique," Steve replied, our standard line when explaining that, no, we use neither the euro, nor the dollar. "It's called the 'pound'. One of our coins is worth five of yours. We're rich! Ha ha ha!"

There was no response, not even the flicker of a smile. Steve was joking, but it was blatantly true. Of course we're rich here, as we are in all of the countries we're visiting – and not just because our currency is so strong. Our mere presence is proof of the opportunities we have, usually above and beyond those of the people we're meeting.

We made a quick and awkward exit, hoping that we hadn't forever scarred our host's opinion of foreigners.

STEVE

It's Peru's Independence Day, but not everyone is in party spirits. For some, like our trucker today, 58-year-old Fabio, there is nothing to celebrate. Fabio, who wore an inside-out white woollen hat over greying hair, told us he hadn't had a holiday in two years. The President, he said, is only concerned with lining his own pockets, and does nothing for the people.

Our driver said he also worries about rising delinquency, particularly in his hometown of Lima, and about young people like his 19-year-old son, who doesn't want to work. Fabio told us he enjoys his job and values a working life, but that some people would rather just steal.

Fabio, who picked us up before we even had time to walk the short distance to the edge of Chala, drove us from 9.30am to 6pm, a full working day. With him, we covered over 500km and passed more coastal desert, the mysterious Nazca Lines and Peru's wine region, the Ica Valley. Seeing vineyards surrounded by sand dunes was another first.

We stopped with Fabio at one of the local *bodegas* to sample some claret. We even bought a bottle … Having opened it, I can promise we won't be doing so again.

Fabio had told us he planned to stop for the night in the town of Mala, 85km short of Lima, and then to continue on to the capital tomorrow. When Mala came and went and a sign proclaimed that we were just 65km from Lima, we began to prepare ourselves for the bright lights. But just as I was congratulating myself on another wildly successful day, Fabio pulled off the highway and dumped us here, in Chilca, a grey sort of town, like Chala, with a lot of dust and not much else. The bright lights will have to wait.

DAY 133: TUESDAY 29TH JULY 2014, 13.56
RESTAURANTE CHARLOTTE, BARRANCO, LIMA, PERU

STEVE

It took us less than an hour this morning to cover the short distance from Chilca to Lima, and a good chunk of that time was spent worrying about our weak hitchhiking position. So worried were we, as we stood on the entry ramp from Chilca to the motorway below, that we abandoned reason and tried our luck on the hard shoulder. We signalled at a few passing cars, as we wandered along, deliberating whether anyone would be foolish enough to stop.

Just the third car to pass contained two such fools. In fact, this couple were so foolish that they saw no reason to pull onto the hard shoulder and simply slammed on the brakes and began reversing back up the inside lane.

Jesús, 65, and Nana, 53, were even loopy enough to invite us back to their lovely apartment in Miraflores, Lima's posh district. Apparently Jesús is a bit of a celebrity here in Peru for his part in a punk rock band in the sixties called Los Yorks. He now works alongside Nana, his partner of 10 years, as a textile designer.

Nana is a wonderfully enthusiastic lady with wild frizzy hair befitting her big personality, and a fondness for tight black leggings and baggy jumpers. As soon as we arrived at her apartment, she told us she planned to smoke a joint, apologised and said we were welcome to join her if we liked. It seemed in keeping with her character, and also with the kind of person who might choose to reverse back down a motorway. She told us it had been her decision to do so; Jesús had been less keen, but she said we looked young and foreign.

Nana, whose real name is Cecilia, also told us that Chilca is well-known for a UFO sighting and ideal surfing conditions. Apparently, people come from all over the world to "connect" with the energy of the UFO and enjoy the coastal waves. I must say that of all the tourist destinations we have visited, Chilca would not top my list of recommendations.

DAY 136: FRIDAY 1ST AUGUST 2014, 18.28
HEBRÓN RESTAURANT GRILL, CHICLAYO, LAMBAYEQUE, PERU

STEVE

Our body clocks are all over the place again. We awoke less than one hour ago, but the sun is already well on its way down. Yesterday, as we hiked for three hours from Miraflores to the *Panamericana Norte*, we hoped only to find a way out of Lima. We never imagined that by lunchtime today, we would find ourselves 750km farther north.

Here in Chiclayo, less than 500km separates us from Peru's border with Ecuador. Thanks to yesterday's progress, the 10 days remaining on our Peruvian visas should be ample.

The litter on the roadside was perhaps the most eye-catching scenery, as we travelled over desert wastelands underneath a permanent cloud. We are told that Lima sits under a cloud for eight months of the year. Until we arrived in Chiclayo and the clouds lifted, we hadn't seen the sun in days. The gloom only added to the bleakness of the scene, as we passed mound after mound of litter-strewn grey earth.

The bulk of our progress, as usual, came thanks to a giant ride with a trucker. But by the time we encountered Eliban, 46, we had already covered more than 100km and been warned about our safety by each of our three pairs of drivers.

Our first drivers, René, 30, and his 40-year-old brother Milton, told us, "just as a recommendation", that we ought not to take our eyes off our bags, at any time.

"Do you know that where we picked you up was a really dangerous part of Lima?" René asked us, as we sipped juice together a few kilometres from the danger zone. "When you arrive somewhere new, make sure you ask around to see if it's safe or not."

René left us by a university, saying that it was a "very secure" place, but that if we encountered any problems, we should call him.

It was a similar story with Percy, 42, and his wife Janet, 33.

"*Cuidado!* [Be careful!]" Percy said, as he dropped us by a set of traffic lights 100km out of Lima and, ostensibly, in the back of beyond.

Our third drivers, Juan, 23, and girlfriend Melina, 27, told us they were glad they found us when they did.

"There are lots of robbers back there," said Melina, before setting us down just 3km farther along, outside the village where they lived.

"Stay here!" Melina ordered us. "Whatever you do, don't walk *that* way," she added, with a nod in the direction in which we wished to travel. "It's dangerous!"

A couple of stray dogs came to comfort us as we attempted to digest all these warnings and the clock passed 5pm. Soon it would be dark and then we'd have to walk *somewhere*.

Luckily for us, it never came to that. In just a few minutes, we were on our way again, and this time we were in it for the long haul. For the next 19 hours, we travelled northward in Eliban's truck, pausing at midnight for just four hours' kip on his double-decker bunks.

And 19 hours gave our driver more than enough time to put the fear of God into us. In almost every town we passed, Eliban spoke of "*delincuencia*". In one town, we tailed another truck and Eliban informed us he was keeping close to ensure no delinquents stole anything from the back of the other truck.

Eliban was also very fond of telling us to guard our possessions. He kept pointing to his eyes and then to each of our belongings in turn, suggesting we never take our eyes off them.

"*Cuidado!*" he said, once more, as eventually we arrived in Chiclayo. "There are *lots* of robbers here, and when they come, it won't just be one; it will be *various*!"

Our fifth and final ride came courtesy of another pair of worriers. Indeed, we wouldn't have encountered Ruru and her teenage son if it weren't for our apparent peril, as we wandered towards the centre of town.

"I'm sorry," Ruru said, "but I simply had to pick you up. There are so many stories of foreigners being robbed here. *Cuidado!*"

This final ride saved us a good hour's walk, but it also ensured that our time here in Peru will end with a similar sense of disappointment to that we felt upon leaving Brazil – a disappointment at the pervading sense of fear, a fear so invasive that, despite singularly positive experiences, we find ourselves looking over our shoulders again.

Jo

Eliban warned us that Chiclayo would be a dark den of delinquency, but so far we've survived unscathed – against what odds, we cannot say. Granted, of the six hours we've been here, four have been spent in our hotel room, having a siesta to recover from our long journey. But still, who knows to what lengths this army of lurking evil men (I'm assuming they're men) will go. Are we even safe in our beds?

It's difficult not to react flippantly to the recent crescendo of warnings. This place must be dangerous, I have to remind myself, for people to mention it so often. We don't need to see something bad happen to believe that it can.

I am still unresolved as to the best reaction, even after all these months of the same conversations coming up again and again. I assume that this fear-fuelled talk is likely to continue until we've returned home, at which point it will become retrospective: "Wasn't it dangerous?" The countries we're inching towards have terrible reputations – Honduras, Guatemala, parts of Mexico – so I won't hope for a quieter time.

I realise that the risks are real and that the warnings we receive are delivered with good intent. However, it would be so encouraging if occasionally we were given a balanced insight from locals: yes, these problems exist, but for the most part the danger is at night, or in a particular location, or between gangs. Then we wouldn't be so tempted to ignore the whole lot.

DAY 139: MONDAY 4TH AUGUST 2014, 20.05
HOSPEDAJE SANTA ROSA, SAN IGNACIO, CAJAMARCA, PERU

STEVE

The Ecuadorian border is in our sights, thanks to a splendid day on the road. Things couldn't have gone much better really, as four rides saw us to within 50km of our penultimate South American country. All in all, hitchhiking in Peru has been a great success. Our early struggles seem a lifetime ago.

We had been told that if we continued on the Pan-American over the supposedly dangerous border near Tumbes, the transition between Peruvian coastal desert and the green fields of Ecuador would be instantaneous.

For us, it took place a lot sooner, as we cut inland from Chiclayo and crossed our latest set of Andean peaks. On one side, it was grey desert; on the other, there were paddy fields, mangroves and banana trees. Everything was green. Not since leaving Cusco had we seen such life.

DAY 140: TUESDAY 5TH AUGUST 2014, 19.40
HOTEL EL EMPERADOR, ZUMBA, ZAMORA CHINCHIPE, ECUADOR

JO

Last night, my opinion of humankind dipped considerably. I felt no love whatsoever for the man down the hallway, who persisted in banging drunkenly on the numerous clangy, cell-like hostel doors around us, before cranking up the television volume to cinematic decibels.

This morning the outlook was just as bleak, as this same man proceeded to retch noisily and as audibly as if he was in our own room. He might as well have been: construction of our hostel seemed to have progressed far enough to provide window frames just below the ceiling, but not so far as to fit them with glass. The combination of echoey acoustics, the Peruvian tendency to watch television loudly and at any given opportunity, and inconsiderate fellow guests, did not make for a restful night, nor for positive judgement of the human race.

It was raining when we emerged blearily to seek breakfast and solace from our unhappy abode. With time enough for a last warning about increased delinquency levels in the area, we ate our *huevlitos* (little eggs), drank our freshly squeezed juice and made for the hills.

Our first driver, Huayna, drove us for 30 minutes, and suddenly we were in the most remote location we'd been in for a long time. We began to walk, knowing that traffic would probably be minimal; as we moved in and out of the clouds, we caught glimpses of extensive hilly peaks, thick with vegetation and throbbing with bird-life.

We flagged down a truck and rode in the back to the next town, before embarking upon a long amble towards the border, occasionally passed by motorbikes or moto-taxis, but otherwise alone. Ninety minutes and four of the six winding kilometres later, we achieved our final truck ride and arrived. The Peruvian immigration officer was on his lunch break, so we had one too; once he had returned, and after a short back-and-forth about whether or not we'd overstayed our visit (he counted that we were three days over; in reality we were six under), we received our exit stamps. Ciao Peru.

12.

DAY 140: (CONTINUED): 19.40
HOTEL EL EMPERADOR, ZUMBA, ZAMORA CHINCHIPE, ECUADOR

STEVE

If hitchhiking in Ecuador is always as easy as it was today, we will have no problems here. Sadly, I fear it may have been an anomaly. We saw just a handful of other vehicles on the winding 23km road from the Peruvian border here to Zumba, and that included two buses and an ambulance. That would have left us with precious few other options for hitching a ride, were it not for Diego and his yellow truck.

We crossed the bridge separating Peru and Ecuador very much alone, so it came as something of a surprise when, while the Ecuadorian immigration officer looked over our documents, we heard a vehicle approaching. It is generally advisable to pay border officials the utmost respect, but I couldn't stop myself from running out of the building to halt the approaching truck.

Fortunately, this particular official was blissfully easy-going and didn't even seem to notice my absence. Meanwhile, I was outside, assuring my new young friend, Diego, a 24-year-old with a decent grasp of English, that we didn't care how many stops he had to make along the way; we wanted in.

It took us four hours to complete the short journey from the border to Zumba. This was partly a result of the dreadful condition of the road, partly down to the weight of Diego's load (filled to the brim with rocks from a river bed), and partly due to the three stops we made to empty, fill, and then empty the trailer again.

The going was slow, but it didn't matter a jot to us. Diego was a charming young man, a recent economics graduate working for his father while he considers his options, and the alternative was a long, hilly trek. If it weren't for Diego, we may still be walking.

Here in Zumba, a small town set among the forested hills that accompanied us throughout our day's journey, we are taking the evening to rest and acclimatise, before pressing on again tomorrow.

Fortunately, there seems little for us to acclimatise to. The scenery is the same, as were the choices of evening meal. Diego told us the greatest differences between Ecuador and Peru are musical tastes, appearance (Diego had an almost Mongol appearance and told us Ecuadorians like him are called "*Chinos*" – Chinese), and better health and education. He said that the ambulance that passed us would be taking a Peruvian patient over the border for the sake of the improved healthcare.

We have yet to experience the difference in musical tastes here, but Diego told us that Ecuadorians love to dance – "We're Latinos; it's in our blood!" – particularly to *cumbia*, Colombian salsa and other Central American steps. Upon reflection, none of the countries we have been to thus far have felt particularly Latino. Perhaps now we have truly arrived in the Latin Quarter.

DAY 141: WEDNESDAY 6TH AUGUST 2014, 13.28
ROADSIDE, VALLADOLID, ZAMORA CHINCHIPE, ECUADOR

STEVE

We're having one of those *poco a poco* (little by little) days. In almost five hours on the road, we have covered just 58km. There has been a bit of walking and a fair bit of waiting, but not too much despairing, for, like yesterday, we lack only for vehicles, not compassion. In fact, I'd wager that we have had an almost 50 per cent success rate with passing drivers today, once you've discounted public transport and those already full, or not going our way.

First there was Jorge, and his wife Daisy, who took us out of Zumba in the back of their pick-up truck. Theirs was the second car to pass.

Next came Fabian, 36, and Carlos, 27, to take us to the town of Palanda. We had waited an hour for that ride, but theirs was only the fifth vehicle to pass and all but one of the drivers had signalled in some way.

That takes us up to two hours ago and our brief stay in Palanda, where we wolfed down some *empanadas* and prepared ourselves for another wait.

Sure enough, half an hour came and went and all we had to show for it were a bus, a taxi, and a pair of uninterested truckers. But then along came a white van and we were in business.

"*Que pasa?* [What happened?]" the driver asked, appearing distressed to find a pair of foreigners looking lost and in need of help.

"Oh, *nada*," I said. "We're just waiting for a ride."

The driver apologised that there was no room in the front, for he was travelling with a companion, but said he was happy to let us ride in the back. He even fastened open the side door to ensure we had a view.

We travelled in the back of the van, alongside bags of toilet rolls and a few brooms, here to the village of Valladolid, where our new friends, whose names we have still to learn, are unloading. In two hours, they have promised to return to take us the remaining 50km or so to Vilcabamba. For now, all we can do is hope that they keep their word. If not, I suppose we shall be in for a little more waiting; the only car to pass in the 30 minutes we have been here was a police car – and it was full.

Jo

"We've not really had a ride like this one before," Steve observed cheerfully, as we approached this tiny village.

No indeed, for we have not yet made a habit of travelling in the back of little vans, surrounded by miscellaneous cleaning products and bumping violently up and down atop makeshift seats (our bags). I would say that for the sake of my spine, it's probably best that this is not a common occurrence – although that may be a lost cause already.

As we become initiated into the intricacies of life in Ecuador, a common topic is that of poverty. Carlos and Fabian, who sped us along the part-excellent, part-under-construction road from Zumba, said that life is expensive for them, and that there isn't much money to be had.

Our drivers were particularly taken with this money theme. The price of this or that item became a recurrent question, and eventually we tried to temper their wide-eyed reaction to how comparatively rich we are by describing how much it costs to rent a house in London (more per month than they earn in a year). This finally stalled their never-ending list, "… And how about a car? And clothes? And a beer?"

DAY 143: Friday 8th August 2014, 10.25
Layseca's Bakery, Vilcabamba, Loja, Ecuador

Steve

Franklin the van driver returned as promised and brought us here to Vilcabamba, or, more specifically, to a hostel on the edge of town where he and his deputy, Nelson, supply toiletries – those same toiletries that were our travelling companions for the first section of our journey.

The second section, the short stretch to Vilcabamba, was not as short as it could have been, for Franklin first took us on a tour of the surrounding area, including a school where he had worked as a teacher in 1978.

We were happy to let him reminisce, although the uncomfortable nature of our seating made the two-hour detour somewhat less enjoyable.

Still, Vilcabamba is the perfect place to come if you're in need of a little recuperation. We are taking a couple of days here in Franklin's friend's blissfully quiet hostel to recover our senses, before we return to the *Panamericana* tomorrow.

Vilcabamba is also a rather odd place. It wouldn't be so very different from the other small towns in this southern region of Ecuador – set inside a valley surrounded by spectacular hills – were it not for its astonishingly large expat community and a recent flood of tourists. The first wave of expats came in the 60s, after learning that Vilcabambans enjoy unnaturally long lives (Vilcabamba is referred to as the "Land of the Centenarians") and that the area boasts a plentiful supply of an hallucinogenic drug made from cactuses.

We find these kinds of places discomfiting – in the plaza where we sit there are more *gringos* than natives – but we cannot deny Vilcabamba's charms any more than we can pretend that we aren't just another couple of those *gringos*.

Jo

"Wow!" said Vincent, an American traveller at our hostel, last night. "That's ballsy! Travelling without Internet? That's really ballsy!"

Vincent had just asked me whether we were finding the hostel Wi-Fi slow, and I had explained that we have neither a smartphone nor a computer in our possession. His reaction was not unprecedented, but we don't think we're being "ballsy" and we're not travelling without Internet to make any particular point. It's just our preference.

It did make me wonder, though, what impact the recent leap in technology – let alone the advances that brought the Internet to us in the first place – has had on those who travel and explore other countries. There are doubtless practical benefits for having the Internet at one's fingertips, but I suspect that smartphones can be disadvantageous too: they surely limit interaction, for why ask a local person the directions and risk an awkward mixed-language conversation when you can find it out yourself? Does not the Internet also water down the thrill of discovery, with so much less left to chance?

… New favourite mistranslated t-shirt just spied: "To be young boy or for young life not to be." That's deep.

DAY 145: SUNDAY 10TH AUGUST 2014, 09.39
HELADERÍA TUTTO FREDDO, CUENCA, ECUADOR

STEVE

We could be in Quito right now. Instead we find ourselves more than 500km south, in the colonial city of Cuenca, after taking the advice of our final driver yesterday, 27-year-old *camionero* Ángel.

Ángel told us that Cuenca is his favourite city in Ecuador and that we mustn't pass up the opportunity to see it. He also said we could always travel the remaining 500km with him one day next week, for he and co-driver, Luis, 54, do the return trip from Quito to Loja three times a week in their bright yellow truck. We have Ángel's number, so there's every chance we may see them again. They will next pass this way, he said, at midday on Tuesday.

In the meantime, we have a few days to enjoy the pretty streets of Cuenca, before heading north again. Ecuador is such a small country – at least as far as South America is concerned – that were we in Quito right now, we would be just a few hundred kilometres from our next border crossing.

It's nice to know that we have a little more time here in the south of Ecuador and, particularly, to think we'll have the chance to travel the mountainous road to Quito in the daylight. The ride here to Cuenca, as well as being very scenic, was made all the more enjoyable by the chatty Ángel, who conversed with us while Luis caught up on some sleep on the bunks behind. Ángel seemed very clued up on much of the goings-on in the world today and asked our opinion on, among other things, conspiracy theories relating to Princess Diana's death and 9/11.

He also reminded us that WikiLeaks founder Julian Assange is still holed up in the Ecuadorian embassy in London. Ángel appeared to take great pride in the fact that a little country like Ecuador was standing up against the bigger world powers in this way.

Like our first Ecuadorian friend, Diego, Ángel said he was very pleased with the changes the current President, Rafael Correa, has made since his election in 2006. Education, tourism and health are on the up, he said, and corruption, although still prevalent in the police, is diminishing. Delinquency is also in decline. We haven't been told to be careful nearly so often here, unless we go to the coast – apparently it's "*super peligroso*" (really dangerous) there.

The President, Ángel said, at least on current form, appears to be an honest man who follows through on his promises. It is refreshing to hear such things about a South American leader and country, having heard so many accounts to the contrary. It has made me wonder how different the continent could be if only each country had such a leader and, slowly but surely, attempted to stamp out corruption.

Ángel said he felt at least partly at fault for corruption's hold on Ecuador.

"We won't be free from corruption," he said, "unless every one of us stands up against it."

Ángel told us that, for him, this would mean making sure all the truck's documentation was intact, instead of simply handing five dollars to any questioning official.

DAY 146: MONDAY 11TH AUGUST 2014, 18.07
PS PETROL STATION RESTAURANT, AMBATO, TUNGURAHUA, ECUADOR

STEVE

It's been a while since we spent time waiting at a service station, but this time we're here on very different terms. All being well, we have just two hours to wait until our new friend, Vanessa, returns to fetch us. Vanessa, 41, our last of five drivers today, needs to pop by the office (she works as a palm-oil saleswoman), but she has kindly invited us home for the evening. She has even agreed to teach us some *cumbia*, Ecuador's favourite dance step.

Here in Ambato, we are but 130km short of Quito, where we will hope to arrive tomorrow. On current form, that should be very easy.

We travelled just 300km today, but none of our nine hours on the road was spent waiting. Our slow progress owed much to the state of our third vehicle, Jorge's rickety old red pick-up truck, in which we spent five hours, which included one breakdown and a thousand jolts between gears.

With Jorge, 52, we rolled over patchwork hills and caught sight of our first Ecuadorian volcano. Apparently there are quite a few of them here ... I'm not sure how many are active.

We were told by Diego, our first driver, that the tourist board has coined the phrase, "All you need is Ecuador", owing to the country's diversity. In one day, you can see coast, mountains and rainforest. We're sticking to the mountain pass, but that is impressive enough.

JO

Let us take this moment, friends, to mark the sad and unfortunate passing of our dearly beloved tent, lost today to the back of Ivan's truck (probably. There or on the side of the road). Newly gaffer-taped to near perfection only three days ago, we must turn our minds away from this deep sorrow and instead remember the special moments we shared: that first (windy) night in Argentina, that second (cold and noisy) attempt in Chile, those (uncomfortable) petrol station car parks in Brazil.

And let us not forget the mosquito net and collection of bits and bobs contained within the tent bag: the head torches, the handy length of pink string, the door wedge (for security purposes).

We bid you farewell, and thank you for your company.

DAY 148: WEDNESDAY 13TH AUGUST 2014, 15.24
JUAN VALDEZ CAFÉ, QUITO, ECUADOR

STEVE

A small child of around eight years just approached us, offering sweets in exchange for a few cents. When we rejected the sweets, he asked for money to buy some food. The same pattern was repeated, as a girl a few years older came our way, offering flowers. Again, we refused. Moments later, we saw the duo being handed a few more goodies by a man lurking nearby.

Our principal driver today, 46-year-old *camionero* Milton, told us there are far fewer child beggars in Ecuador today than in years past. He said that nowadays, if parents are caught using their child to make money, that child is taken away from them. As with many of the problems from Ecuador's past, it seems this unpleasant phenomenon is on the wane.

Four days since first encountering a driver heading to Quito, we arrived here this morning thanks to a long ride with Milton, sandwiched between two smaller rides.

We delayed our departure from Ambato by one day to visit Baños, a spa town recommended to us by almost every Ecuadorian we've met. Vanessa and her husband, Ángel, were no different, insisting we stay an extra night to give ourselves the opportunity to enjoy the hot springs there. Enjoy them we did, although as often seems to be the case when we visit somewhere scenic, it was cloudy all day, so we missed the chance to view the volcano that looms over Baños.

The same was true today, as we passed numerous volcanoes enshrouded by clouds on the road to Quito. If we're lucky, the clouds will lift just long enough for us to view the famous Cotopaxi volcano on Quito's horizon, before we depart the city tomorrow.

DAY 150: FRIDAY 15TH AUGUST 2014, 16.25
LA CASA DE INTAG, OTAVALO, IMBABURA, ECUADOR

JO

The past couple of days have brought us into contact with several President Correa detractors, providing a more balanced view of the political situation in Ecuador.

Sister-of-a-friend Beth and her Ecuadorian husband, Oswaldo, took us out for dinner in Quito, and were quick to disclose that they are not supporters of the current leader.

"He's coming down really hard on the free press," Oswaldo explained. "There's a story almost every week about the President suing someone in the media."

Oswaldo told us about the editor of a popular newspaper, who, having published a column criticising Correa, was given three years in prison and a fine of 40 million dollars – payable to Correa himself.

"He's being very clever," Beth added. "Better roads, more jobs – those are the things that poorer people care about. Why would they be interested in freedom of speech? It doesn't impact them so directly. Also, the propaganda machine is very strong: the President says that unemployment is down to 5%, but that's because people who work as street sellers are counted as having employment."

Oswaldo told us that within his company, government corruption is plain to see, with underhand payments leading to the securing of contracts.

"We were very optimistic when he was elected," said Beth. "But he could have done so much more."

STEVE

On this, our one hundred and fiftieth day on the road, we crossed the halfway mark, at least geographically speaking. The Equator lies just 25km north of Quito and it took us little time to reach it this morning.

As we began our walk along the Pan-American Highway, which runs through the city, we were preparing ourselves for at least a couple of hours of trekking before our first ride. In actual fact, it took us less than 15 minutes, thanks to a chance meeting with José, 32, at a junction on the other side of Parque La Alameda.

Seeing his smiling face through the window of his pick-up truck, I wagged a hopeful thumb in his direction.

Winding down the window, he asked: "*¿Adónde vas?* [Where are you going?]"

"*Norte* [north]," I responded.

"OK, *vamos!* [Let's go!]," he said, beckoning us in.

At first we thought we were to part on the other side of another park, Parque La Carolina, a few kilometres farther north, but having picked up his older sister Esther, 34, from her work at the United Nations, José told us he'd take us to the edge of town.

"He's always helping foreigners," said Esther. "It's just a shame he can't speak any English."

At 10.30, we were bidding our new friends farewell. We hadn't expected to arrive there until at least midday, so this was bonus territory.

By the time the clock reached 12, we were in our fifth and final vehicle of the day and were well on our way here to Otavalo, but before that we experienced our first quibble in Ecuador over paying for transport.

"It will be four dollars to the *peaje* [toll]," said the driver of a little red car.

"Oh, sorry, we can't pay anything," I responded.

"OK, two dollars," he said.

"No, really, we can't pay anything," I said.

And that was that. Bags out. Relationship over. And off the little red car sped.

But it wasn't long before our second José of the day came along and we were back on track.

It was so early when we arrived here in Otavalo that we have already had time to browse the artisanal market for which the town is famed, and feel ready to move on again tomorrow. We have just 150km to go to Tulcán, northern Ecuador's border town, after which there will be just one country separating us from our next continent.

DAY 152: SUNDAY 17TH AUGUST 2014, 14.05
GUADALQUIVIR CAFÉ, PASTO, NARIÑO, COLOMBIA

JO

About once a week, it occurs to me anew that the life of a hitchhiker is a ridiculous one. This week, the realisation dawned somewhere in the middle of Laguna de Yahuarcocha, where our driver, Jersson, 38, had taken us for a little trip in a pedalo. I relaxed in the back of our oversized green turtle, while Jersson and Steve battled the elements; at one point it seemed feasible that we would need to be rescued by a motorboat (the fate of another group on the lake), so gusty was the wind. What's more, Jersson had brought his iPhone along to provide us with a blaring soundtrack of 1980s pop classics.

"How on earth did this come to be?" I mused, as I surveyed the situation. There had been no warning from Jersson that this was his plan; I had thought he was helpfully driving us away from the town, until we started making a detour for this watery excursion. It was all a bit difficult to keep up with.

STEVE

Just 12 days after arriving in Ecuador, we departed yesterday, although it wasn't until after breakfast this morning that we waved off our latest Ecuadorian chum, Lorena, 36, and her Chilean husband Erasmo, 45. This delightful couple found us at the Colombian border late yesterday afternoon and took us with them to visit a quite astonishing church built into a mountainside, before bringing us here to the city of Pasto.

Our last day in Ecuador passed much like those before it. We enjoyed swift pick-ups and several of our drivers went out of their way to show us the local sights. Our penultimate ride came courtesy of 50-year-old farmer Justino, who gave us perhaps our greatest introduction to Colombia thus far. Justino, a Colombian driving a beaten-up blue van, told us he travelled over the border regularly to purchase Ecuador's subsidised supplies of petrol and gas. We had been told by another driver that the Ecuadorian government had recently banned vehicles more than 15 years in age. It seems Colombia doesn't share this law, for Justino's old banger was made in 1987 and the fumes, which travelled straight from the exhaust pipe, through the driver's window and into our lungs, ensured we were feeling queasy by the time we arrived at the border. I also had a malfunctioning passenger door (and, of course, no seatbelt) to worry about, but luckily we weren't rounding any bends on the two occasions it swung open.

It was around 5pm when Erasmo and Lorena found us, and some five hours later by the time we had checked into a hotel here in Pasto. For a 13-hour day, we might have hoped to travel more than 250km, but we are just happy to have crossed another border, another marker on our journey north.

We can't report much about Colombia just yet, other than that they seem to use "*mucho gusto*" (nice to meet you) to mean absolutely anything; there are quite a few policemen with guns; and they have a few more noughts on the end of the notes. Our hotel costs 45,000 pesos a night. Ouch.

13. FARC-LAND

DAY 154: TUESDAY 19TH AUGUST 2014, 09.50
RESTAURANTE JENGIBRE, POPAYÁN, CAUCA, COLOMBIA

STEVE

It's so far, so good from a hitchhiking perspective here in Colombia. There were a few moments yesterday when we feared we might struggle, but in the end our first full day on the road must go down as a success. The statistics speak for themselves: three rides, 250km and not more than 20 minutes waiting in any one spot.

It seemed we were off to a flyer when, wandering out of Pasto, a car appeared to pull over for us, but we reached the vehicle to find it packed full, and the driver looked surprised to see us.

"Oh, you're full," I said.

"*Si, pero adónde van?* [Yes, but where are you going?]" he responded.

"Er, Cali," I said, wondering why he had asked.

"OK, *vamos*," he said. "My children are staying here."

It seemed too good to be true, and it was. Five minutes later, having watched the four children pile out of the back seats, and replaced their belongings with ours, he raised the dreaded question: how much were we willing to pay?

"Ah, *nada*," I said, and that was that.

This experience had done little for our confidence, but it was soon bolstered by Alfonso, 27, and mother Patricia, who genuinely pulled over *for us* and appeared hurt when I asked if they were a taxi.

They left us in a petrol station on the edge of town, and life was rosy again.

Twenty minutes passed and our confidence had taken another dip, but then along came Wilber, 40, his wife Saida, 47, and sister Marilyn, 38, providing us with our two hundredth ride since Ushuaia, and our spirits were lifted.

This trio were utterly charming – the kind of friendly Colombians we had heard so much about – and went out of their way to take us to a petrol station around an hour north of Pasto.

But there, as another 20 minutes came and went without anything to show for it, we began to worry again.

Once more, we needn't have done so. Franklin, 28, our first Colombian *camionero*, soon came to the rescue in his yellow truck, and we were on our way to Popayán. Here, we find ourselves apparently just three hours short of Cali, where we hope to arrive later today.

We still don't feel entirely used to this new country, but perhaps a few days dancing salsa in the unofficial Salsa Capital of the World will help. For now, our main observations about Colombia are still the number of armed soldiers on the roads (who, we saw yesterday, provide thumbs-up gestures if all is well on the road ahead) and a return to being told to watch our backs.

To be fair, we had anticipated this aspect of Colombia. It is, after all, as Saida put it, what Colombia is most known for around the world: problems with guerrillas and the drugs trade (although Wilber told us the situation has improved in the last four years). Anyway, we had heard as many reports about the friendliness of Colombians as we had about our chances of dying here.

Jo

Rumour had it that Colombian Spanish is the easiest to understand in South America.

Rumour was wrong.

Most people we've interacted with so far have spoken at such a sprint that barely one word in 20 registered. It's as if someone has turned on a high-speed fan and poured Spanish into it: the words tumble out and spin around our ears, just out of reach of comprehension.

It's a bit of a blow, but for the time being I will stick to the technique of answering the question I think I have been asked, while smiling sweetly in the face of impending confusion.

Coca tea

Hitchhiking in Bolivia

Our fellow stoaways on the road to Santa Cruz

A rooftop ride in Bolivia

Mennonites

The Pantanal, Corumbá, Brazil

Mih

Hitching with the goats

A Brazilian breakfast

A long wait outside Criciúma

World Cup fever with Bruno, Olga and family in Belo Horizonte

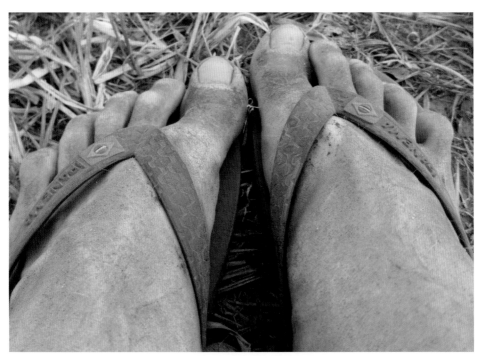

Never hitch in flip-flops

Bedding down in a *posto*

Cusco

Guinea pig in Cusco, Peru

A load of rubbish outside Lima

DAY 154 (CONTINUED): 20.10
ANDERSON AND LUZ DANY'S HOUSE, MIRANDA, FARC TERRITORY, CAUCA, COLOMBIA

STEVE

The FARC, Colombia's infamous rebel group, came up in conversation for the first time today. Apparently we drove down the "most dangerous road in Colombia", right through the heart of FARC territory, at least according to our ultimate drivers and hosts tonight, Anderson, 29, and partner Luz Dany, 24.

As we passed through the town of Corinto, sitting in the back of their jeep with six-year-old Denilson and Scott the poodle, the tinted windows were wound up and we drove that little bit quicker.

"This is the centre of the drugs trade," said Anderson. "The FARC runs its operation from *those* mountains."

Those same mountains lie behind us tonight, as we shelter here in Miranda, just a few kilometres from Corinto and FARC-land.

DAY 155: WEDNESDAY 20TH AUGUST 2014, 09.14
ANDERSON AND LUZ DANY'S HOUSE, MIRANDA, CAUCA, COLOMBIA

JO

Our breakfast this morning was a traditional spread: scrambled eggs with chopped tomatoes, square crispbreads, homemade hot chocolate, and the trillionth discussion of how many places on our itinerary are dangerous and/or deadly. Steve has now been whisked away on a new secret mission with Anderson. The last one involved the covert purchasing of cannabis; I found that I was not surprised.

For my part, I am sat in the middle of a dog face-off: Choco, the pit bull and man of the house, versus Scott, the new pretender. Scott spent his first night in the house rifling through rubbish in the kitchen, so his cloud of poodle fluff is no longer as gleaming as it once was. Choco has an aversion to all other canines and is uttering a low, rumbling growl as Scott tiptoes around in his peripheral vision. I don't think this will end well.

This is not the first animal-related incident since being invited to the home of our first Colombian hosts.

"Please can somebody tell me what's happening?" I wondered silently yesterday afternoon, as I sat on a sofa with a parrot on my shoulder.

There was no way of divining how much longer I was to be favoured by this creature, and though I tried to pretend we were forging a strong relationship, my stiff posture most likely gave me away. The pet parrot had arrived on its perch uninvited and promptly pooed onto the cushions below. Mercifully, it missed my clothing.

... Scott the dog has lost the fight. Something in his timid, poodle ways tipped Choco over the edge and he just gave a squealing Scott a nip on the face. Now Scott sits nursing his wounds pitifully, vainly attempting to reach the bloody streaks on his snout with his tongue.

DAY 155 (CONTINUED): 10.05
ANDERSON AND LUZ DANY'S HOUSE, MIRANDA, CAUCA, COLOMBIA

STEVE

Our hosts have informed us that later today they plan to drive to Cali, where Luz Dany is a student, so it would appear that our passage there is assured.

In the meantime, I have become much better acquainted with Anderson, thanks to two short trips with him on his motorbike. During these excursions, first to a local lake, and then to a river, Anderson lit up a joint (he told me not to tell Luz Dany) and spoke about his life.

It seems Anderson is in a much better place today than in years past. He told me that his family is mixed up in one of the world's biggest drug cartels and that his cousin is currently serving 45 years in a New York jail for drug trafficking.

Here in Miranda, Anderson has chosen to follow a different path, away from his family and a lot of old enemies in Cali.

"My wife and son are studying," he said. "It's a better way to live."

While they are in Cali, Anderson is all on his own in Miranda and secretly smokes dope with a set of new friends.

"I'm alone here. It's just a hobby," he said, apologetically.

DAY 155 (CONTINUED): 20.44
HOTEL FARALLONES, CALI, VALLE DEL CAUCA, COLOMBIA

STEVE

We're on lockdown here in Cali. Almost everyone we've spoken to has insisted we shouldn't go out after 7pm – "I suggest you don't do anything at all," said the lady at reception – so we haven't. We even got a taxi from the restaurant on the other side of the city centre to avoid the long, perilous trek home.

Personally, I can't see what all the fuss is about. Cali feels no shiftier than Córdoba in Argentina or Chiclayo in Peru, but it's difficult not to be affected when everyone goes on about the danger all the time.

We arrived here at around 3pm, just the sort of time we had anticipated arriving, but not in the way we planned.

Anderson's promise of a ride swiftly evaporated when he failed to locate his driving license – he told us he couldn't drive without it. So, instead, we were plonked on the edge of town beside some military police officers and wished the best of luck.

It was a shock to the system to find ourselves alone again and still with some work to do, but we received an almost instant lift from Wilson, 52, and 19-year-old apprentice Sammy. They took us only as far as a bridge on the near side of the next town, named Florida, but we were glad just to be moving again.

Wilson had told us the bridge was "very dangerous" and that on no account should we cross it alone. We were still in FARC territory.

When we crossed the bridge, we were safely behind the tinted windows of a car belonging to a man who lived in the heart of FARC-land. I wondered whether Camilo, 31, whose eyes were shielded behind sunglasses, was part of the rebel group, especially when he asked us whether we had any drugs or felt at all scared to be doing what we were doing in a "very dangerous" place.

When we responded negatively to both questions, he informed us that we were "*loco*" (insane).

Camilo then proceeded to tell us that Cali was also very dangerous and that we should be very careful. He repeated these words a few times. As we arrived in the centre, he repeated them again and reiterated his opinion that we were mad.

After checking into the nearest hotel, Jo began to cry.

DAY 161: TUESDAY 26TH AUGUST 2014, 15.05
PANADERÍA Y PASTELERÍA EL COQUITO, BOGOTÁ, DISTRITO CAPITAL, COLOMBIA

Jo

This "rule of thumb" business – creating a continuous line of hitching or walking between Argentina and Alaska – really scrapes its nails down the blackboard in cities like Bogotá.

When we were deposited several kilometres outside the capital city yesterday at 5.30pm, I threw a small yet (mostly) controlled hissy fit at the prospect of making our way on foot under an already darkening sky. We weren't even into the city, let alone near our host-to-be in a northern neighbourhood. But drivers were looking at us warily, and no-one was stopping to help as we hovered near a set of traffic lights.

Before we finally abandoned prospects of further progress, Steve intercepted Carlos as he was pulling out of a petrol station. Carlos was going to the city centre (part of his 90-minute-each-way commute as a vet on a chicken farm) and though he took us with him obligingly enough, his opinion about our escapades was clear. Yep, I hear you, we're crazy. Uh huh, *really* crazy. Oh I see, time to mention it again, eh? Now you're on the phone to your wife, telling her how crazy we are. And that we speak "*bien poco español*" (hardly any Spanish). Enough to understand *that*, chum!

It was with these rays of light shining upon us that we were let out onto the big, bad streets of Bogotá. Later, we took a bus to where we had been invited to stay, and so, for integrity's sake, today has been spent walking back to where we were dropped off. We began just before 10am and arrived at 2pm, which I think can be labelled reasonably as A Lot of Walking.

I have hereby vetoed going to the capital cities of Guatemala and Mexico, both of which have reputations as nasty metropolises, and neither of which I have any desire to visit. Alas, both are on our route, and there seems a certain amount of inevitability we will end up there.

DAY 164: FRIDAY 29TH AUGUST 2014, 08.08
HOTEL PRINCIPE, BUCARAMANGA, SANTANDER, COLOMBIA

STEVE

Our progress northward continues, but the going is slow. Colombia seems to be built upon one giant mountain – yes, we're in the Andes again, and here in Colombia the range is split into three branches. We're currently on the eastern branch and in the past two days have managed to travel less than 400km, leaving us more than 500km from Colombia's Caribbean coastline. In other countries, we would be confident of crossing that distance in one day. Here, we're not even sure we'll make it in two.

If it weren't for our third and final ride yesterday, in Juan's super-speedy blue BMW, I imagine we'd have even farther to go. Juan, 32, left Bogotá at 10am yesterday and, despite being the fastest car on the road, it was 6pm by the time we arrived in Bucaramanga.

He found us after lunch in the town of Oiba, where we had been waiting for just two minutes since our previous ride. In fact, we must have endured only an hour of waiting during the whole day. Still, it took us as much time yesterday to reach Bucaramanga from Arcabuco, where we had finished the previous evening, as it did for Juan to cover the full distance from Bogotá. I'm not sure if that says more about his driving, or the slog that is hitchhiking here in Colombia.

DAY 164 (CONTINUED): 19.00
HOTEL SANTORI, PELAYA, CESAR, COLOMBIA

STEVE

We're in the danger zone again. Here in the tiny town of Pelaya, we stand but a stone's throw from the border with Venezuela and, we're told, Colombia's coca-growing region.

Robert, 50, and wife Rosio, 32, told us all about it on our journey north from Bucaramanga.

"For one kilo of cocaine, they can make 1,500 dollars. Why would you choose another profession?" said Robert.

It had been a bitty, and hot, start to the day, as we trekked out of Bucaramanga. Rodrigo, 35, shortened our walk by a few kilometres to leave us in a good spot on the edge of town, but there we endured a strange half-hour in which we were approached numerous times by unmarked cars hoping for some cash in return for a lift to the next town. We hadn't experienced the like anywhere else in Colombia, so it was hard to know what to make of it all.

Fortunately, Carlos, 47, and wife Joanna, 36, wanted nothing to take us, and it was in this next town that Robert and Rosio found us, but only after another painful 45 minutes in which Jo declared herself exhausted by our week's exertions. I was just glad she chose to focus on the week, rather than the previous five months.

There was to be no such waiting for our fourth and final ride of the day, with 35-year-old Leesa, the latest Seventh-day Adventist to have helped us on our way.

"I couldn't just leave you there," she told us. "It's too dangerous for you to be walking on your own here. There are lots of bad people around."

I wonder where they're all hiding; we are yet to encounter any.

JO

It must be tropical here. There's a gecko on the wall, the air around us is heavy with heat and at any given moment I am adorned by four or five intrepid insects. Earlier, Steve even conceded that his cold shower "wasn't too bad".

My enthusiasm for hitchhiking was at best half-hearted during our wait outside Bucaramanga. The arrival of Robert and Rosio interrupted my moping, but after the usual early pleasantries and getting-to-know-yous, I sank into a mild heat-of-the-day-induced torpor.

I was roused from my reverie by an unexpected occurrence. We were approaching an unremarkable stretch of road when a woman appeared, waving at our car and looking stricken. We slowed as we drove past, and there the cause of the woman's anguish came into view: a huge, galloping pig making a gleeful bid for freedom.

We overtook the gallant creature cautiously so that we would not inhibit its determined course of action. I swivelled round in my seat, and was granted the memorable sight of this huge swine being chased by three grown men, their arms flailing and eyes bulging. I am convinced that as we rounded the corner, I caught a grin on the pig's face.

When not distracted by adventurous animals, my passion for the road is at a low ebb; I think it is the same for us both. I am slower to shake myself from sleep in the mornings; my aching legs never seem to recover from one long walk before the next; my capacity for keeping up with Spanish is faltering. It was encouraging to be told by Juan yesterday that our grasp of the language is *grandissimo* (have *that*, Carlos of *bien poco español* opinion!), but at times my aptitude is feeble.

Steve suggests that our interest in South America might be waning. In general, the experience of hitchhiking in Colombia, and the feel of the place, are not remarkably different from Ecuador and Peru, and progress has felt slow of late.

Additionally, I am forecasting impending doom regarding our approaching passage from Colombia to Panama. It has been in the back of my mind since before we left England: the only way to go is over the water, assuming we're ignoring the guerrilla- and jungle-lined 99-mile stretch called the Darién Gap (which we are). We know of boat crossings from Cartagena and also of a shorter passage from a port named Turbo farther down the coast, although we suspect distance will make no difference. We heard rumours of two people who had managed to hitch on boats, but it transpired that both had just negotiated cheaper rides.

Stupid, inconvenient ocean!

DAY 166: SUNDAY 31ST AUGUST 2014, 08.02
HOSPEDERÍA CASA FAMILIAR, SANTA MARTA, MAGDALENA, COLOMBIA

STEVE

One hundred and sixty-five days after leaving the Beagle Channel in Ushuaia, we arrived yesterday at Colombia's Caribbean coastline. We have just two remaining stops in Colombia – Barranquilla and Cartagena – before we will be bidding farewell to South America.

Ushuaia feels like a lifetime ago now. Yesterday's passage alone seemed to take an eternity.

When a car pulled over after just 20 minutes of waiting on the edge of Pelaya, it seemed we had made a strong start. But then the owner of the vehicle, a chap named Wilson, began talking about his work in the transport business and we were promptly released to continue on our own.

Our very short ride in Wilson's unmarked taxi had at least taken us to a far preferable spot, at a toll controlled by a squadron of youthful military police officers. Juan and Justin, both 19, took a particular shine to us and were soon stopping vehicles on our behalf. It felt a little like being two cows in a cattle market, as our advocates pointed to us, drivers looked us up and down, and then decided, for whatever reason, that we didn't cut the mustard.

But it wasn't long before one took pity on us. Big Pedro, a 29-year-old *camionero*, was heading for Cartagena and agreed to take us to the crossroads dividing north and west in the town of Bosconia. Our final destination in South America was in our grasp, but we rejected the offer of a ride due to prior engagements. We have a friend here in Santa Marta, you see: Facundo, Flor's brother, whom we met on just our second day on the road, in El Chaltén. Then there's another Tearfund project to visit in nearby Barranquilla, before we set our sights on Cartagena and the minor challenge of attempting to hitchhike on a boat.

Pedro dropped us just 150km from Santa Marta. At 1pm, we fancied our chances. Pedro had told us that it would take four hours in a *mula* (the Colombian word for "big truck"), or three hours in a car. By 2pm, we were on our way, although at first we didn't know where we were heading.

A trucker had stopped for us, but, aware of the traffic behind, he ordered us to climb quickly onto his trailer. We did so, and soon found ourselves bumping along on top of a few empty wooden pallets, hoping our driver was going to Santa Marta.

We were soon joined by another couple of hitchers, or *Colombianadas* as Pedro would call them. These two young men, both of African descent, spotted us as we passed through a little village, and seized the opportunity, running after the trailer and leaping on. We had seen a number of these opportunists already in Colombia, and Pedro had told us they were a trucker's nightmare – dangerous thugs who often steal things from the trailer and never ask permission before clambering aboard.

Our time with these particular *Colombianadas* was short-lived. Our driver, having pulled over in the next village, came to beckon us for a drinks break and was far from pleased by the sight of two unexpected additions.

While Jo and I sipped coffee, there was an awkward standoff between driver Raúl and the stowaways. At first they seemed determined to remain on the trailer, despite Raúl's repeated orders for them to disembark, each of which included the word "negro", spat out with contempt. Eventually, they got the message and disembarked with a scowl and some saliva projected in Raúl's direction.

One thing we had learned from our short time with the *Colombianadas* was the joyful news that Raúl was on his way to Santa Marta. I'm not sure how they had known it, but Raúl confirmed it and, after a break in excess of an hour, we were back on the pallets and I was declaring excitedly, "Next stop Santa Marta!"

But of course, things are never that easy. At around 6pm, just before sunset, we made another stop in another little village. Raúl, a frenetic sort, moved to and fro between truck and village shack for a while until, around 20 minutes later, we were informed by his travelling companion that this was as far as Raúl could take us. We didn't entirely grasp the reason, but the word "*combustible*" (petrol) was used, and so, with precious few remaining minutes of light and no clue how far we remained from Santa Marta, we were on our own again.

Raúl's friend climbed on a bus and offered to pay for us too. We thanked him, but shook our heads and wandered solemnly in search of a spot where vehicles might be going slowly enough to see us.

By the time we'd found one, it was dark and our plight seemed hopeless. As music blared out of a nearby bar, we were facing the awful possibility of having to spend the weekend there (given we never travel on Sundays), in a dingy village, distinguishable only by the presence of numerous bars pumping out unnecessarily loud music. And bad music, at that.

"Hang in there," I said to Jo, who was close to tears.

A truck was parked just in front of us. It seemed our last hope.

Inside, a young man was fiddling with the controls on his dashboard, as I knocked on the window.

I had to restrain myself from kissing him when he agreed to take us.

An hour later, it was with some relief, as well as joy, that we glimpsed the Caribbean coast for the first time.

DAY 167: MONDAY 1ST SEPTEMBER 2014, 08.13
HOSPEDERÍA CASA FAMILIAR, SANTA MARTA, MAGDALENA, COLOMBIA

STEVE

Every now and then, we come across a story that forces us to reconsider our happy-go-lucky attitude to security in South America. Last night, as we caught up with Facundo, we encountered another.

Facundo has been through a rough time lately. Four months ago, he bought a bicycle, intent on continuing his journey to Alaska by pedal power, once he had saved enough money.

Roll on two months and everything had changed. Walking home one night with a friend, Facundo was subjected to a violent attack. His neck was cut and his lips split open. A passerby took pity on him and picked him up on his motorbike to take him to hospital, but on the way they were struck by a car. Facundo's right leg pressed against the bike's exhaust and he was badly burnt. It took 25 days, he said, before he could walk without pain.

The incident also had an impact on his livelihood. Facundo works as a tour guide, taking groups on four-day hikes. After a month without work and no insurance to cover his losses, Facundo was ready to return. He needed to. The medical bills alone had left him penniless. And then, on the morning he returned to work, his bicycle was stolen.

Now, poor Facundo is trying to work out a new plan. He has just two months more on his Colombian visa and little money. There is a court hearing in a few days to decide the fate of his muggers, and a small chance they will choose to pay damages instead of facing a jail sentence. Perhaps this would enable him to dream again. In the meantime, our friend tells us that he has had enough of South America, but doesn't have the means to leave, nor the energy to continue his journey north.

Facundo's story is a sad one and enough to make us stop and think. Last night, as he walked us back to our hostel, we felt very aware of the dangers around us.

"I'm sorry for scaring you," he said. "It was just one incident in four months. You're not in any danger here."

The tragedy is that it takes just one event for everything to change. It will be some time before Facundo is able to move on from that attack and all that followed. We are very thankful that we have made it thus far without mishap, and pray that continues. If something happens, you can bet that we too will feel differently about security in South America.

DAY 168: TUESDAY 2ND SEPTEMBER 2014, 17.17
CENTRO COMERCIAL AMERICANO, BARRANQUILLA, ATLÁNTICO, COLOMBIA

Jo

Earlier, as I scooped perspiration from my forehead and flicked it theatrically to the floor, I surmised that hitchhiking is a comfortable activity only during a certain few weather conditions.

Winds of Patagonian velocity, for example, make standing still with one's thumb out a difficult prospect; rain forces us to don our all-black waterproofs, cloaking any distinguishable features and rendering us none too appealing to potential drivers; the cold is not a welcome companion during long waits; brightness makes our expressions squinty; heat saps the soul. But, then again, "comfortable" is not usually a word associated with hitchhiking.

I have also realised that for a few drivers, picking up hitchhikers is a wholly matter-of-fact, unemotional act, one from which they desire nothing in return. They don't want to find out about us and they don't want to be found out about, as with Jhoni today, who drove us and his truck of cows to Barranquilla: once we're in, the music is turned up, and everyone settles down to the rhythm of his or her own thoughts. It is a rare eventuality, but we don't mind if drivers don't want to talk: it gives our Spanish brains a rest for a while.

STEVE

We have been doing a bit more research on the boats-to-Panama front and I'm not overly optimistic of our chances of hitching a ride. The majority of boats seem to be $500-per-person cruises via the islands of San Blas, and a free ride on a boat other people are paying for seems no different to a free ride on a bus. Anyway, blagging free rides isn't really why we're doing this thing.

That leaves the option of hitching a ride on a cargo ship, of which there are also apparently a few, but I know from past experiences in Bangladesh that the rules regarding passengers can be prohibitive.

To be honest, I'm not really too concerned if we can't find a free ride. It isn't our fault there isn't a road connecting Colombia and Panama, and, however we arrive there, we will still be able to ensure that we hitch the entire length of road from Ushuaia to Alaska, even if there's a Darién Gap-shaped hole in the middle. Of course it would be nice if we can hitch across the ocean, but as I see it, there is little point in taking it too much to heart should we fail.

DAY 171: FRIDAY 5TH SEPTEMBER 2014, 10.08
HOSTAL CASA VIENA, CARTAGENA, BOLÍVAR, COLOMBIA

JO

Since Ecuador, it has been noticeable that the average age for starting a family has decreased: applying quick maths to the age of the driver and how long they've been married usually reveals betrothal at 16 and children not much later. The topic is a regular feature in our conversations, and I am so accustomed to the way that the dialogue proceeds that I now find myself pre-emptively adopting a mournful tone: no, we don't have children, and isn't it a shame that we have confused our priorities in this way.

Manuel, the trucker who brought us most of the way to Cartagena, was 40-years-old and had five children, the oldest of whom was 24.

"Do you have grandchildren?" I asked.

"No!" he exclaimed. "I'm too young for that!"

This struck me as a strange response from someone who had had three children by the age his oldest daughter is now, but I didn't comment.

Our arrival in Cartagena means that it's official: we have achieved our final hitch in South America. We celebrated with cocktails in the historic centre last night, and tried to ignore the perspiration hosting its own gathering on our foreheads.

The heat in this part of Colombia is like a straitjacket. Any patch of shade becomes a long-lost friend not to be parted from. Fans and air-conditioning are lingered under using any pretence necessary: yes, I am indeed interested in this excruciatingly expensive jewelled necklace. Sun cream forms oily beads of sweat, unable to be absorbed into already sodden skin.

Wet patches on clothes are the new accessory – everyone has them, apart from the rich ladies, somehow even now floating along in their clouds of white silk. When an earlier downward glance revealed a burgeoning stripe of perspiration conquering the lower half of my t-shirt, I resigned myself to the fact that I am not one of those ladies.

DAY 171 (CONTINUED): 13.20
CAFÉ SERRANO, CARTAGENA, BOLÍVAR, COLOMBIA

STEVE

We have a boat, although unfortunately it wasn't acquired in quite the way we would have liked.

This morning, after visiting Cartagena's yacht club and cargo port, it became apparent that we were not going to be able to find ourselves a free ride. But as I said, finding ourselves a free ride wasn't really what we were after. We hoped only that by some chance a ship's captain might be so enamoured by the tale of our adventure that they would happily take us aboard, more as new friends than as a couple of freeloaders. But it was not to be.

Instead, all we found were Spanish-speaking captains who had seen many of our kind before and, understandably, wished to charge the usual fee. And when it came to the cargo ships, it was simple: no passengers allowed.

Well at least we gave it a try. But now it is clear: we will sail to Panama and, like everyone else, pay for the privilege. From Panama, we will recommence our hitchhike north to Alaska.

Perhaps, then, our journey could be considered a two-part affair. The first ended yesterday, after a day that could be seen as a microcosm of our adventure to date. First there was the super-quick ride, which made us believe the day was sure to be a success. But then came the long wait, in which life seemed hopeless and we feared we may never reach our target in one day. For almost two hours, we waited and wandered on the edge of the town of Baranoa. Then, as all hope faded, our rescuer arrived in the form of Manuel the trucker. With him, we travelled the remaining distance to Cartagena, where, as we began the trek into the centre, we waved hopefully at passing cars and were immediately invited into the plush Toyota Hilux belonging to an old chap named Jaime, who told us that he too had hitchhiked when young and that he thought our trip was *excelente*.

Gracias amigo, your help made for the perfect end to part one of our adventure. Now we head for pastures new. There is to be no heroic boat-hitchhike, but we press on, with heads held high and, we believe, our mission firmly intact.

14. BORDER HOPPING

DAY 181: Monday 15th September 2014, 17.26
Casa Sucre Coffeehouse, Panama City, Panama

Jo

As we sit sipping our mugs of Panamanian coffee, my mind lurches in motion with the sea that is no longer beneath us, and sporadic waves of tiredness break over me. I can't explain why I feel so exhausted – there was a lot of sleeping on the boat – but maybe it's all this adjusting to *terra firma* after six nights offshore.

We have arrived in Panama – land of "abundant fish", according to the translation of the name – and so the next chapter begins. I am definitely rested: standing at the edge of the small port town of Portobelo this morning, I felt that if we were in for a long wait I would be able to cope. The boat crossing is behind us now and only land lies ahead.

In the end, we didn't have to wait long for our first ride in Central America. A father and son from Madrid passed us on their way to Panama City and brought us to the outskirts. A tremendous downpour ensured that the entire contents of our bags were sodden after our hour's walk to the centre, but otherwise we are none the worse for wear as we assimilate to this new continent.

DAY 184: THURSDAY 18TH SEPTEMBER 2014, 21.02
HOTEL PLAZA, SANTIAGO, VERAGUAS, PANAMA

STEVE

Panamanians are the happiest people on the planet, or so we were told today by two of our drivers. It's a far cry from what we had heard about Panama from the Turkish captain of our ship – that culture is lacking and that it generally feels a little soulless. But in a recent poll, apparently Panamanians came out on top, with Costa Ricans a close second. Given that we're now halfway between Panama City and the Costa Rican border, it seems we are well placed.

There was plenty of soul among our drivers today – all six of them – although we endured a few nervous moments during our second ride.

I should have sensed it earlier. There was definitely something business-like about the way Eddy, 25, pulled over and carefully placed our belongings in the boot of his car. But it wasn't until we were inside and noticed two additional female passengers on the back seats that the situation became clear.

"Is this your family?" I asked Eddy, in hope more than expectation.

"No," he responded, looking confused.

"Ah, this is a taxi, isn't it?" I said.

Eddy nodded.

"Ah, we don't have any money."

Giggles from the back.

"Is that going to be a problem?"

More giggles.

"You see, we're travelling *aventón* [for free] from Argentina to Alaska!"

Howls of laughter.

Thankfully, this was to be our last misunderstanding of the day. Perhaps by way of payback, Eddy left us in a rotten spot, right in the middle of the next town, but after a two-hour walk to relocate the main road, it was all plain sailing.

Seventy-one-year-old gran Mary Cruz was a particular gem, with her fabulous black hair-net and disregard for driving regulations. We were glad of the presence of her young neighbour, 13-year-old Magnolia, who was playing the fundamental role of co-pilot to ensure Mary Cruz didn't change lanes at the wrong time. (She didn't seem to have discovered the wing mirrors.)

Our next driver, Will, a thirty-something American-Panamanian, told us the road ahead was dangerous but that we had "good energies" and would therefore "probably be OK".

And then it was the turn of the happiness brigade, as our final two drivers informed us of Panama's chart-topping stats.

"I love Panama," enthused 19-year-old Mary Lisa. "People are just really happy here. We have everything!"

If the happiness rating correlates with ease of hitchhiking (and I reckon it should), then I suppose we will indeed "probably be OK" here.

DAY 185: FRIDAY 19TH SEPTEMBER 2014, 21.02
MULTI CAFÉ, DAVID, CHIRIQUÍ, PANAMA

JO

I was so full of beginner's optimism on our first day hitching in Panama that I feel slightly guilty confessing to the unshakeable tiredness I'm now burdened with, a mere five days later. It must be psychosomatic – there is no other reasonable explanation. We have just had a 10-day hitching break, and it would feel pathetic to point to the sultry heat or cumulative time on the road as excuses. Surely we're acclimatised to those by now.

Real or imagined, the tiredness pervades, and on our walk through the town of Santiago this morning I had to resort to counting my steps to ward off negative thoughts. I reached three thousand nine hundred and ninety by the time we arrived at the spot where we were later picked up. The total distance was probably a cool (or, rather, inescapably hot and sticky) five kilometres. At least my subsequent tiredness was legitimate.

STEVE

There may be a lot of happy people here in Panama, but we were not two of them this lunchtime. A swelteringly hot morning, combined with a lot of walking and no pick-ups, left us exhausted and rather short of optimism, as we took shelter from the sun at a roadside cafe and the clock struck 12.

No Panamanians stopped for us this afternoon, either, but thankfully a few fellow foreigners did. First there was gentle George, an American retiree with a bumper sticker that seemed slightly at odds with his character: "Gun control means hitting your target ... Have a nice day!"

But it was a pair of Peruvians who truly saved the day. Edison, 50, and his son, Edison Jnr., 18, brought us 95 per cent of the way here to the city of David, ensuring the day was not a total failure and that we are just 40 minutes short of the border. We will head that way tomorrow and hope for a little more happiness.

DAY 186: SATURDAY 20TH SEPTEMBER 2014, 15.26
TORTILLA FLATS, DOMINICAL, PUNTARENAS, COSTA RICA

STEVE

Well, I suppose that if you're going to pass through Costa Rica, a country whose very name translates as "rich coastlines", it would be rude not to visit one. So here we are, on the Pacific coast again, and the surfer's haven of Playa Dominical. To be honest, we'd never heard of it, but this is where our fourth and final driver of the day, Jazz, was headed. Having breezed through Panama in just three days, we have already crossed about a third of the length of Costa Rica, and we've only been here a few hours. Central America is small.

Our passage to the border this morning was quick and the crossing straightforward. Much had been made of Costa Rica's strict borders – so much so that we had two fake plane tickets in hand (as proof of onward travel) – but we needn't have worried.

On the other side, the clocks were an hour behind, meaning that it was just 10am as we waited for our first ride in Costa Rica.

We received little recognition early on, but Mauricio, 29, and girlfriend Virginia, 22, took us to Neily, the next city, and it was there that Jazz found us and brought us here, to a town full of *gringos*. The bar next door is screening American football and there is more written, and spoken, English here than Spanish. Well, I guess it'll give us a few days off.

Oh, and on our hotel room door, "Avoid stopping when a stranger asks you for a ride" features in a list of "Tips for having a great and safe vacation in Costa Rica and the rest of the world". Let's hope this view isn't shared by all Costa Ricans.

Jo

Since landing on Panama's shores two weeks ago, we have never been far from thick vegetation – all around are deep green forests and mountainous horizons. It is no wonder the colours are so verdant: the rainfall is incredible.

Magnificent deluges, such as the one we were caught in on our walk into Panama City, are typical events, and predictable almost to the minute: mornings are blisteringly hot, and then at around 1pm an almighty storm breaks. Rain launches itself at the ground with grim determination; thunder and lightning throw punches at each other across the menacing sky. We humans are mere pawns in nature's play: whatever the means of protection, one still gets wet – really, really wet.

At least we still have our waterproofs. We are not doing well with retaining our belongings; our total inventory of lost or misplaced items currently stands at: one jumper, one top, one pair of pants, one pair of trousers, three socks and a pair of flip-flops. (And, of course, the tent.) If only we'd left them all in the same place, someone could have gained a whole – if unusual – outfit.

DAY 189: TUESDAY 23RD SEPTEMBER 2014, 10.58
SIEMBRAS & COSECHAS, MASAYA, NICARAGUA

STEVE

When hitchhiking through countries the size of those in Central America, if you're not careful you can pass right through them without really trying. Such was our fate yesterday, as we bade farewell to Costa Rica before we'd even had time to try the national breakfast, *gallo pinto* (rice and beans). Fortunately, it exists here in Nicaragua too. In fact, the Nicaraguan who brought us here, 25-year-old *camionero* Lester, claims it originated here.

Our short stay in Costa Rica meant we had little time to get to grips with the country. We learnt only that the new President is popular and said to be willing to follow through on the great advances he has promised, such as improvements to infrastructure. Perhaps we will have more to say about Nicaragua. Thanks to 10 hours with Lester, we have already heard about a faltering economy and unpopular government.

Lester told us that Nicaragua has the best resources in the whole of Central America and that the country would prosper if only a good man would lead it. Asked when the next elections were, Lester told us it didn't matter because the country is bound to remain unchanged.

"It's like a dictatorship," he said.

But hope lies in plans to build a canal through Nicaragua that could rival Panama's famous waterway. This year is the Panama Canal's one hundredth anniversary and it is clear what a great effect it has had on the country's economy.

Despite our success yesterday in travelling more than two thirds of the length of Costa Rica and a good few hours into Nicaragua, there were moments we thought the day might prove a disaster.

After Mauricio had transported us 40km to Quepos in his minivan, we spent the next two hours there, wandering around the perimeter of the town in search of a good spot. Eventually we found one, but only after the help of a chap named Jorge, who took us to the far side of town.

There, we were soon picked up by José, 25, an auditor, and when he told us he was driving a good distance, Jo's fears that we might stay in Quepos forever were blown away.

Indeed, from that moment on, the day was an unmitigated success. An old man named Rafael helped us to rejoin the *Panamericana* running north, where we spotted two parked trucks about to pull out. As we passed them on the inside and Jo questioned which was more likely to run us over, I waved at the driver of the one at the rear and was beckoned over. We had hoped to journey just an hour or so farther north to a spot on the coastline where a friend lives, but the offer of a ride to the border seemed too good to turn down.

We spent the next 10 hours driving, waiting in queues at the border, and then driving some more, until, at 1am, we arrived on the edge of the city of

Masaya and, after passing half a dozen seedy-looking motels, eventually found a respectable hotel where we could crash for the night.

DAY 190: WEDNESDAY 24TH SEPTEMBER 2014, 15.57
EL SESTEO, LEÓN, NICARAGUA

STEVE

Hitchhiking is easy again. Thank you Nicaragua for refreshing us with your friendly faces and quick pick-ups. In securing three rides today, we didn't once have time to lay our bags to rest before a driver pulled over.

First, an elderly couple named Dolores and Antonio took us the remaining 30km to the capital, Managua. We thought we might spend the day there, but Dolores told us we needn't bother.

"It's not a tourist city," she said. "León is much nicer."

That settled it. It was just 10am and León was only 90km to the west. Oscar, 47, took us to the start of the right road and there we were picked up by the first black trucker we have seen, 43-year-old Crisanto. We were in León by lunchtime and now lie just a few hours' journey from our next border. Tomorrow, we will set our sights on Honduras.

JO

Our daily hunt for juice (an easily satisfied craving in these countries of plentiful fruits) led to a chance encounter this morning. My nose to the wind, I sniffed out a shopping centre that seemed certain to have a *jugueria* (a juice-lover's haven) somewhere inside. We were directed to the fourth floor, and while Steve scouted the food hall, I bumped into a fellow backpacker.

"Hello," he said. "Are you Australian?"

"No," I replied, wondering if I should be. "English." He confessed that he was no good at accents.

The traveller revealed himself to be American, and asked where we were heading. I said that we had only recently arrived in Managua ("Me too!" he interjected) but that we were now heading off.

"We're hitchhiking," I said, as if that might explain our rapid departure.

"ME TOO!" he exclaimed.

And then it all came tumbling out. This was a hitchhiking aficionado by the name of Adam, on an adventure like ours but from north to south: he had departed from Georgia in the States and was gradually making his way to Argentina. Not only that, but he was doing it with no money to his name.

"I'd heard of people who leave home with $1,000 and are still travelling 10 years later," he said. "I figured they must work something out, so I gave all my money away and left."

He made it sound remarkably easy.

"People are incredibly generous with food, and so many of them insist on giving me money," he added. "I just keep it until I find somebody who needs it more than me. I've got $140 in my giveaway fund at the moment."

I could have quizzed Adam for hours about this "moneyless experiment", as he called it. He's been living this way for over a year now and it doesn't seem to have dented his enthusiasm. What an insight into both his own resourcefulness and the generosity of the world around him.

I found our meeting encouraging for another reason. Adam has just hitchhiked through the countries we're heading towards – the "dangerous" ones – and had only positive reports. Hearing that it's all possible, and having concrete evidence there in front of me, made a big impact. Alaska suddenly doesn't feel so unreachable.

DAY 191: THURSDAY 25TH SEPTEMBER 2014, 13.29
JHONI'S TRUCK, FRONTERA EL GUASAULE, NICARAGUA

STEVE

We sit at one border, knowing we have already secured our passage to the next. Here, at Nicaragua's border with Honduras, we await *camionero* Jhoni's paperwork to be completed, before we set a course for El Salvador. In fact, Jhoni, 35, has invited us to join him on his journey all the way through to his native Guatemala, but we think it might be rather remiss to skip through too many Central American countries in one go. Saying that, we don't mind missing out on Honduras. No-one seems to have much good to say about it. Even Elias, our first *camionero* today, who hails from Honduras, said he prefers his life in Nicaragua, away from the "*delincuencia*" of his native land.

"There's too much *delincuencia*," he told us, pointing his fingers to his throat in the shape of a gun. "Honduras has the highest crime rate in the world. I don't miss living there very much."

Jhoni seems to be of the same mind.

"Honduras is *feo* [ugly]," he said. "I don't like it. Nor the food."

Jhoni, who lives in Guatemala City, admitted his own country is blighted by the same "*delincuencia*", but he maintains that it is beautiful and well worth a visit. We have heard the same from many others and look forward particularly to the oft-recommended former capital, Antigua Guatemala. But for the time being, our sights are set on El Salvador. Jhoni told us he knows a nice place on the Pacific coast, a port town named La Libertad, where he plans to drop us. All being well, this time tomorrow we'll be enjoying another dip in the Pacific Ocean.

DAY 192: FRIDAY 26TH SEPTEMBER 2014, 04.30
POLICE STATION, JÍCARO GALÁN, VALLE, HONDURAS

STEVE

It's 4.30 the next morning and we find ourselves in a police station in Honduras. How did we end up here?

I guess it all began at around 2.30 yesterday afternoon, as we stepped out of Jhoni's truck to pass through immigration.

"I'll see you on the other side in around 30 minutes," Jhoni had said.

Well, 30 minutes came and went, and there was no sign. Another hour passed and still nothing.

When the clock reached 5pm and the sun started to fade, we began reassessing our options. What could have become of our driver? We knew borders could be tricky places, particularly for truckers, and we felt sure he had been genuine in his invitation to see us on the other side, but it would soon be dark. We couldn't wait indefinitely.

On my regular laps of the vicinity to see if Jhoni may be lurking somewhere, or looking for us, I befriended another *camionero*, Paulo, 33, who offered us a ride to a police checkpoint five kilometres from the border with El Salvador.

When, at 6pm and now dark, Paulo passed in his truck and extended his invitation anew, we felt we had to accept. He told us we'd be at the checkpoint by eight.

We arrived at nine and thanked Paulo for his help, but then we got chatting to the police and discovered the border was in fact still more than an hour and a half's drive away. Not five kilometres, after all. We were also told that no trucks would be passing that way until the following morning.

The peculiar Sergeant Espinoza plonked us on a bench made in the shape of two love hearts, and we were forced to watch as truck after truck went by and the sergeant let them go without a word. I tried waving at a few of them from our perch on the other side of the road, but it was hopeless.

When, at just before 10pm, a heavy thunderstorm struck, we decided to cut our losses and, with no hotel in sight and no Honduran currency to pay for it anyway, asked if we could spend the night at the police station. Sergeant Espinoza nodded and pointed us to a corner, where we could lay our mats.

So, here we are, six hours later, awaiting the dawn, as a man mops the floor by my head and a new round of officers watch cartoons on the TV next door, making it impossible to sleep. With a bit of luck, we'll make it to the border for breakfast. Who knows, perhaps we'll even see our friend Jhoni again.

DAY 192 (CONTINUED): 14.23
PLAZA LIBERTAD, SAN SALVADOR, EL SALVADOR

JO

Last night's storm was humungous. The warning signs had been there since sundown, with flashes of lightning dancing around us as we travelled. When Sergeant Espinoza stopped being distracted by his phone long enough to talk to us, he told us we could sit inside when the rain came.

Whatever was going on up in the heavens, it involved deep fury. Seconds after the first droplets, the rain cranked up to power-hose strength, and from there – seemingly impossibly – it only got heavier. The roof of the police station was made of corrugated iron, intensifying the percussive cacophony, and then the thunder muscled in to voice its indignation. Soon there was a veritable crowd sheltering in the station: us, the absent-minded police chief and about 10 soldiers shaking the rain from their machine guns.

"A good night to smuggle drugs," Steve said. "The country's military are all hiding from the rain."

We laid our roll-mats on the tiled floor, carefully avoiding the path of red ants trooping along the skirting board, and caught a few hours' kip.

We weren't the only waifs and strays. Opposite us, a man and his son were sprawled across an ancient mattress. As we packed our bags this morning, the man's wrinkly face creased into a sleepy smile, and, pointing at his bare feet, he asked: "*Tienes zapatos?* [Do you have shoes?]"

"For you?" I asked. He nodded hopefully.

"Ah no, I'm sorry my friend, we only have these ones," I apologised.

Why was this man at the station, and why did he have no shoes? He didn't look upset that we couldn't help, but I found it sad all the same.

DAY 192 (CONTINUED): 18.14
JUAN VALDEZ CAFÉ, CENTRO COMERCIAL GALERÍAS, SAN SALVADOR, EL SALVADOR

STEVE

At 5am, as the sun started to rise, I woke Jo and we staggered blearily outside to recommence our journey to El Salvador. It was chastening to think that by rights we should already be there, snoozing in a comfy hotel beside the sea. As it was, we were still a way from the border and faced a new day of fresh challenges.

Pablo, 47, another *camionero*, got us off to a good start, but he was driving only to the next city, Nacaome, and left us in arguably a worse position, on a main road where cars flashed past.

As we wandered in search of a better spot, we waved at passing vehicles, but few drivers seemed even to notice us. We plodded steadily on and turned at the sound of each vehicle. We almost missed one, but caught it just at the last minute and the driver skidded to a halt.

Dany, 40, and fellow mechanic Alexis, 46, were going to a job near the border and went out of their way to take us the remaining distance. Dany also provided us with a different account of life in Honduras. He said that life was certainly challenging, with low salaries and high unemployment, but that it was a shame we didn't have time to explore the country further. The north, he said, is completely different from the poorer south – more commercial, a different culture and, sadly, higher crime rates too.

Juan Carlos, 40, another Honduran, who brought us from the border here to San Salvador in his swish Toyota Hilux, said the level of "*delincuencia*" in some Central American countries was "a great shame".

"Nicaragua, now there's a special country," he said. "No *delincuencia* and it's beautiful too. In Honduras, and even more so in Guatemala, there's too much *delincuencia*."

Juan Carlos told us he had once worked as a *camionero*, but that he had stopped after experiencing an assault in Guatemala.

"Don't go there!" he warned.

Well, whatever the state of Guatemala, we will be going there. After getting to grips with El Salvador, Guatemala is next on our itinerary and, as in Honduras and Colombia, I imagine passing through the country won't feel half as bad as we were told it should.

Dany asked what my biggest takeaway was from the trip so far.

"That the world is full of good people and that danger exists far more in the mind than in reality," I replied.

I should think we have some way to go before people will stop warning us about our safety, with Mexico still to come, followed by the mean streets of the USA and a people fed on horror stories. But I have a sneaky feeling we'll pass through it all without mishap.

Jo

Steve and I have deliberately sought out a shopping centre: not a normal activity for us, especially in a different country. These places are stripped of local character – we could be anywhere in the world in this air-conditioned capsule – and they dull one's awareness of the actual economic state of a country. We were told today that El Salvador is Central America's second poorest country (Nicaragua is at the top), and yet here we are, surrounded by international brands and expensive-looking people. It's a bubble.

This afternoon, after a healthy nap to recoup last night's broken sleep, we went on a foray into the *centro histórico*, a thriving jumble of tin-roofed market stands. I've never seen such a spread, each street ringing with the resounding chorus of vendors half-singing, half-shouting about their wares.

We ate a traditional lunch of *pupusas* (a sandwich of fried tortillas filled with meat and beans) for the staggering price of 30p.

However, it wasn't the kind of place to hunker down and write awhile – we would have been getting in the way of business – and we couldn't find anywhere else conducive to writing (and coffee drinking). That's what brought us here; we don't feel pressured to hasten our departure from a Colombian coffee chain in a gigantic mall.

DAY 195: MONDAY 29TH SEPTEMBER 2014, 13.22
RESTAURANTE LA TERRAZA, LA LIBERTAD, EL SALVADOR

STEVE

Hitchhiking in the past week has been a stroll in the park. It makes such a difference. We could be sitting here, tired and jaded, but instead we're feeling fresh after another easy day on the road.

We travelled just 35km today and I'd wager that more than a quarter of those were covered on foot, but by the time we reached the *autopista* (motorway) running south, it was blissfully straightforward.

Two short rides helped us on our way, and then along came Francisco, 27, in a van headed for the market in La Libertad, where we were set to come last Thursday with trucker Jhoni. Well, eventually we've found our way here and have another chance to glimpse the Pacific before we set our sights on Guatemala and the gargantuan Mexico.

JO

On Saturday, we met Jimi. We were ambling past the cathedral in San Salvador when a man leaning against a railing greeted us with an American accent. We stopped to chat.

Our conversation revealed Jimi to be a desperate man. It was in his eyes as well as his words.

"Life here is hard, man," he told us, having explained that he'd lived in California for 30 years but was back because of difficulties with paperwork. He put himself in a different category to those whose whole lives have been spent in El Salvador.

"People here are not civilised like us," he said. "You might not see it because you're just passing through, but this is a developing country. People aren't educated, systems don't work. I want to leave, I want to get to Guatemala or Costa Rica, where life is better, and wait out my time until I can get back to the US."

It was clear Jimi felt he had fallen flat by having to return to El Salvador. He referenced education several times, and the lack of opportunities in his home country. We wondered later why he didn't try to find a job teaching English, considering his proficiency, though he hadn't sounded keen to make roots.

Wil, one of our inner-city taxi drivers, reiterated the idea that life in El Salvador is more difficult after time spent in the US.

"It's dangerous," he said, when we asked him about life here. "Not for you or other tourists – the danger won't touch you. It's different for us. There are gangs, and if they know that you've lived in the US, can speak English and are educated, they assume you have money and the risk is even greater."

Wil seemed to put his finger on the reality that most of the risks we are told about affect only local people and not those passing through. The targeting of tourists for petty theft may be common, but generally we're not likely to encounter the violence and gun crime associated with Colombia, for example, or Mexico. We get an easy ride.

DAY 196: TUESDAY 30TH SEPTEMBER 2014, 17.07
SEÑOR CHAI, ANTIGUA GUATEMALA, SACATEPÉQUEZ, GUATEMALA

STEVE

We enjoy hitchhiking for two primary reasons:

1. Because it allows us to get to know people and to hear their opinions on life in their country.
2. Because it's fun.

Today featured little of the former, but plenty of the latter. For five of our seven rides, we were in the back of trucks (four pick-ups and a *camión* filled with rubble). Inside our first car, with Julio and cousin Ricardo, who took us over the border into Guatemala, we heard more from the subwoofer in the boot than our drivers, and spent the rest of the time trying to work out if the next corner would be our last. Julio was a 200km/hr kind of guy. I had always feared we might die in Guatemala, but "road accident" did not top my list of potential causes.

In reality, the early signs are that we have little to worry about here. For one thing, we currently have a 100 per cent hitching success rate: two waves at passing cars; two pick-ups.

Sergio, a 21-year-old student, was the first and told us to avoid Guatemala City. But other than the capital, Sergio said he loved everything about his country – the people, culture, food, and sights.

Our seventh and final driver, Elber, who travelled with aged father Rafael, told us Guatemala was "the best".

Like I said, early signs are good. The former capital, Antigua Guatemala, is picturesque and lies beneath three giant green volcanoes. It makes for quite a backdrop.

DAY 197: WEDNESDAY 1ST OCTOBER 2014, 16.18
CAFÉ BARISTA, ANTIGUA GUATEMALA, SACATEPÉQUEZ, GUATEMALA

JO

Antigua has been an instant hit. I am particularly taken by Volcán de Fuego (Volcano of Fire), which periodically puffs out plumes of smoke, just to remind us little people of our mortality.

We have achieved my previously stated aim of not visiting Guatemala City; I needed some time off tramping the endless streets of large cities, and besides, the general consensus is that the majority of crime and violence in Guatemala takes place within the capital. Wandering through Antigua's historic streets, with charming, crumbling churches around every corner, our primary concern is whether we're going to escape the next thunderstorm.

It was even cool enough last night to make us wonder whether we might need to put on warmer layers, for the first time since Bogotá – at which point Steve discovered that his one and only pair of trousers is no longer in our possession. How these things happen is a mystery. Steve would probably happily carry on with just his swim shorts, if there wasn't the chill of an approaching American winter to consider.

DAY 198: THURSDAY 2ND OCTOBER 2014, 14.02
LAGO ATITLÁN, PANAJACHEL, SOLOLÁ, GUATEMALA

STEVE

We lost our 100 per cent hitching success rate with passing Guatemalans today, but only just. We were told it would take around three hours to travel to Lago Atitlán, a large lake overlooked by another trio of green volcanoes. It took us just two and a half. As in Chile, Argentina and Ecuador, in this part of Central America, hitchhiking is not only the best way to travel; it's also the quickest.

At one stage, with our third driver, it seemed we were about to pass the lake by. Jaime, 59, a travelling vet, was heading farther east to the city of Quetzaltenango, or "Xela" for short. When asked if we wanted to travel with him all the way, we had been indecisive. Having spent only two nights in Guatemala, we were wary of moving through too quickly and had heard of the beauty of Atitlán. But as the lake passed out of sight, we assumed the decision had been made for us.

"Well, I suppose we'll just have to come back to Guatemala," I reflected. "At this rate, we might be in Mexico tonight!"

But then we rounded a corner and Jaime pulled over at a junction at the top of a hill.

"The lake's down there," he said. "Enjoy it!"

From the junction, we were taken the remaining distance by a young Guatemalan couple, Pablo Javier, 25, and Amy, 24, who told us that a lack of jobs, not crime, is their country's greatest problem.

Pablo Javier has been through university, but, when he finished, he said he couldn't find work, so he started trading cars. He said many of his friends have done the same.

Amy is in the final year of a law degree, but she too fears she will struggle to find work – or at least work that pays sufficiently.

Guatemala boasts a great many tourist attractions. Pablo Javier and Amy were disappointed when we told them we have no plans to head to the Mayan ruins farther north. Tomorrow, we will leave the lake and set our sights on the border to the west and our final Spanish-speaking country. Tomorrow, we hope to arrive in Mexico.

15. A WHOLE LOTTA TORTILLAS

DAY 199: FRIDAY 3RD OCTOBER 2014, 21.03
HOTEL PLAZA MAZARI, CIUDAD HIDALGO, CHIAPAS, MEXICO

STEVE

Just 19 days after arriving on the coast of Panama, we have passed out of the last of the mini Central American countries into the giant Mexico.

This particular part of Mexico is still considered Central America, but there will be no more border crossings for a while. We have just three remaining borders before we will be in Alaska. That doesn't sounds so bad, given that we've changed countries seven times in less than three weeks, but the scale will be rather different from here on in.

We're staying the night in the border town, while we try to get to grips with our latest new country, and currency. It's back to pesos again, although we can't work out if Mexico is going to be expensive or cheap. Our hotel was relatively pricey, but dinner for us both came to less than two pounds.

If we hadn't heard otherwise, nothing about our time in Guatemala would have led us to believe the country suffered from high crime rates and violence. It's funny what a country's reputation does to one's thinking. Even here in the state of Chiapas, we have been told to watch out. I'm just hoping it doesn't mean we'll struggle to find rides because of the fear drilled into people. With any luck, it will have the opposite effect and people will be begging us into their cars to save us.

Once we're through Chiapas, I'm hopeful we won't be warned of danger for a while, although goodness knows how we'll cope once we start to close in on the notorious northern border.

We arrived at our fourth-to-last border in good time today, with a day of easy hitching to put a nice seal on our sprint through Central America.

Three rides took us back to the Pan-American and then came our first of two truck journeys, with Francisco, 30. With him we climbed westward over a range of hills, which, he told us, are known as "the vegetable patch of the Americas" – or words to that effect. Plantations were everywhere. As we drew closer to the border, the lush green hillsides and fresh air were replaced by a return to sea level and hot, hot, hot.

We had been planning to stick to the Pan-American and a border a little farther north at La Mesilla, but Francisco was heading south and dropped us at a place he said was just an hour's drive from the Tecun Uman border.

Our next driver, Ronald, 30, told us the border was in fact four hours away. When we passed a sign indicating we were just 72km from the "*frontera*", I asked him whether the road was particularly winding.

"No, just like this," he said, pointing in a straight line along the very straight road we were on. We wondered how 72km could possibly take four hours. Perhaps he thought we were walking.

Contrary to Ronald's prediction, we arrived at the border a little over an hour later, thanks to a final ride in 44-year-old Oscar's truck.

And that brings us here, to a border town whose name we don't yet know. Judging from a sign on a passing bus, we think it might be called "CD Hidalgo" – we're guessing "CD" is short for "Ciudad", although we haven't seen that anywhere else in Spanish-speaking America. I make this our thirteenth Spanish-speaking country, and we still have things to learn.

DAY 200: SATURDAY 4TH OCTOBER 2014, 10.50
PAULINA'S TYRE WORKSHOP, TAPACHULA, CHIAPAS, MEXICO

STEVE

We find ourselves in an office surrounded by tyres. I'm currently leaning my head against one, while we wait for our second driver of the day, Paulina, to finish a few jobs before she takes us to the next town, Huixtla.

We met Paulina, a slim 28-year-old with jet-black hair, about half an hour ago, as we walked along the hard shoulder of the motorway on the outskirts of the city of Tapachula, where we had been dropped by our first driver, *camionero* Carlos, 34.

Carlos, whose truck was the first vehicle to pass us on the road from the border, told us that Chiapas is the most interesting part of Mexico (although he confessed that he hasn't ever visited another part), and that all the other states are just desert wastelands.

He also told us that there is no respect for the police in Mexico, who, he said, are "all corrupt".

In most of the countries we have visited, we have watched as bribes changed hands for minor driving offences – such as speeding or a cracked windscreen – but, other than that horrible man in Rio, we are yet to experience any hostility from law-enforcers. Could the Mexican police prove our undoing?

DAY 201: SUNDAY 5TH OCTOBER 2014, 19.03
HAMMOCK, PAULINA'S HOUSE, HUIXTLA, CHIAPAS, MEXICO

STEVE

Our decision to wait an hour in Paulina's tyre workshop proved unexpectedly rewarding. After less than an hour, Paulina ushered us back into her silver 4x4, where we were joined by her husband-to-be, Samuel, 26, and taken to Huixtla, as promised. We were dropped on the edge of town at a spot where lots of *camiones* were parked, and wished the best of luck.

But, as we waited to wave them goodbye, the passenger door swung open and Sam asked if we'd like to join them for lunch.

"We know an excellent place where they serve quesadillas," he enthused.

We couldn't refuse, and soon an offer of quesadillas had turned into a place to stay for the weekend.

Here in Huixtla, with Paulina, Sam, family and friends, we have been treated to a host of wonderful Mexican dishes, and an introduction to Mexican fiestas.

It just so happened that we arrived in Huixtla on the most important day of the town's calendar, 4 October, the day of Huixtla's patron saint, San Francisco de Asís. To celebrate, we joined our new friends at the local Catholic church and waited for Mass to finish and the festivities to begin. *Arroz con leche* (rice pudding) was handed out while a marimba player led the party outside and a group of mariachis (a Mexican string band), complete with matching outfits but sadly bereft of sombreros, marched into the church to kick off the party inside. We split our time between the two and were wowed by the talents and enthusiasm of both, as well as the camaraderie of the locals. Here in Huixtla, everyone knows everyone and we were soon made to feel part of the town.

With the party still going strong, I was invited back to Sam's friend's house for a late-night barbecue, some beers and my first tequila slammer, while Jo went for a girls' night with Paulina and friends.

The festivities continued today with a trip to a nearby river, accompanied by several more beers and more tortillas than I've ever seen. Oh, and Samuel presented us with a bottle of *mezcal* (a spirit like tequila) to drink when we arrive in Alaska, and invited us to their wedding in March. All in all, it's been a wonderful beginning to our time in Mexico. We haven't enjoyed this level of hospitality since southern Colombia.

And tomorrow it's set to get even better, as Jesús, Paulina's father, takes us to Tuxtla, the capital of Chiapas and a good few hundred kilometres towards our target.

Paulina told us her father once ran for a seat in the local government, but that the opposition bought votes to deny him a chance of victory.

"Mexico is the number-one country for corruption," she said. "And fat people."

This last part came as a shock. We haven't noticed many obese people here yet and it would take some doing to beat the Brazilians, or indeed the Americans, on that front.

Jesús spent this morning offering us advice on the best routes through Mexico. It seems we have two options: west to the Pacific coast and straight on up to California, or north alongside the Gulf of Mexico to the closer border with Texas. The accompanying dangers of the border crossings was mentioned as part of his spiel, but Jesús told us he'd driven the road to California and seemed confident we'd survive whichever way we went. First, we'll head with him tomorrow to the mountainous heart of Chiapas, which everyone has been telling us so much about.

DAY 202: MONDAY 6TH OCTOBER 2014, 10.29
PAULINA'S HOUSE, HUIXTLA, CHIAPAS, MEXICO

Jo

It's a bright, sunny morning in Huixtla as we embark upon our first full week in Mexico. (A full week in a country! It's been a while.) We are wonderfully relaxed at this moment; I am reclining in a cream-coloured hammock, Steve is on a comfy chair near the courtyard. If only waiting for the next lift always looked like this.

The promise of a ride is not always reliable, in our experience. Details don't filter through; people change their minds about when or where they're going; unexpected obstacles arise. We've had Anderson in Miranda, not able to find his driving licence; Raúl the trucker, unilaterally deciding that he was stopping in the middle of nowhere for the night; Jhoni, who promised a ride to El Salvador, if only we hadn't lost him at the Nicaraguan border. Could it be that Paulina's father will end up not driving us to the capital (not Mexico City, as I had excitedly thought, but the state capital, Tuxtla) so that instead of relaxing coolly in our civvies, we will be back in grotty t-shirts and sweating profusely on the side of a road somewhere? It's possible, but I'll just keep on enjoying my hammock for now.

Our Spanish education continues: here in Mexico, we have been thrust into a new set of vocabulary. Even Spanish-language television programmes from other countries display subtitles in Mexican Spanish, such are the differences. A *torta* here is a sandwich, where previously it was a cake; a cake is a *pastel*, which was a fried, usually savoury, *empanada* in Brazil; an *empanada* can be found in all manner of different forms, and as yet we don't know if they exist here. We're being kept on our toes, as ever.

DAY 203: Tuesday 7th October 2014, 20.29
Hotel Catedral, Tuxtla, Chiapas, Mexico

Jo

Jesús did follow through on his offer of a ride to Tuxtla – though we hadn't realised he was not to be the chauffeur. Just before lunch, Paulina's mum, Celia, drove us all to a ranch just outside Huixtla, whereupon we swapped cars, and drivers, to travel with Cesar, a colleague of Jesús'. A quick tour of his ranch had revealed that no expense had been spared on furnishings; this was a man with money to his name, and his character was as big as his bank balance.

"Do you like the monarchy?" Cesar asked us, shortly after our hurtle to Tuxtla had begun. "We Mexicans don't," he said, before I had time to respond. "The private jets; the castles; all that money they cost."

I wasn't sure how many Mexicans held this opinion, nor whether it was against the British monarchy or monarchies in general, but I tried to give a positive review of Queen Elizabeth and what a pillar of moral uprightness she is for Britain.

My view seemed to be of little consequence.

"And what about Charles' wife?" Cesar demanded.

"Camilla?" I asked.

"Yes, *Camillasita*. Do people like her?"

I assured him that most people probably do not have much of an opinion at all.

"But after Lady Diana was killed by the secret police for being pregnant with Dodi Fayed's baby, don't they hate her?"

This was not the first time we had been offered conspiracy theories, and I chose this moment to declare that I was not one for indulging in such talk. Unperturbed, Cesar continued with the theme of Diana's fate and Camilla's popularity rating.

"Look!" I said finally, having been asked whether people bow or boo when Camilla walks past. "Camilla is not thought of as a bad person in England, and anyway, most people don't care. And while the rest of the world continues to think that Diana was marvellous, it's not the same in England. I didn't like her!"

I announced this last statement with a triumphant air and a "case-closed" flourish. It wasn't the whole truth, but Cesar's binary manner had rubbed off on me, and my patience for the conversation had run too thin to scrabble for the Spanish for "divided opinion", "courted the media" and "tensions within the royal family".

For a moment, all was quiet and I worried I might have caused offence, but then I realised that Cesar was probably busy muttering "bloody monarchists" and congratulating himself on being such a successful republican.

The roads were quiet and well-maintained, such that Cesar's habit of driving at 150km per hour was undeterred. That was until one particular stretch where a police car stationed under a bridge came into view, and we were flagged down.

"I work for the government," Cesar declared, before the policeman had uttered more than "good afternoon". At the time, I wasn't entirely sure if this was true, though he certainly sounded authoritative.

"Oh ... I see, sir. I apologise, I didn't know," stuttered the policeman pathetically. From this point on, we all knew the conversation was just hot air, and moments later he sent us on our way with a plaintive, "You *were* going quite fast. Mind your speed, then."

The incident made not an iota of difference to the speedometer.

DAY 205: THURSDAY 9TH OCTOBER 2014, 19.43
LA CASA DEL MEZCAL, OAXACA, MEXICO

STEVE

In hitchhiking terms, the past two days were like chalk and cheese. On the first – yesterday – we endured a good deal of time waiting and an equal length walking. Today, there was very little of either. Yesterday, we were given six rides and spent the duration of each conversing with our drivers. Today, we had only three and spent them in the back (of two trucks and a 4x4) and thus out of earshot of our drivers. Yesterday, we struggled for optimism, as we journeyed just 200km during a full day on the road. Today, it took us only five hours to complete the 300km remaining to Oaxaca, the home of *mezcal*, a spirit with an older tradition than tequila and made from the same *agave* plant.

We saw a great many of those cactus-like plants on our journey today, the bulk of which was spent in the back of Efrain and Patricia's 4x4. The road was long and winding, and we endured an unfortunate length of time in the sun, but otherwise had no complaints from the moment Efrain pulled over, more than 250km from Oaxaca, and told us he'd take us all the way.

Our first two rides had served only to undo the detour of the night before, when, after dark and desperate to make some ground, we travelled in Gerardo's truck for 50km farther than needed, and in the wrong direction.

Gerardo had found us in a somewhat bedraggled state in the village of

Rizo de Oro, which, as precious little traffic passed, felt to us like the middle of nowhere and certainly miles from where we wanted to be. We had been there for 90 minutes, since a short ride in Wilber's truck, and had spent an hour before that waiting for Wilber.

Even before those long waits, our day's progress had been minimal – less than 100km in more than five hours with four different drivers, including two truckers (on whom one can usually rely to cover great distances).

Yesterday's toils added an extra layer of sweetness to today's successes. Here in La Casa del Mezcal, we sip two generous shots of the honey-coloured spirit in celebration, while considering whether we will continue on towards Mexico City tomorrow, or rest here for another day.

Jo

Steve and I are on the crispier side of sun-kissed this evening: despite liberal and repeated application of factor 70 sun cream (factor 70! Who knew that existed?), the sun still managed to have its way with my left hand and Steve's knees during our five-hour back-of-a-truck hitch to Oaxaca. There was a wonderful breeze throughout, which helped us keep our cool, but whenever the vehicle slowed, we could feel the intensity of the sun's rays.

Yesterday, as the sun began to set on the day's stops and starts, we drove with Gerardo through an entire city of wind turbines. That's what it felt like, anyway. It wasn't like the majority of English wind farms, with their handful of turbines; there were hundreds and hundreds of them. To the left and the right, the rows stretched on and on, and just as we thought we'd reached the end, more rose up in the distance. It brought to mind sci-fi films, in which cities are razed to the ground and angry robotic sentinels guard the land where the buildings once were; here, we were swapping robots for colossal windmills.

"Sometimes you can see trucks lying on their side, pushed over by the force of the wind," Gerardo said as we oohed and aahed. Until then we hadn't noticed the gales, sheltered as we were in the truck cabin, but then Gerardo opened the windows so we could feel the full effect. The wind whooshed in, bullying its way into every space and whistling boisterously in our ears. The gusts were warm and therefore not as cruel as those in Patagonia, but still, one did not doubt the wind's power.

Gerardo took us to the lorry depot of his employer, Cruz Azul, in Lagunas, and it appeared as if the entire town was sponsored by this cement company. A large blue cross stood as a monument in the centre, and we were fairly confident it wasn't a Christian symbol – the supermarket and bus stops were branded in the same way.

As we departed this morning, we strolled parallel to the railway line used to transport cement to different locations. We hadn't been walking long before a train chugged by, beginning its own lengthy journey, and we soon noticed that each carriage had a huddle of people hanging onto, or seated outside, the containers. We waved, and the return greetings were rather more vigorous than ours.

"Come with us!" a voice shouted over in English. This cry was taken up by various others.

"Quickly, quickly!" they urged us.

We were unmoved by the calls of the *migrantes*, not inclined to jump trains ourselves, but it is well-known that people from all around Central America ride trains in this manner – often with America as their final destination. Several drivers have asked us if our passports are in order, presumably influenced by a heightened suspicion of foreigners in Mexico's border states.

"My dad has an El Salvadorian friend he used to drive to work," Paulina told us last weekend. "Eventually his friend confessed that even though he has been living in Mexico for 10 years, he's never had the official paperwork, nor has he ever been caught when going back and forth between the countries. After that, my dad was so nervous when approaching the police checkpoint that he would divert through the restaurant car park behind it and out the other side!"

DAY 207: SATURDAY 11TH OCTOBER 2014, 17.53
PLAZA DE LAS TRES CULTURAS, CIUDAD DE MÉXICO, MEXICO

STEVE

Here we are, in the heart of the one of the biggest metropolises in the world, and it wasn't even especially hard to get here, or at least not to the centre.

Arriving on the outskirts at around 2pm, a passerby told us, thanks to the GPS on his smartphone, that we were 17km, or three and a half hours' walk, from the centre. Somehow, it didn't sound so bad. At least, we figured, we'd arrive in daylight.

But then it got a whole lot better. First, a delightful taxi driver named Juan, 49, who spoke some English and looked like Elton John, gave us a free ride to the Calzada Ignacio Zaragoza, the main road heading into the centre. And then, as we walked along with thumbs outstretched, a second driver came to our aid. We didn't work out where Arturo, 43, and his two sons, Mauricio, 18, and Eduardo, 15, were planning to go, but they took us all the way to our destination, the Tlatelolco district, where our next friend-of-a-friend, Farid, lives. Our three-and-a-half-hour walk had taken just an hour.

But that's not quite the whole story of our journey here to District Federal, or "DF" ("Day Effay"), as they call it here. The longer version involved a full day on the road yesterday, including three rides in the back of 4x4s, and thus a good deal of sunburn, and today our first taste of the Mexican *autopista* and a reminder of what it is like to travel *inside* vehicles – much cooler, and less burny.

We have passed two milestones this week: 30,000km since leaving Ushuaia, with over 300 drivers. Unfortunately, our three hundredth driver was a bit of a disappointment, quite like number 100 had been in Brazil. Edgar, 36, yesterday and Talvas in Brazil seemed to share a similar view on life: that danger is everywhere and that we had been very lucky to escape unscathed thus far and should be very careful in future. Edgar spent the duration of our journey together telling us about the dangers of Mexico, particularly DF.

When Jesús, 39, our three hundred and second driver, started on similar lines, I cut him off. "Well, we've been to São Paulo, Rio, Bogotá and Cali, and nothing happened. It never does!"

I felt a little bad about the outburst, but enough was enough. Here in Mexico City, we feel as safe as we have everywhere else and have experienced only kindness. Special thanks to dear Juan, and Arturo and sons, for saving us a serious walk. Our legs, and backs, are very grateful.

DAY 209: MONDAY 13TH OCTOBER 2014, 19.21
PIIX CAFÉ, QUERÉTARO, MEXICO

STEVE

They call this place "Mini DF" for its similarity to the historic centre of the capital city. On first impressions, that seems generous to DF, which, although impressive, did not match the beauty of Querétaro: cobbled streets, painted houses, beautiful churches, green plazas. It's one of the most striking places we've been, and I say that after less than two hours here.

Our journey here from DF, just 200km away, was long but without cause to grumble. Silver-haired Mario set us on our way, rescuing us from the hard shoulder of the lengthy Avenida de los Insurgentes, where we still found ourselves after an hour's trek from Tlatelolco. Mario was one of those Mexicans who spoke as though it were a song. We have noticed a wonderful tunefulness in many Mexican voices, which rise at the end of each sentence and carry the final note for an extra few syllables.

Our time with Mario was followed by a ride with Edgar the trucker, who found us at a *gasolinera* (the preferred Mexican term for "petrol station"). Edgar, who looked much older than his 28 years, travelled in a cab hosting a myriad of lucky charms. The most striking was a figurine resembling the Grim Reaper. Santa Muerte (Saint Death), believed to be the protector of people who work during the night, seems to be popular here. There's a statue of her in our hostel too, and we have passed a handful more of them in the shop windows of Querétaro. Perhaps it's part of the Halloween decorations, although I think there might be more to it.

Edgar also had a dreamcatcher, a native Indian charm believed to ward off bad dreams, and a wooden cross, which, he told us, had the specific purpose of preventing the spirits of dead truckers from entering his cab.

Our superstitious driver dropped us at another *gasolinera* just 15 minutes' drive, he said, from Querétaro. An hour later, after a ride with a pair of brothers, Cairo, 25, and Diego, 24, we were told for the second time we were just 15 minutes from the city. It was 5.30pm by then and we feared we may not reach Querétaro before sunset, but fortunately here in the south of Mexico, the clocks are an hour ahead of the other Central American countries and the sun doesn't set until after 7pm. This gave Armando, 30, sufficient light to see us, and drive us the final distance to the centre, pointing out beautiful sights along the way, including a striking brick aqueduct.

We were interested to hear from our friend Farid in DF that Mexico seems to be regressing. The Partido Revolucionario Institucional (PRI), which ruled for 70 years before the turn of the millennium, was voted back into power two years ago and, according to Farid, is up to its old tricks again. We learned that the square we visited on our first day, Plaza de las Tres Culturas, is known as a scene of massacres: first by the native Indians; then the Spanish; and latterly, in 1968, by the PRI government. With the Mexican Olympics approaching, a protest in the square angered the President, Gustavo Díaz Ordaz, and it is widely believed that he gave the final order for the bloodshed that followed, as around 300 people were killed.

Roll on to the present day, and history seems to be repeating itself, if not this time in the same location. Forty-three student teachers went missing two weeks ago after a protest in the southern state of Guerrero. Mass graves have been discovered and efforts are being made to identify the bodies. The military are thought to have been behind the disappearances, but someone must have given the order and fingers are again pointing to the top.

Economically, too, Farid says the country is going backwards.

"The President is selling off all of our assets overseas, including to Britain," he said. "Pemex [the national oil company] is currently being sold off to foreign investors. It's terrible."

Mexico is also struggling with a growing reputation as the world's new drug-trafficking hub. During our time in Huixtla, Sam told us that Mexico has become the "new Colombia", with drug lords holding the real power in the country and taking prominent places on the list of the World's Most Wanted.

Only in February, "El Chapo", the most wanted man in the world, was arrested. His capture reminded me of the hunt for Pablo Escobar, Colombia's infamous former drug lord. Yet El Chapo's incarceration is thought to have had little impact on the movement of cocaine over land and sea.

Still, despite political problems and an irrepressible group of cartels, Mexico is another land generally misunderstood by the wider world. We met some friends from the United States for dinner last night and they explained that their families had pleaded with them not to "risk their lives" by flying to DF for a holiday.

In reality, as with many of the other countries we have passed through, perceived danger seems grossly overestimated. We have seen little sign of it here. Perhaps as we journey northwest towards the much-maligned state of Sinaloa, our minds may be changed. We plan to head that way in the coming weeks, hugging the Pacific coast until we arrive in California, although our journey today presented us with a tempting alternative. As I write, Edgar the trucker is driving towards Monterrey in the northeast. If we had so desired, we could have found ourselves just a few hours' drive from Texas this time tomorrow. But when it came to it, we didn't feel ready to say goodbye to Mexico just yet.

Jo

In Central America, we became accustomed to the simplicity of the menu. Each country had a couple of main course dishes comprising meat in a sauce with rice and tortillas, and there was not much else on offer. The menu in Mexico, by contrast, contains jaw-dropping variety.

This is particularly noticeable when considering the *antojito* ("little craving") section, otherwise known as a list of snacks based upon the ubiquitous tortilla. Certain *antojitos* have garnered international popularity – tacos, quesadillas, enchiladas – but these are the tip of a huge culinary iceberg. Dishes we've sampled lately include *flautas*, *fringas*, *sincronizadas* and *tostadas*; the difference lies in the ingredients used for the tortilla, or the filling, or whether the tortilla is fried, or folded, or open, and so on. Every day we see words we don't yet understand included in this list – *tlayudas*, *enfrijoladas*, *gringas*. All credit to the Mexicans for harnessing the versatility of the humble tortilla.

DAY 212: THURSDAY 16TH OCTOBER 2014, 21.26
HOTEL HI!, GUADALAJARA, JALISCO, MEXICO

STEVE

Jo and I knocked back a couple of tequila slammers tonight. We had to: we're in Guadalajara, the state capital of Jalisco, which is to tequila what Oaxaca is to mezcal. In both, we have been presented with an extensive list of choices, and not known where to start. I thought tequila was tequila. Well, clearly not. Anyway, Jose Cuervo seems to be the brand of choice here, so we sampled a couple of his most popular blends. They tasted much the same: fiery, and helped down with some lime and salt.

We arrived here in Guadalajara in the same spectacularly easy fashion as on our journey from Querétaro to Guanajuato on Tuesday. It took us just five hours today to cover more than 250km, including the hike out of Guanajuato to the *autopista* – these *autopistas* are working a treat.

Camionero Jonathan, 31, was our fifth and final driver of the day. He is able to drive solidly for 30 days at a time with the help of co-driver Martín, 33, who was asleep for most of our journey. (He does the night shifts).

Jonathan left us at the exit to the road to Tepic, the next state capital. From there, the road runs north to Sinaloa (Jonathan reiterated our need to be careful there) and on to the Sonoran Desert and northern border. With two days left this week, we may yet be in the USA by the end of it. It's still some 2,000km away, but Jonathan told us streams of truckers head that way, and we're on the right road now. The Arizona border town, "NOGALES", is even on the signs.

DAY 214: SATURDAY 18TH OCTOBER 2014, 15.03
CAFÉ PARIS, CIUDAD OBREGÓN, SONORA, MEXICO

STEVE

We haven't done an all-nighter in a while. In fact, we've never done one like last night's, without a moment's rest – at least not for our driver. Jo and I took shifts staying awake with *camionero* Cornelio, 27, with whom we travelled for almost 24 hours straight, from 1pm yesterday, and during which time he didn't get a wink's sleep.

Sometimes, Cornelio told us, he will go for days without sleep; he'll simply unload, take on fresh cargo and set off again. He told us that he can be away for two months at a time and never knows where his next job will be: "My boss will just call me and say, 'You know what, now we need you to go *here*'."

Perhaps it is little wonder Cornelio subsists on a diet of coffee and caffeine pills, although it seems he's getting used to it.

"The night is mine!" he said, when I asked how he manages to stay awake.

Cornelio, who has a wife and two kids, reminded us once again how tough the life of a *camionero* can be. He has been doing the job seven years now and has never had a holiday. When we asked him what happens at Christmas, he said, "If I'm in Mexico City with my family, great. If I'm not, I'm not."

When Cornelio found us early yesterday afternoon, we were in a sorry state. The morning had been a drag. We had unwittingly found ourselves on the *libre* (free road) again and after three rides had travelled just 70km from Guadalajara. The latest of these, sharing the back of Héctor's pick-up truck with a giant petrol tank, had landed us in a *gasolinera* on the edge of the town of Magdalena, where we had been waiting longer than has become our custom. After just 15 minutes, Jo declared that she didn't want to live there.

I reminded Jo that it was still early days and that, even if we made it only to Tepic, we could consider the day a success.

"Who knows?" I added. "We might yet finish in the States. It only takes one ride!"

So we didn't quite get that far, but here in Ciudad Obregón in the state of Sonora, we lie just 500km from the Arizona border. Even to the Tijuana border with California in the far west, we are just 1,000km short. Cornelio's ride made a world of difference to our outlook and prospects for the next week.

The journey itself, all 22 hours of it, provided us with a welcome change of routine. We had become a little bored with our recent pattern of travelling a steady few hundred kilometres each day and then finding ourselves a hotel in which to rest before returning to the road again. We had been doing that a lot of late, and, while we are surely glad how easy it is to hitchhike here, we were secretly longing for a little more excitement.

Yesterday's ride certainly provided it. Not only was the scenery striking – from Tequila's *agaves* to mangroves, volcanoes and then the vast Sonoran Desert, but we were also given the thrill of a night-time ride through Sinaloa.

Our time in Sinaloa, famed as a lawless hub of drug trafficking, passed much like our time in Honduras: rapidly, mostly in the dark, and without incident. We are unable to judge whether everything they say about Sinaloa is true, but Cornelio certainly believes it.

The entire state, he told us, belongs to one man: El Chapo. "All of this is his," said Cornelio. "And that includes the police, the military, the government. In Mexico, if you have lots of money, no-one will touch you, and El Chapo is one of the richest men in the world. There are many places in the desert full of drugs, and no-one does or says anything. They can't. If they did, he'd kill them. He's done it before."

Nowhere is Mexico's drugs trade thought to be stronger than in Sinaloa. We're glad to be safely out the other side, although we're not out of the woods just yet. The entire stretch along the border is thought to be dangerous and Cornelio told us a chilling tale about the neighbouring state of Chihuahua, home to the notorious Juárez crossing.

"There are people in Chihuahua who will stop your vehicle and demand that you pay them 'rent' of 2,000 pesos [around £45]. If you don't have it, or refuse to pay, they'll chop off one of your fingers for every 100 pesos that's missing."

When, over dinner, a colleague of Cornelio's revealed a bandaged hand, I gulped. Just beforehand, Cornelio had stopped to do a seemingly dodgy deal involving the roadside selling of four jerry cans of diesel for 1,000 pesos.

"*Dinero* express!" exclaimed our friend, with a wink.

Well, at least we were halfway towards our rent payment, I thought.

Jo

Our latest marathon journey has brought us to Ciudad Obregón, which, even early this morning, was stiflingly hot – the kind of heat that waits impatiently for an open door, so it can push its way in and meddle with tranquillity. We're shielding ourselves with the use of air-con in our hotel room, and enjoyed an hour's nap to boost the few hours' sleep we cobbled together in Cornelio's truck.

We were the lucky ones.

"It's like this all day, every day," Cornelio said blithely, once I'd taken Steve's place in the passenger seat, so he could take a nap. We switched places throughout the night to relieve our drooping eyelids – and all the while Cornelio was driving, driving, driving.

"Didn't you sleep in Guadalajara last night?" he asked us. We confirmed that we had. "Then why are you tired?"

It was a fair question coming from someone whose past seven years have been filled with these 24-hour drives every few days. I am convinced that truck driving is one of the most unforgiving careers in existence, at least as far as work-life balance is concerned. How do these men do it?

As we drove through ill-reputed lands, Steve kept joking that everyone we passed was a drug dealer: "Is *he* a narco? Is *he* a narco?"

Trucks are rarely the target of the dangers associated with this part of Mexico, so we weren't especially perturbed, though it struck me that it's a delicate world when violence and corruption hold the power. Cornelio is safe driving these empty roads in the small hours – until someone sees fit to target him, and then he's utterly vulnerable.

DAY 217: TUESDAY 21ST OCTOBER 2014, 07.44
MOTEL SAN FRANCISCO, SANTA ANA, SONORA, MEXICO

STEVE

Here in the little town of Santa Ana, we have a decision to make. The road before us splits into two. One heads north to Nogales, just 100km from here. The other runs west towards Tijuana in Baja California (literally "Lower California"). The distance to the latter is greater (around 600km), but a good deal of traffic is said to journey that way and we would then lie just half an hour's drive from San Diego, California.

Yesterday, as we crossed 400km of Sonoran Desert, we wondered whether the decision might be made for us. If, we said, a driver was heading for Nogales, we would join him. If to Tijuana, the same. But after *camionero* Héctor, 45, brought us to Sonora's state capital, Hermosillo, and we had navigated our way to the exit road, our next drivers brought us here.

Manuel, 21, and Edgar, 19, two young mechanics, brought us to this motel, our first of the trip. We are assured it is of the American type (i.e. a cheap hotel), rather than anything untoward. It certainly feels OK; in fact, it looks just like all the American motels in the movies – two floors of identical basic rooms.

When Jo wakes up, we will go for some breakfast, and then it will be decision time. Our thoughts are still split, but I think we are leaning towards the desert drive to Tijuana in the west.

The desert here is unlike any other I've seen. No wide open stretches of sand; the land is barren, but speckled with wispy, pale-green shrubs and yellow grass. There isn't much in the way of agriculture, but we passed a few vineyards yesterday (our first since Peru). The road is flat, but in the distance jagged rocky mountains climb from the ground to add to the vista.

DAY 218: WEDNESDAY 22ND OCTOBER 2014, 08.37
SORIANA, MEXICALI, BAJA CALIFORNIA, MEXICO

STEVE

A strange discriminatory process takes place in the moments before we're picked up. The driver must search our appearance and decide, in a matter of seconds, whether we present a threat, or are safe to help. I suppose many factors will help them choose: are we clean? What might be in our bags? Are we a couple? And, perhaps most importantly here in Latin America, are we foreign?

Well, from here on in, that particular aspect is unlikely to help us. In a few minutes, we will walk the remaining six kilometres to Mexicali's border with the States, and thereby end our time in Spanish-speaking America. On the other side, back in a country better resembling home, I suppose a new set of criteria will come into use, and "being foreign" is unlikely to help us, nor is it likely to be particularly obvious. Ever since arriving in Mexico, and a good few times before, people have assumed we are Americans. Many times, they haven't even asked. They've just asked us which state we're from.

And the uncomfortable truth is that, for some reason, our status as foreigners has most certainly aided our cause throughout our journey to date. Numerous times, our drivers have told us so.

"I wouldn't have picked you up if you weren't foreign," they have said. "Foreigners are safe. A Mexican [or native of any type] might rob us."

Yesterday morning, as we walked out of Santa Ana, we spotted two unkempt Mexicans slumped by the side of the road. They were trying to hitch a ride north, but saw no purpose in flagging down vehicles. They knew how hopeless that would be. Instead, they occasionally approached parked trucks in an attempt to prove their harmlessness and to ask for help. In our time alongside them at a *gasolinera*, we watched them approach two truckers. On both occasions, the answer was the same: a shake of the head. Such was their proximity to us and their obvious negative effect on passersby, we decided to move on. On the other side of a bridge, free from the distraction of dangerous-looking Mexicans, we were picked up in an instant.

Our ride with Juan, 38, a *camionero*, was not without its own problems on account of our status as foreigners, but these were of a different kind.

Being so close to the border, security is much tighter. We passed five police checkpoints yesterday and had our bags searched three times – more times than on the journey as a whole. On one of those occasions, we were frisked.

During the first check, with two particularly shifty policemen, it seemed we might be ordered to leave Juan's truck and continue on a bus. Fortunately, our driver pleaded our case, assuring the police there was no problem with our travelling together and that he was not trafficking us over the border. Our papers were intact, and no money was being exchanged. He was no "coyote", as they call the people-smugglers here.

During the other checks, it was our status as *mochileros* (backpackers) that caused most concern. The police told Juan that most *mochileros* use marijuana. Was he sure, they asked him, that we didn't have any on us?

As with the first check, Juan endured a painful few moments while our passports were scanned for defects and our bags searched. If they found anything, we wouldn't be the only ones in trouble. Juan could lose his job, his freedom, everything. We realised at that moment how great a risk he had taken, and indeed, how great a risk all our drivers took on our behalf.

At the fourth checkpoint, just 80km from Mexicali, we joined a long queue of trucks. Juan, who was driving only a few kilometres farther, told us he'd be there for two hours and asked if we'd like to find another ride.

We thanked him, and walked to the far end of the queue, where our bags were searched again and we hoped for one final ride, to the border. Our final hitch in Latin America came courtesy of Roberto, 52, a fine upstanding Mexican gentleman with a fine moustache to prove it. Roberto was travelling with his employee, 30-year-old Ramón. The four of us squeezed into the front of their pick-up truck (Roberto said the police wouldn't allow us to travel in the back) and travelled here to Mexicali. The border, we're told, is just an hour's walk away. For 200km of our journey yesterday, it was even closer. The border fence was in sight for most of our afternoon's passage through the sprawling Sonoran Desert.

With Roberto and Ramón, we left the desert behind and entered Baja California. The difference was apparent immediately. Cotton fields lined the roads. No more wasteland; like the American farmers who flooded to California during the great Depression, we had reached the Promised Land. Indeed, it will feel like our own Promised Land when, all being well, we arrive on American soil in just a few hours' time.

Jo

Borders are such arbitrary lines. We skirted the US *frontera* for several hours yesterday – sometimes a simple wooden fence; sometimes a tall wire structure (allegedly with motion-detecting ability); sometimes right beside us and sometimes far off in the desert distance.

We soon saw signs for the town across the border from Mexicali: Calexico. I can only assume that, when this border was drawn up, some suited American chap in an office said, "Right, everyone, we're upsetting a fair few Mexicans by ruthlessly seizing their land, so to appease them we're going to ensure that the towns on both sides of the border include part of the words 'Mexico' and 'California'. That's your task for this morning. Off you go."

As arbitrary as a line in the sand might appear, this hasn't prevented a bubble of nerves collecting in my stomach as I anticipate reaching the gates to America later this morning. Yesterday's three bag searches have compounded the feeling; they weren't particularly unpleasant and there wasn't anything to find that shouldn't be in our possession, but the underlying suspicion affected me.

"Mexico is beautiful, but it's dangerous to walk around here," one officer warned us, with a fatherly tilt of the head to insinuate he was saving us from deep and grave danger.

I assume that working as a police officer searching trucks and people all the livelong day can only nurture dislike for one's fellow countrymen. The female officer who searched me seemed genuinely surprised to find nothing wanting.

"You really *are* just adventurers," she said, mainly to herself, after I'd removed my shoes and shaken them out to prove their emptiness, done the same with my socks, emptied my pockets of telephone and tissues, and even unwrapped the scrap of paper that contained discarded chewing gum from the day before.

"You can throw that on the floor," she said, and, despite my aversion to littering, I thought it best not to object.

16. THE LAND OF THE FREEWAY

DAY 219: THURSDAY 23RD OCTOBER 2014, 14.28
NOSH DELICATESSEN, SAN DIEGO, CALIFORNIA, USA

STEVE

We're in America! Well, actually, I know quite a few South and Central Americans who'd tell me off for saying that. As our old friend Federico told us in Santiago, we've been in America all along. But now we're on US soil, it's abundantly clear that an extra linguistic distinction is needed, even if "America" isn't the best way of going about it. It isn't only the language that's different; culturally, economically, politically – in fact in almost every way – the USA-ers are a different breed.

The transition was softened by the fact that our first drivers in the USA were Mexican-Americans. Victor and Mike, both 28, and Pennie, 25, are all from Mexican families. The same is true of Budiee, 30, a friend of theirs, who kindly invited us to stay.

We have been made to feel very welcome in our first 24 hours in the States. Since being driven all the way from Calexico to San Diego, we have been treated to beers, nachos, doughnuts, coffees; we had breakfast made for us this morning and were brought downtown this afternoon. Budiee's going to take us for a walk along the beach later. We're feeling very spoilt.

We're especially grateful for the help, given the size of San Diego, which is in the top 10 largest cities in the States. In a country of large cities, that tells you that San Diego is pretty big. The buildings are big here too. Skyscrapers aren't really a thing where we're from, and we haven't seen too many on our journey here. But now we're in the States, I suppose we'd better get used to them. Indeed, I guess we'd better get used to big things in general. That seems to be the USA's speciality.

Jo

I spent much of the hour-long sweat to the border conducting a rigorous and harsh mock-interview with an imaginary border guard, interwoven with trying to name the 50 states in case they came up in some sort of entry examination. With every unsatisfactory answer or missed state, my heart beat that little bit faster.

The situation worsened when we discovered that the computer system at the border wasn't showing up our online visas. The office we were referred to was a little too reminiscent of the Rio federal police office, but fortunately the officer on duty was an amiable man. By 1pm we had made it to the "Land of the Free".

San Diego has stirred up the thrill brought about by bright lights and big cities. Everything is manufactured on such a vast scale – the roads, the buildings, the doughnuts – and there is magnetism in its message of capitalist success. It's a fallacy, of course; we've seen several "Help me, I'm homeless" signs already and spent five minutes talking to one homeless man struggling to get by. In a place as shiny as San Diego, the contrast between the haves and have-nots is somehow even more palpable.

What a novelty to be back in an English-speaking country! It's as if the curtains of linguistic comprehension have been flung open. Our Spanish had progressed to the point where a one-to-one conversation was almost always successfully understood, but we still struggled to pick up on background chatter. Now, we can focus in and out of what's being said around us and the words make sense!

We weren't, however, so naive as to think that the language barrier would be completely eliminated here. Already our alien accent has provoked guesses of Australian, Welsh and Eastern European heritage (the latter surely insinuating that we do not speak English properly). At a bar in San Diego yesterday, the situation became faintly ridiculous.

Man from nearby table: "Are you guys moving on?"

Me: "Yes, we're about to go."

Man: "Can you grab us when you're leaving, so we can have the table?"

Me: "Of course. Where are you guys sitting?"

Man: "I'm sorry?"

Me: "Where are you?"

Man: "What was that?"

Me: "*Where … are … you … sitting?*"

Man: "… '*Why*' what?"

Steve: "WHERE. ARE. YOU. SITTING?"

Man: "Ohh – '*where*'. Your accent really got me there."

… Come now. It wasn't that hard.

The other major adjustment is remembering to put toilet paper in the toilet bowl. After seven months' conditioning, my hand is magnetically drawn to the bin, before I remember that the drainage system here can cope with tissue. It feels quite strange.

DAY 222: SUNDAY 26TH OCTOBER 2014, 13.19
ADAM'S APARTMENT, COSTA MESA, CALIFORNIA, USA

STEVE

We're staying with the Energy Guy. Adam is his name. We met him yesterday in bizarre circumstances at the home of our third and final driver of the day, Jen. Adam was doing the rounds of the local Laguna Niguel neighbourhood, selling government-sponsored solar panels.

"The government wants a third of California to be using renewable energy by 2020," he told us. "So they'll set it up for free."

It sounded like a good deal, but, unfortunately for Adam, Jen isn't a home owner at present. She's just renting the property, a typical American house with wooden panelling and a sloping roof, as she recovers from a messy divorce.

"But why don't you stay for a drink?" asked Jen.

"Hell, it was getting late anyway!" said Adam, a 21-year-old from the mean streets of Chicago (complete with gangster accent and swagger), as he pulled up a chair and helped himself to a glass of wine and some nibbles. Paul, a sommelier and Jen's kind-of other half, had just come back from the shops and was raving about the combination of salami, cheese and melon.

"Take your salami and cheese and wrap the melon inside it," he told us. "Then when you're just about to swallow the last bit, sip some of the Pinot Noir. It will blow your mind."

Paul and Jen, who were just returning from their very first date (Jen later told us she'd been longing for some support), picked us up at 2pm and invited us back to Jen's to do some laundry. We had hoped to make it to L.A. by the end of the day, but Jen kindly offered to pay for us to stay in a nice hotel for the night. We were sold. The new couple, both in their forties, were in fine spirits. It was clear they'd been drinking, although Paul promised he'd "only had a glass or two".

It was as we waited for the clothes to dry that Adam joined the party. We chatted together on the patio, while inside the house Paul and Jen had their first fight. Paul, a former football (that's American football) player, had claimed that lacrosse was for "pussies who didn't make the football team". Given that Jen's oldest son plays lacrosse and was last season voted his team's "MVP" (Most Valuable Player), it was an unwise suggestion.

As the two of them argued drunkenly inside, we got better acquainted with Adam, who told us he had a place for us in Costa Mesa if we needed it.

Roll on 24 hours and here we are, at Adam's. The hotel didn't work out (Jen lost her credit card), but we were able to crash at her place until, sobering up this morning, she asked where we wanted to be taken. They were her first words, so it was pretty clear that the party was over. Her kids were due back in the evening, she said, and she wanted the house to look as though nothing had happened.

Adam's housemate Jack just came in and it looks like we've got a ride to L.A. tomorrow. Things are working out well, despite all the warnings we've received about the perils of hitching here and how we might struggle for rides. Indeed, our first ride out of San Diego yesterday, with a former hitchhiker named Frank, came just five minutes after a gentleman had pulled over to tell us we might find hitching difficult in the States.

"Have you much experience of hitchhiking here?" he asked.

We shook our heads.

"Well it isn't as easy as it was when I was young," he said. "There are too many wackos. Just yesterday, we had a school shooting in Washington." He paused, perhaps sensing our discomfort. "... You know, just so you're prepared for a bit of waiting."

Jo shed a few tears in the aftermath of the conversation, as we waited by a petrol station for just our second ride in the States. She shed a few more a little later, as we walked along the hard shoulder of the five-lane "I-5" (Interstate 5) running north, looking for the next exit.

Jo

The attractive self-confidence and glossy veneer of the American city quickly loses its charm when attempting to hitchhike. It's as if the town-planner promised a bonus payment to anyone curtailing the ease of hitchhiking, to be spent on a brand new super-sized car – which would at least explain the need for six lanes in each direction at certain sections of the freeway.

I burst into tears when it became apparent during our first days' hitching in America that Ming, our second driver yesterday, had dropped us in a terrible spot. From the high-speed slip-road where we were standing, we could either walk back up the freeway from whence we'd come, or onto the one ahead of us. The latter it was.

It was the most intense and terrifying walk of this entire trip. The roar of hundreds of vehicles tearing past was deafening, and though I placed myself at the very far edge of the hard shoulder, it simply was not far enough. We walked for no more than 10 minutes before we came upon the next entry ramp, but I cried myself through the entire experience.

DAY 224: TUESDAY 28TH OCTOBER 2014, 09.44
La Vista Motel, Los Angeles, California, USA

STEVE

The United States of America is not a country well set up for hitchhiking. We were lucky yesterday that Adam's friends Jack and Pete brought us all the way here to L.A., but our ease of passage in no way alleviated our fears for the coming days. Jo's concerns were outspoken and tearful; mine hidden, but still very much alive.

The problem is that there just aren't any good hitchhiking spots, at least not in sunny California, where the volume of traffic, people and houses seems to render "the edge of town" an outdated concept. There appear to be two options: freeway or coastal highway. Freeways are five-lane monstrosities where hitchhiking is prohibited and also nigh on impossible. There are no service stations, so the only option is hitchhiking illegally on the hard shoulder (hugely impractical) or finding an entry ramp. We tried the latter with some success on Monday, but still endured some hard-shoulder wandering to get there. And, perhaps more relevantly, we achieved only 65 miles for our day's troubles. The problem with entry ramps is that those entering them tend to live nearby and, at least as current form suggests, don't tend to be travelling very far.

There is also the issue that freeways run right through the heart of cities, meaning a lot of people use them daily to go very short distances. I suppose in the long run the I-5, which runs all the way to Canada, will prove our best option, but progress is likely to be slow.

The second option is the coastal road. The Pacific Costal Highway (PCH) also ends in Canada, but it is considerably longer. Now, this would be OK if we could be sure of securing long rides on it, but surely most people driving long distances would be more likely to use the freeway. And, while on freeways there is some escape from Southern California's never-ending network of towns, the coastal road seems to blend them all together. The chances of finding someone travelling even two towns on the coastal highway seem slim.

All in all, it appears we have our work cut out. Here in L.A., on Lincoln Boulevard, we happen to be on the PCH, but we walked about 7km of it in the wrong direction yesterday to find a cheap motel and don't look forward to the return leg, nor did we see any good potential spots during our walk. We mean to check later if we're close to any freeways, but if not – and perhaps even if so – tomorrow promises to be a punishing day. If we make it to San Francisco, 400 miles away, in one day, it would be a minor miracle. And after everything we've been through, our appetite for the long slog is at a low ebb.

Jo

Most of our drivers over the past few days have alluded to a severe drought gripping California, and Central America too. We hadn't heard about it previously, and with the regular tropical storms in Central America it wasn't obvious that there were any problems. Here, though, the landscape is noticeably parched.

An advert we saw recently on television offered a solution to the problem. "Spray your grass healthier!" the voice-over proclaimed excitedly, to images of a man improving the look of his drought-weary lawn with green spray-paint, before taking on the challenge in his appreciative neighbours' gardens.

Adam informed us that Southern Californians have a reputation for superficiality and that their values system is based on appearance and dollar signs. Whether or not this is the case, it strikes me that no-one begrudges a brown lawn during the worst drought since the 19th Century, and that this might be a step too far.

DAY 225: WEDNESDAY 29TH OCTOBER 2014, 21.37
MELODY RANCH MOTEL, PASO ROBLES, CALIFORNIA, USA

STEVE

Well that really wasn't so bad, after all. There was a slight scare first thing, as after breakfast we endured a 30-minute wait by a set of traffic lights somewhere near Venice Beach and were informed by a well-meaning female passerby that we might struggle to hitchhike in America. But from the moment we received our first ride, from 23-year-old hippie Paige, we never looked back.

In securing three further rides, we must have waited a total of 10 minutes and travelled 200 miles. And, what's more, we even finally located "the edge of town". We first saw it somewhere on the other side of Malibu, where second driver Enrique, 18, dropped us. As we journeyed with Ben, 29, a professional "handicapper" (apparently this is someone who advises betting companies on what odds to place on sporting contests), we finally said goodbye to Southern California's endless sets of neighbouring towns and entered desert and wine country.

Our decision to opt for the PCH proved fruitful, although perhaps we'd have had a better chance of making it to San Francisco in one day on the freeway. Instead, for the best part of four hours, we enjoyed coastal roads with Ben, who told us he planned to drive no farther than Santa Barbara, but took us another 60 miles to San Luis Obispo. He said he had just woken up and fancied a drive, and didn't have any reason not to go a little farther.

We ended the day with Matthew, 33, a film producer and former traveller, who said he'd been in three car accidents overseas and was once kidnapped in Senegal. Matthew dropped us here, in the small town of Paso

Robles, just in time to catch the final game of baseball's World Series. The San Francisco Giants beat the Kansas City Royals to take the series 4-3. Perhaps we'll be in San Francisco in time to welcome home the returning champs tomorrow. If not, we'll surely be there for Halloween on Friday.

DAY 227: Friday 31st October 2014, 09.08
Café Rosalena, San Jose, California, USA

STEVE

Perhaps I spoke too soon. In every way that Wednesday reassured us that hitchhiking here might be OK, yesterday forced us to reconsider. After waiting without success for more than three hours for our second ride – at a freeway entrance beside the tiny town of San Miguel, just a few miles out of Paso Robles – we were informed for the second time that our efforts were hopeless and told to walk on the freeway. And so we did.

This was just a two-laner, which made it somewhat less daunting, but it was still discomforting to walk down the hard shoulder with thumbs outstretched, as cars passed at 70mph. Our first driver, Mario, had told us there was a "rest area" five miles along, and it was to this prospect we clung as we walked, as close to the barrier as we could.

We had never seen a rest area in the States, but it seemed our only hope. In other countries, we'd encountered drivers who were crazy or kind enough to pull over on the hard shoulder, but surely not in the States …

Well, we were wrong about that. After almost an hour's walking, the unthinkable happened. Caitlin, a 23-year-old yoga instructor with dyed-black hair, metallic blue nail varnish and tattoos, was exactly the kind of crazy person we were looking for. She had never picked up a hitchhiker before, she told us, but after passing us, she had seen the apparent look of misery on our faces and turned the car around at the next exit. We told her she must be an angel.

JO

My first least favourite moment of yesterday was being forced to accept that I had become *that* person – the person who, if I'd have seen them walking along the side of a freeway, would have caused me to mutter, "What an idiot! Don't they know that's utterly stupid and completely dangerous?"

What's more, there was no valid justification for why we were walking on the freeway. I don't think "We had no other choice, officer" would have been received very sympathetically, even if we did have our reasons.

We don't know why people were so convinced that the spot outside San Miguel was so terrible, but we were warned twice that we might be waiting there for weeks, rather than hours.

"Are you opposed to breaking the law?" our second advisor asked me, as I collected lunch from a cafe.

"You mean walking on the freeway?" I asked. Steve had been trying to persuade me to do this for about an hour and I had been staunchly opposed, the prospect filling me with nerves.

"Yup," my advisor replied. "You might get picked up by the highway patrol, but even that would be better than being stuck here."

In the end I conceded we should give it a go.

So there we were again, strolling along a freeway. It wasn't especially busy, but it still made me shudder every time a truck thundered by, or yet another spotless supercar rocketed past.

"Who on earth would stop in a place like this?" I wondered. But then Caitlin did, and the world was brighter.

STEVE

Caitlin had transformed a day of just 10 miles progress into one of 150 miles. As we arrived in San Jose at 4pm, with two hours of light remaining and just 50 miles from San Francisco, our target was in reach. At our new spot beside the entrance to Interstate 280, a car soon pulled over and it seemed we might be on our way. But no, the driver was going only two junctions and suggested we were in a good position and should wait for a longer ride. The clock was ticking, but we felt hopeful.

But the next vehicle to stop wasn't exactly what we had in mind. A policeman approached on a motorbike, pulled over just beyond us, dismounted, turned on the flashing lights and reached for his baton.

"You're breaking the law," he told us, as he swaggered towards us with baton aloft and sunglasses shading his eyes.

"Oh, I thought it was OK to hitchhike at freeway entrances," I replied.

"Look, we can argue about this all day, but the law is the law!" he said.

I wasn't quite sure how my statement could have been mistaken for an argument, but this policeman was of the type we had dreaded we might meet in corrupt South America.

"Where *can* we hitchhike?" I asked, hoping for some reassurance.

"Five hundred metres from any freeway," came the cold reply.

As if hitchhiking here wasn't hard enough already, we now had a new problem. The freeway was our only way out of San Jose, leaving us with a choice: give up, or wilfully break the law. We had never envisaged that we might need to do that on our journey to Alaska, but now it seemed the parameters had shifted, and for me there was only one option, and giving up wasn't it. We were just going to have to persevere and hope that other officers would take a different view of our efforts.

With the policeman out of sight, I returned to the road and recommenced hitching efforts. Jo didn't follow.

"I can't do it!" she protested.

Jo's reaction to spending hours bumping about in the back of a van filled with toiletries

All you need is Ecuador

Shoe shiner, Ecuador

That time Jersson took us for a spontaneous ride in a pedalo

Anderson, Luz Dany, Denilson and Scott the poodle

The young Colombian soldiers who flagged down a truck for us

Santa Marta

Arriving in Panama on the Delfin Solo

Walking into Panama City

A night with the police in Honduras

Hitching in Nicaragua

Mariachis in Huixtla

Paulina and Sam

"Well, what other option do we have?" I asked. "We *have* to hitch and if we don't do it here, we'll just be walking to an equally illegal spot somewhere else. Let's just get on with it and hope we get a ride quickly!"

Jo didn't buy it. Walking on the freeway had already taken its toll on her nerves; the prospect of intentionally breaking the law and facing possible arrest was too much to bear.

And so, with more than an hour's remaining light and San Francisco within touching distance, we shouldered our bags and walked away from the freeway. In my mind, we were only putting off the inevitable, but Jo was keen to explore other options.

We have a friend in San Francisco and Jo dialled his number.

"Vijay, we need some help," she said.

Vijay, who works in San Jose, said he'd see if he could find us a ride with one of his colleagues. In the meantime, he said we should log on to the Internet and type our request into the "Rideshare" section of the website, Craigslist. I was dubious, but it was worth a try.

Roll on to the next morning, and here we sit in a popular breakfast bar, awaiting a call from our next driver. We awoke to find a message on our phone: "Still need a ride to SF?" I called the number immediately and the offer still stood. I don't even know the name of our prospective saviour, but he agreed to meet us here in a few hours to take us with him to San Francisco. Now we wait and hope he keeps to his word. If not, I'm not sure Jo will be able to cope with Plan B: walking back to the freeway and hoping we find a ride before a cop shows up.

Jo

My second least favourite moment yesterday was on the entry ramp in San Jose. I noticed the highway patrol motorbike before Steve, and would have rolled my eyes at the ceremonious way in which the policeman readied himself with his baton, had not all my energy been redirected to the sick feeling in my stomach.

The scene played out for a few minutes, the policeman evincing a totally unnecessary combative demeanour while we worked out that we were stuck.

"There have already been calls about you," the officer said, slightly unconvincingly. "People die every day walking on the freeway, you know. And good luck finding a spot, because 500 metres in every direction from here is back onto a freeway – ha ha!"

Steve wanted to ignore him, but I simply couldn't. We had been breaking the law on the freeway; it was now transpiring that at least 50% of the places where we've found rides in the US have probably been illegal; and now this aggravating officer was bullying us away. That was quite enough illegality on my conscience for one day.

DAY 227 (CONTINUED): 17.33
VIJAY'S APARTMENT, SAN FRANCISCO, CALIFORNIA, USA

STEVE

OK, so we made it to San Francisco, but what a palaver!

After waiting two hours for our Craigslist contact, and unable to reach him on the phone, it became clear he was never going to come.

Completely drained of energy, we hastily but reluctantly accepted the kind offer of a lift to the freeway from a passing elderly lady named Peggy. It was past midday and we had made zero progress, but at least Peggy's ride helped us to avoid a long walk to the freeway, and kept our minds on the job in hand, rather than our disappointment.

An Indian man called Umesh picked up where Peggy had left off, taking us out of the rain on a short ride to the next city, Sunnyvale. We were just grateful to be out of San Jose. At least this way, we figured we were unlikely to be told off by the *same* policeman again.

A police car appeared, with sirens flashing, as we waited by our next freeway entrance, but we were happy to watch it drive on past. And as we wondered whether it might return, a car pulled over and we were finally on our way to San Francisco. Tania, 22, and her girlfriend Anicia, 21, were heading to the city to catch the final moments of the Giants' homecoming parade and the evening's Halloween festivities. After buying us a beer, they kindly dropped us at Vijay's door. Tonight, we are heading out to enjoy our first ever American Halloween and to forget about hitchhiking for a while. It's been a long week, but, thank goodness, it's over now.

JO

I'll admit that I'm more teary than usual – it isn't taking much to set me off. I had steeled myself against the possibility that our promised ride might not turn up, so it wasn't the slow death of hope that tripped the switch today. Instead – following the actions of a kindly old man outside the breakfast bar, who insisted I take $10 to buy a couple of coffees ("Make sure you spend it all," he said), and Peggy, who bought us "scones" (or shortbread, to us Brits) and lifted our crushed spirits – it was the gift of a packet of crisps.

"Are you hungry?" a Mexican man asked me, as he exited the petrol station where we were gathering our thoughts.

"Ah thank you, but we're OK," I replied; the day's events had already squashed my appetite and we'd given my scone to a homeless man.

But he didn't take no for an answer.

"Here, take one of these," he said, proffering two large packets of crisps that he'd just purchased to share with his colleague. I did, he left, and I cried at the kindness of strangers.

DAY 229: SUNDAY 2ND NOVEMBER 2015, 21.18
VIJAY'S APARTMENT, SAN FRANCISCO, CALIFORNIA, USA

JO

This weekend, we have been introduced to life in Silicon Valley. Our friend-of-a-friend host, Vijay, works for eBay, and on hearing about his experience of life in San Francisco, we have gained insight into this hub of high-tech and savvy companies, and its abundance of wealthy young entrepreneurs.

Friday night was Halloween, and while spending time with Cleopatra, Santa Claus, a sheikh and a medley of other people dressed as whatever they fancied, I discovered just what a different world this group inhabits. One house we visited was owned by a 30-year-old and had cost $3 million; another was on one of the most renowned streets in San Francisco. Somehow I don't think we're in the same wage bracket.

Vijay took obvious delight in telling his friends about our travels, and (much the most important detail) that we're travelling without a smartphone.

"Can you believe it!" he marvelled repeatedly. To this group, whose lives and careers revolve around being at the cutting edge of technology, it was clear that our choice betrayed our identity as aliens, or anarchists, or something like that.

"We're not trying to make a point!" I blurted out several times, attempting to reign in the impression that we are anti-technology cave people. I'm fairly convinced it made no difference.

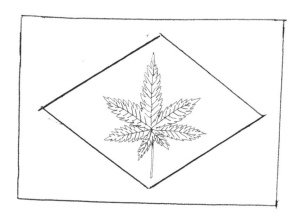

17. TRIMMIGRATION

DAY 231: TUESDAY 4TH NOVEMBER 2014, 21.06
HOTEL ARCATA, ARCATA, HUMBOLDT COUNTY, CALIFORNIA, USA

STEVE

California has an interesting relationship with marijuana. During our first week in the state, we met two people with medical prescriptions for the drug. Neither one was necessary. In Venice Beach, we passed a shop advertising "medical marijuana evaluations" – yours for $40. One of our drivers last week, Ben, told us he had taken an evaluation as an experiment. He said he was asked just two questions: "Is your blood pressure always this high?" and "How did you hear about us?" And that was that. Prescription prescribed.

Everywhere we go, the smell of marijuana seems to follow. And nowhere more so than here in Humboldt County, apparently one of the marijuana capitals of the world – or so said our driver today, 40-year-old Colin, a giant of a man.

So prevalent is the drug here in Humboldt, Colin told us, that new words have been created to refer to its adherents. The first new word Colin taught us was "trimmigrant". This term refers to people from all around the world who travel to Humboldt to work as "weed trimmers".

"By trimming marijuana plants, you can make $600 a day," Colin told us.

The second new word was devised specifically for a subsection of the population here in Arcata, where Colin went to college. "Plazoid", Colin said, refers to the innumerable dopers who linger on the plaza, day in, day out. Our hotel overlooks the plaza, and we can report that there have been at least a dozen plazoids, and the accompanying scent of marijuana, ever since we arrived.

So big was the plazoid problem that a few years ago Arcata passed a law banning all smoking within two blocks of the main square. It doesn't seem to have had much effect. Colin told us that smokers' immediate reaction was to find new hangouts in the surrounding residential areas. Perhaps this undesired effect is the reason the police don't tend to be too heavy in handing out the $130 fine for breaching the ban. For now, the plaza belongs to the trimmigrant plazoids.

The third addition to our vocabulary was "tweaker", reserved for those unlucky folk (many of whom seem to congregate in Humboldt) who have lost their minds to crystal meth. We saw one such man pushing a shopping trolley along the 101 through Eureka.

"He'll fill that up with recyclable materials every day, sell it and get his fix. Then he'll start over again," Colin told us. The vacant expression on the face of a tweaker resembles that of a zombie. It's tragic.

Colin told us that in Humboldt you can gauge a person's level of craziness by looking at his or her hat. We soon passed a man with a plastic cup glued onto the top of his baseball cap. It confirmed the theory.

Here in Arcata, we are just 100 miles from the state line with Oregon. We have been in California for almost two weeks – as long as we spent in Chile and longer than we were in Ecuador – which gives some idea of the size of it.

At one stage this morning, it looked as if we might be here for a good deal longer. When Colin found us, at our latest freeway entrance on the 101 north outside Healdsburg, it was 11.30 and we had been waiting for two hours. Before that, we had waited half an hour at a different, less-used freeway entrance, before a passerby suggested we try the next on-ramp.

We fared slightly better yesterday. After trekking out of San Francisco and over the Golden Gate Bridge, past a multitude of signs declaring hitchhiking illegal, we received five rides in four hours to take us, bit by bit, 50 miles farther north, and ended the day in Healdsburg and the heart of California's wine country.

One of our drivers yesterday, another Colin, aged 34, also tall but a good deal slimmer than today's Colin, provided us with another living example of California's love of weed. Colin, a former ice-hockey hopeful, described his journey from personal trainer to self-proclaimed "shaman" and "Wizard of Herb" (it says that on his business card). It all started, he told us, because one of his clients, "the Michael Jordan of poker", had taught him a great deal about "intuition".

It was intuition, Colin said, that had led him to stop for us, despite never having picked up a hitchhiker. It was also intuition that had led Colin to fill his car with personal items, including a stack of about a dozen old hockey sticks formerly used by the San Jose Sharks.

Each item, he told us, had been placed in the car for a reason, although he didn't know what reason yet. Colin said he had a feeling the hockey sticks would find a new home by Wednesday.

Just before he dropped us off, Colin asked us if we smoked (he meant marijuana).

We shook our heads.

"Oh, that's a shame. I was going to give you a little package to take on your way," he said, handing us a business card instead.

… Only in California.

Jo

"Do you feel like the challenge is over now?" a friend asked me last week. "You've made it to America, after all."

If only the distance, which is indeed relatively short now, was the only factor to consider.

I have started (inadvisably, no doubt) to let myself wonder what it would be like if we were home already. What if we'd decided to travel just to the end of Spanish-speaking America, or if Mexico had conveniently repositioned itself at the top of the continent? Or I think about how much better I would feel if all that lay before us was 3,000 miles of favourable ground: roads built for hitching, weather made for standing – just keep on doing what you're doing.

Instead, I see nothing but challenges. The clocks have changed, so it's getting darker earlier. The issue of US road layouts is well documented. I have only just begun to relax about policemen. Then there's Alaska, which looms in my mind as a darkness-filled, snow-covered monster waiting to devour us and our naivety at the earliest possible opportunity. According to our ideal schedule, we need to be on a flight home in no more than a month, and my brain can't accommodate how that might be possible.

This melancholy outlook reached its peak yesterday, when the memories of last week's difficulties were combined with fatigue after the morning's six-mile traipse to cross the Golden Gate Bridge. My legs were exhausted, my feet strained and my emotions worn thin. In the end, I had to shut off my thoughts (unhelpfully revolving around the theme of wanting to go home) by reminding myself that walking over one of the world's most iconic bridges is no insignificant event and ought to be appreciated.

I did allow myself one final grumble, though, that an adventure should sometimes be such plain old hard work.

DAY 232: WEDNESDAY 5TH NOVEMBER 2014, 21.14
ELK HORN BREWERY, EUGENE, OREGON, USA

STEVE

In a fitting end to our time in California, today we received lifts from a cowboy, a tweaker, an old rocker (and stoner), a hippie and a trimmigrant.

And if the trimmigrant, 22-year-old Caleb, is to be believed, we're in for much of the same here in Oregon, where marijuana was legalised just yesterday, following local elections.

"Oregon's much easier for hitchhiking," said Caleb, who was driving home from a spot of weed-trimming in Garberville, a town that seems to subsist only on marijuana. "You can walk on the freeways here and people are really nice, like the people in northern California."

Here in Eugene, Caleb's home, we were told the crowd is similar to that in Arcata. To us, that means stoners, tweakers and hippies. Well, they're certainly an interesting bunch. Our drivers today kept us entertained from the word go.

First there was Neil, 33, a cowboy (complete with boots and hat) on his way from Arcata to his job as a builder of luxury beachside homes. He dropped us beside his latest home-in-the-making in McKinleyville and pointed us towards a coastal trail that would eventually lead us back to the freeway.

After a nice stroll through a hazy forest, we returned to the 101 and, traffic being light, decided to walk on the freeway instead of waiting at a barely used on-ramp. Our tactic worked, as soon we were running to catch up with Bonnie's reversing jeep, which had skidded to a halt on the hard shoulder. Bonnie, 49, was almost certainly one of Colin's tweakers. It was the twitches that sealed it. Throughout our journey together, as she swerved towards her home in the rural town of Orick, Bonnie would regularly brush her bristly hair behind her ears, with a jerk, then frantically wipe her face. Of all the drivers we have travelled with, Bonnie was probably the one in whom I had the least faith. Lovely though she was, her mind was not all there – not the sort of person you want to be driving with on a freeway, particularly one known for its jaywalking elk herds.

But of course we were still very grateful for Bonnie's help, not least because she left us in a perfect spot. In her small town, in the middle of the beautiful Redwood National Park, the 101 goes down to a single lane. We took up our position on the edge of town with renewed confidence and soon bundled into our next vehicle – that of old rocker, David Shane Duke, another about to celebrate his fiftieth birthday.

David, with his long brown hair, grey beard, mild manner softened by years of marijuana, and southern drawl, charmed us from the off. Treating us to a soundtrack of country music from some of his pals in Alabama, David took us on a scenic tour of the Redwood Park, stopped at a native Indian museum, bought us clam chowder at Crescent City beach and then set us down on the 199 running inland towards central Oregon.

Vanessa, 32, a Mexican-American hippie travelling with her two young children, Zion (seven) and Malachi (five months), took us a little farther, through another patch of giant redwoods, and then it was time for trimmigrant Caleb to rock up. The mess and stale smell inside his pick-up truck betrayed the fact that Caleb had used it as a bed for the last 10 nights in Garberville. Caleb himself, a bone ring through his nose and tattoos up his arms, was by no means smelling fresh, but we were in northern California, so it was little surprise.

Jo

It had just struck 2pm when, as we were standing in a shady patch surrounded by lofty pines, a highway patrol car pulled up in front of us. I fleetingly wondered whether my heartbeat was as audible to everyone else as it was to me.

The two officers exited the car, appeared to hover for a moment ("Assembling their batonry?" I wondered) and then began the approach. If time had been slower and had provided the opportunity to scientifically analyse my legs, I feel sure they would have most resembled the cell format of jelly.

"Hello," we all said at once, to get the formalities out of the way.

One of the officers caught my eye, and said, "Don't worry, you aren't doing anything illegal."

His sentence didn't actually finish there, but it might as well have. My blood pressure began righting itself, there was instantly a higher likelihood I would remain on my feet to the end of the conversation, and I may even have attempted a smile.

"… We just wanted to check you guys were doing OK."

I couldn't believe what I was hearing. Struck dumb with relief, it was down to Steve to respond that everything was fine.

"Well, that's OK then," the officer said. "Maybe just step a little farther away from the white line to be on the safe side. Have a good day."

With that they headed back to their car, as a lady driving past pulled an entertaining "Now, what is going on *here*?" expression.

This interaction with the police was exactly what I needed. Our tête-à-tête with Officer San Jose last week had still been affecting my nerves, but this was a fresh reminder that he's been the only cop we've had a negative conversation with in the US. What's more, now we know that walking on the freeway isn't prohibited in Oregon, I won't have to worry if we have to.

DAY 235: SATURDAY 8TH NOVEMBER 2014, 15.02
POWELL'S BOOKS, PORTLAND, OREGON, USA

STEVE

As we approach our end goal (it's still over 2,000 miles away, but we're getting there), we are receiving a great many more raised eyebrows when we tell our drivers we plan to hitchhike in Alaska as autumn turns to winter. It isn't only the freezing temperatures; it's the lack of light too. In just a few weeks, the northern part of the state will be entering total darkness and, although we've heard that the snow and moonlight provide some visibility, I'm not sure how that will hold up when we're waving our frostbite-endangered thumbs on the side of the road.

When we look at a map of northern Canada and Alaska and see a whole lot of nothingness, Jo imagines our being stranded out there, but I try my best to reassure her that people don't just drive to nowhere; they drive to places. As such, rather than worrying about the nothingness, I am hopeful of some fairly significant rides when we start hitting no-man's-land.

Here in Oregon, we have no such fears. Even in the high desert north of Redmond this morning, traffic was free-flowing in the five minutes we waited before Michael, 45, a software engineer originally from England, pulled over.

Our journey from Eugene to Redmond on Thursday wasn't as straightforward, but it was certainly entertaining. The highlight was our time with Todd and Arien, who were on their way to some hot springs just off Route 126 and invited us to join them. It was only after we'd arrived that they dropped into conversation that the hot springs were generally frequented by naked people. It made for quite an intimate introduction, even if *we* remained partly clothed.

The same was true of our introduction to our next drivers, Dennis and Anastasia, an ageing couple we met in the open-air changing hut on our way out. I wondered whether to wait until they were fully clothed before asking them if they'd drive us back to the main road, but in the end I decided they probably wouldn't mind. It was that kind of place, and they seemed to be those kinds of people.

When we returned to the forested main road, it was 2pm and pouring with rain. Cars passed at some speed and seemed barely able to spot us before they were on top of us. For several of them, the shock led them to lean heavily on their horns.

The 30 minutes that we waited there weren't some of the happiest of Jo's life. We were saved by Nancy, a retired Polish-American on her way over the McKenzie Pass. The journey over the mountains led us past lava fields, and, on the other side, the rainforests of western Oregon were replaced by Wild West country as we crossed into central Oregon's arid high desert.

DAY 237: MONDAY 10TH NOVEMBER 2014, 18.51
NICK AND NAT'S HOUSE, REDMOND, WASHINGTON, USA

STEVE

On Saturday we received an offer of a lift to Seattle in quite incredible circumstances. During a conversation with a shop assistant named Dan, as we bought winter clothes for our journey north, I casually asked: "You wouldn't happen to be driving to Seattle on Monday, would you?"

Dan chuckled and said that he wasn't but added that he might know someone who was. Two hours later, we were drinking beers with Dan, a 21-year-old from Chicago, and his college friends at his apartment in Portland. Among them was Punneh, an Iranian-American from Seattle. She had wanted to meet us before agreeing to give us a ride, and it seemed we had passed the test.

As we prepared to leave, Punneh promised to call us on the morrow. She told us she planned to leave around 5pm and would pick us up on her way out of town.

We left the gathering in high spirits. A shopping trip had turned into the promise of a ride to Seattle, our ultimate destination in the lower 48 states of America.

At around midday yesterday, with no word from Punneh, we sent her a message to double-check arrangements. There was no response. We tried calling. There was no answer. Perhaps she was still asleep, we thought.

When the clock struck 5pm (Punneh's scheduled departure time), I sent a message to Dan to ask if he'd heard from her. The response read: "I called her boyfriend. He says she's sleeping and will call you soon."

Panic over.

Four hours later, though, the panic had well and truly returned. Jo was crying in bed and attempting to read a book to take her mind off things. I was deliberating whether to try to call Punneh again.

Eventually, at a little after 9pm, I received a message: "Sorry, been out of it all day. Going to leave early tomorrow morning. Probably around 5.30."

Panic over again. I sent a message back pretending all was well and asking if she could pick us up on the way out.

No response.

Finally, after an additional hour of fretting, another message came through: "So sorry. Work wants me to stay for another day. Not going until Tuesday now. I'll try to put you in touch with someone else driving to Seattle tomorrow."

We never heard from her again.

After our experience in San Jose with Craigslist, we had been panicking for most of the day and felt utterly spent. When our host, a friend-of-a-friend named Josher, offered to drive us to the I-5 on his way to college early the next morning, we leapt at the chance. An early start would do us good after a tumultuous day.

Following a short ride with a redneck named Rick, who joked that he was going to take us somewhere deep into the woods (we didn't laugh), we met Steve, 30, a recovering alcoholic and recent divorcé, who was on his way to visit his parents in Seattle. In the end, we arrived here just five hours later than we might have if Punneh had picked us up at 5.30 this morning. For the second time in the States, we were left wishing a hollow offer had never been received. Josher told us that people on the West Coast of the United States have a reputation for being "flaky". We certainly wouldn't argue with that.

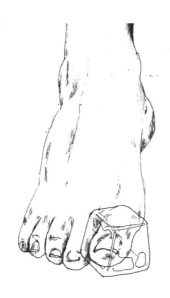

18. COLD FEET ON THE HIGHWAY OF TEARS

DAY 240: THURSDAY 13TH NOVEMBER 2014, 18.07
CHOCOLAT, VICTORIA, VANCOUVER ISLAND, BRITISH COLUMBIA, CANADA

STEVE

"Hitchhiking is illegal in Canada," we were told as we crossed the border yesterday after a long day on the road. And here in Canada, it's illegal to *pick up* hitchhikers too.

We managed to avoid the law at nine different freeway entrances in the USA yesterday, but the process during our 11-driver day – as we travelled just 140 miles – took its toll on Jo. Only in Washington State had we seen signs specifically prohibiting hitchhiking. A series of no-thumbing signs were pinned up close to others that read:

**FREEWAY
ENTRANCE**
PEDESTRIANS
HITCHHIKERS
BICYCLES
PROHIBITED

I attempted to persuade Jo that the signs must just be referring to the point on the freeway beyond the sign, but I don't think she bought it. I had hoped that here in famously friendly Canada we might find a more lenient approach to our pursuit, but apparently not. Here the signs say:

NO
HITCH-HIKING
PICKUP
IS ILLEGAL

It is hard enough knowing that our journey is now most certainly in defiance of the law; it is worse still to think we will now be begging passersby to join us in our law-breaking. The border official said the laws are there to protect people and prevent accidents. I can understand why they might ban hitchhiking on freeways, or at freeway entrances where there is not sufficient space for drivers to pull in safely. But at other freeway entrances, where there is plenty of space and cars are moving very slowly, I cannot see why our pursuit should be prohibited.

I can only hope that Canada's reputation as a country of "nice people" will save us. Early signs are good. After crossing the border, it took just a few minutes before we were picked up by Dennis, 61, a stereotypically pleasant Canadian, who even offered us a place to stay.

We spent the evening enjoying Canadian hospitality courtesy of Dennis, wife Marcy and 28-year-old daughter Sam. A personal highlight of the evening was Sam's frequent use of the Canadian "eh?" to end sentences, and Dennis's pronunciation of the words "out" and "about" as "oot" and "aboot". On first impressions at the very least, everything they say about Canadians is true. And, as Dennis said, "It's better to be known for being too nice than for being a real so-and-so".

We are taking the rest of the week off to connect with long-lost family members in Vancouver, and here on Vancouver Island. We will recommence hitching efforts on Monday and have no more planned stops before our final destination, 3,000km away: Alaska.

DAY 245: TUESDAY 18TH NOVEMBER 2014, 08.53
PRINCE MOTEL, PRINCE GEORGE, BRITISH COLUMBIA, CANADA

JO

It was a further incident with the police yesterday that finally pierced the bubble of anxiety that has encircled my head for the past three weeks.

Our long weekend was punctuated with bouts of worry. Left unchecked, my thoughts would wander to one melancholy theme or other, and my enthusiasm for food and cheer remained diminished. Diversionary tactics were occasionally successful, but ultimately the knot in my stomach refused to untie.

As we made our way yesterday to Canada's Highway 1 running west towards the mountains around Whistler, we walked straight into some sort of spot-check involving a collection of cars, drivers and policemen.

"Wonderful," I thought. "The cops aren't having a slow start to Monday morning, then!" (This had been my hope for aiding a quick get-away, but apparently the police hadn't received my memo.)

As we continued, we found ourselves (probably illegally) walking along a busy road with no pavement, which had run out without warning. A slight turn of my head suddenly revealed a police car at my side.

"Here we go," I thought. "Well, we might as well get it over with."

But although the car had slowed down, it soon sped up again and moved off. We had been granted a brief reprieve.

Steve and I established ourselves at the side of the road, just shy of the "ANY VEHICLE LESS THAN 60 MPH PROHIBITED" sign, and awaited our fate. Several streams of cars went by, and then I spied another patrol car.

"*Calm ... calm ...*" I vainly instructed my heart.

And nothing. The police ignored us. Around 10 minutes later, the same happened again. Finally, it dawned on me.

"HITCHHIKING *ISN'T* ILLEGAL!"

My heart soared, my stomach tingled and my shoulders felt young and free again. We were not breaking the law! The sign we had seen before must have been on a freeway. Here, on an approach road, we were free to hitchhike at will, just like in the US.

Immediately, my approach to our situation switched from "just waiting to be arrested" to "just waiting for the right person to see us", and that changed everything.

STEVE

Worries about the police behind us, we became more concerned with staying warm. As we wiggled our toes, we thought back to our weekend in Vancouver and, particularly, to the Gastown district, where the city's significant homeless population congregates. We were told that many of Canada's homeless head for Vancouver in winter for its relatively mild climate. As we stood shivering after just 30 minutes standing still, we wondered how the poor folk survive.

Another feature of Vancouver's population is its large Asian community (partly a result of the thousands of Chinese workers once drafted in to build a railway across the country), so it was no surprise when our first driver, Ellen, 35, introduced herself as a Filipino.

Slightly more surprising was Ellen's opening gambit: "Oh, I thought you had a baby."

We weren't sure what had given her that impression – perhaps it was all our layers of clothing – or indeed which one of us was supposed to have been carrying the phantom child. But considering it had led to a lift, we wondered if we should try travelling with a pram in future.

However, we were not to endure another wait until our very last ride of the day, and by that time we had already travelled in excess of 350km – way beyond our expectations.

It was quarter to four when our penultimate driver, retired forester Ralph, pulled over at a crossroads and offered us two options: either we could try our luck there (we had about an hour left of light), or he could take us 11km in the wrong direction to the next town, Cache Creek, where we could be sure of finding food and accommodation if required.

We weighed up the options. On the one hand, our first golden rule for the remainder of the trip is to ensure we are never stranded in the middle of nowhere. In below-zero temperatures, this could prove critical. But on the other hand, we had enjoyed a very successful day on the road; Canadians had so far been quite willing to pick us up; and there were a few houses nearby. If it came to it, we figured, we could always ask for help and lodgings there, or, at worst, make the 11km trek to Cache Creek. It was decided: we would take a chance at the crossroads.

Forty-five minutes later, we were starting to fear we had made an error of judgement. Light was fading; even in our many layers of clothing, we were struggling to stay warm; and, despite a surprising number of vehicles, they were passing too quickly to notice us, or to care.

"Maybe we should just give up and hitch the other way," said Jo. We had seen several cars pulling out of the junction opposite, but all were heading towards Cache Creek. "We don't want to run out of options."

I had it in mind to cross the road and start hitching that way, while Jo hitched the other, but then salvation came. Shane, 43, told us he had felt bad after driving past us and noticing that it was -9°C, so he spun his car around and came back for us.

We were surprised to learn it had been quite so cold and felt reassured that our clothing might yet prove sufficient to take us through to Alaska. We felt encouraged, and that was before our new friend told us he was driving all the way to Prince George, 400km farther north.

By the time we arrived here, autumn had been replaced by winter. Snow clung to the branches of the pines and cedars flanking the roads. The leaves we had seen carpeting the floor that morning were but a distant memory.

Here in Prince George, in what Shane called the last "reasonable-sized city" before Alaska, the 2,000km or so before our final border crossing suddenly doesn't seem so great.

Jo

"Anything down to -10°C is just kinda 'meh'," Shane said, with an accompanying shrug of the shoulders.

Steve and I, revelling in the delight of having bagged a 400km ride, had begun quizzing him about life in the low temperatures. Shane had served in the military and had experienced much colder climes in Canada's north.

"When you get to -18°, -20°, that's when it starts to bite," Shane said. "The hairs in your nostrils begin to freeze, your eyeballs hurt, that kind of thing."

I wondered silently what other kind of thing he might be referring to.

"Minus 30°C, that's painful," Shane continued. "You can't have any flesh showing at all, or you're in trouble. You can still do everything, you can still live, but it is hard work."

"Presumably it feels a bit better if you're moving about?" Steve asked. Both of us were secretly imagining what it might be like to hitchhike in these temperatures.

"Well … no," Shane replied, and we all laughed, some more nervously than others. "It doesn't make a difference. The coldest I've experienced is about -45°. It wasn't fun."

As I sat in the car, trying to contemplate these temperatures, I realised that I couldn't imagine them. Minus 30? Minus 45? It sounded horrendous.

"The old guys gripe about how things are changing," our second driver of the day, Ross, had told us, in relation to his neighbours in the northerly Yukon Territory to which we are heading. "They say, 'It only gets to -50°C these days. It used to be -60°C'."

Concerns about global warming aside, I cannot work out how people survive in such conditions, or, more to the point, why they would want to. We complain about dreary British winters as much as any Englishman, but I know which I'd prefer.

Forecast checks have become a new hobby, and from what we have seen, we shouldn't experience lower than -10°C in the daytime before we've finished. "Meh," as Shane would say.

DAY 245 (CONTINUED): 19.18
IDYLWILD MOTOR INN, HOUSTON, THE HIGHWAY OF TEARS, BRITISH COLUMBIA, CANADA

STEVE

Here in Houston, British Columbia, we find ourselves midway along the "Highway of Tears". We had been warned about Highway 16 during our time in Vancouver, and, for the locals here, it is even more of a hot topic. They say that on the road between Prince George and Prince Rupert, a stretch of around 700km, 20 female hitchhikers have gone missing in the past 40 years. The perpetrator has never been caught. All but one of our drivers mentioned it on our way here from Prince George today, and several passersby took the time to warn us that what we were doing was "very dangerous here".

"This is a bad highway," said Lisa, 40, our penultimate driver. "I only picked you up because I promised myself I would always do everything possible to keep hitchhikers safe on this road. It's something we locals have to do."

It is difficult to know what to make of it all. Undeniably, tragedy has struck hard on this road, but I have learned to put my trust in strangers and don't wish to stop now.

This morning, as we left our motel in Prince George, we had a choice of two routes to Alaska: via the infamous Highway 16 running west, or the slightly longer route via Highway 9⬦ to the north. Having been told that the scenery was more interesting and the road shorter via the 16, I saw no reason to avoid it, and after a day on the road, I don't regret the decision. We endured around two hours of waiting in sub-zero temperatures over the course of the day, but otherwise had no cause for complaint.

Alex, a middle-aged man with native Indian blood, or "First Nation" as they call it here, set us on our way. Then followed our first wait.

After more than an hour, we felt sufficiently cold to give ourselves a short break in a nearby petrol station, where we downed some soup and asked the temperature outside.

"Minus seven," we were told. This piece of information was followed by one warning about the Highway of Tears and another about our slim chances of catching a ride.

"We had another couple of hitchhikers here two weeks ago. They were here for three days," said one lady.

We have heard similar things on several occasions and have seen a collection of abandoned cardboard signs displaying messages such as "BEEN HERE FOR DAYS. PLEASE PICK ME UP", but, for whatever reason, we always seem to have better luck.

"See you later," said another of the ladies behind the till, as we left, hands and feet almost thawed.

"I hope not," I replied.

Minutes later, we were on our way, thanks to Scott, 34, the first driver we have had who travels with a fitted breathalyser.

"It's a long story," said Scott, after we watched him blow into the device.

Scott told us he was caught drink-driving a year ago and had been forced to pay a princely sum for the breathalyser to be fitted for a year after the event, or a further year after any failed test. He told us he has since failed twice, so he still has some way to go.

After Scott came Lisa, a quirky lady with a hearty laugh that erupted after almost every sentence – except the ones about our impending doom. It was 2.30pm by the time she dropped us at a petrol station in the small town of Fort Fraser. We had been on the road for more than four hours and covered less than 150km, but in our line of work, one more ride can make all the difference and it came in the form of our first truck-ride since Mexico. Gary, with whom we hope to reconnect tomorrow, is on his way to Terrace, a further three hours west, but stopped here for the night on account of rumoured bad weather up ahead.

"There's some freezing rain on its way. Better to travel through such conditions in the daylight," Gary said.

We agreed to meet him back at his truck at 7.30 tomorrow morning to recommence our journey together. Now, our record on such pre-arranged journeys is not favourable, but we live in hope.

Jo

My outfit today consisted of: thermal headband, knitted hat, thermal long-sleeved base layer, t-shirt, alpaca jumper, down jacket, fleece-lined normal jacket, thermal ski gloves, thermal long johns, normal trousers and thermal socks – probably the most items of clothing I've ever worn. If this is what is required for -7°C, what on earth does one wear at -40°C?

As we stood waiting for Gary to return from his toilet stop, a car stopped beside us.

"Are you hitchhiking?" the female driver asked.

"Yes," we replied. "We've just got a lift in this truck."

"I see," said the lady, and paused. "Don't you know how dangerous it is here? This is the 'Highway of Tears'."

"Yes, we have heard that," I replied. There was an awkward silence.

"We've hitchhiked here from Argentina!" I added cheerily, thinking it might make it better.

It didn't.

"My mother said I should drive over and take a good look at you two, in case we see you on the news," she said.

The undertone of this statement was so ominous, and yet it was delivered so politely, that I didn't know what the appropriate response should be. I glanced at the shrivelled, toothless old woman in the passenger seat, who had been the apparent instigator of our meeting. She wasn't saying anything now.

"Oh, right, yes. Well … thank you," I said, and with that they drove off, perhaps now satisfied that they could identify us should we too end up on the history pages of this horrid highway.

DAY 246: WEDNESDAY 19TH NOVEMBER 2014, 21.56
PRINCE MOTEL, PRINCE GEORGE, BRITISH COLUMBIA, CANADA

STEVE

It's 10pm and we have just arrived at the Prince Motel in Prince George. No, we haven't gone back in time; we've just done a lot of backtracking. Four hundred and eighty-five kilometres of it, to be precise. And it wasn't Gary's fault – he kept to his word and took us right to the start of the Stewart-Cassiar Highway running north. Nor was it the spectre of the Highway 16 killer, about whom we continued to be warned in person and on signs that read: "HITCHHIKING: Is it Worth the Risk? Ain't worth the risk, sister".

No, the real reason for our turning around was the promise of a whole lot of nothingness between us and the next landmark, Watson Lake, 750km farther north. And no-one to take us there. We tried for two hours to talk to truckers at the petrol station where Gary had left us. Many of them were going all the way to Alaska – it was tantalising – but the message was always the same: "The road's too dangerous in these conditions and my insurance doesn't cover me for extra passengers."

A few car drivers pulled over to offer a ride, or some advice. None of them was going more than 15km and one of them told us he thought we were crazy for attempting to hitchhike on the Stewart-Cassiar Highway, along which there was nothing – not even a hotel – for hundreds of kilometres.

"I've done a lot of hitchhiking myself," he told us. "But I'd never do what you're doing. I've never met anyone trying to hitch from here all the way to Watson Lake."

We were starting to consider Plan B, when a smiley trucker with a long white beard and stars-and-stripes bandana rolled by, heading in the opposite direction. Out of his open window, he apologised that he wasn't going our way.

After Jo and I had held a short conference, I went to ask his opinion on our predicament.

"How long you been standing there?" asked the driver, who, it struck me, looked a great deal like Santa Claus.

"Two hours," I replied.

"Then, I'd head thataway!" he said, pointing back towards Prince George.

So it was that, at midday, just two hours after arriving, we were turning around and heading back in the opposite direction. It was a truly horrible feeling to pass back over all of that ground we'd already covered, wondering why we'd bothered. I tried not to think about it, while Jo took regular naps – her own avoidance therapy.

The going was slow. Rosco's truck was heavy-laden with logs, and, by 6pm, we had managed only to undo all of the good work Gary had helped us to achieve.

Pulling into the very same petrol station where we had met Gary more than 24 hours prior, we wondered whether to laugh or cry. When Rosco's truck decided to choose that location to break down, it was decided: crying it would be, at least for Jo. I just kept it all bottled up inside, attempted to reassure Jo that everything would be OK, and felt too sick to eat, and certainly too sick to consider the prospect that the next day we might still need to hitch our way back to Prince George.

It was too much to bear. In the petrol-station restaurant, as we attempted to force down some soggy lasagne, I asked the lady behind the till if anyone else might be heading to Prince George that evening.

"Just the bus," she said.

We jumped at the chance. We'd already hitched the road once anyhow; this was just backtracking, so we couldn't see any reason to prevent us from taking the bus, especially given the breakdown saga and how, by rights, we should be in Prince George already.

I was about to splurge the required $70 to pay for our tickets when I decided to check with Rosco, one last time, to see if he'd had any luck with the truck. It seemed so unlikely, but as I approached, the engine was running and Rosco was sitting there with a broad smile and a thumbs-up. We were back in business.

I skated over the icy car park to collect Jo, adrenaline pumping through my veins.

"Thank the Lord!" I said, as we hurried back to the truck. "I was feeling really low back there. Even the prospect of getting the bus had given me a lift, but now I feel great!"

Jo smiled weakly and said nothing. Her emotions had been through the mill. It was bad enough that we had essentially wasted two days on the road, without the breakdown to throw into the mix. But it's over now, at least for today. Who knows what new trials await us tomorrow?

DAY 248: FRIDAY 21ST NOVEMBER 2014, 07.59
AIRPORT INN MOTEL, DAWSON CREEK, MILE 'O' ON THE ALASKA HIGHWAY, BRITISH COLUMBIA, CANADA

STEVE

So I guess it's true what they say about Prince George. On our way there (the first time) with Shane, we were told all about its reputation as a "rough" city.

"The further north you go in Canada, the rougher it gets," Shane said. "And Prince George is right up there."

Since then, having twice hitched out of the city – to the west and then, yesterday, to the north – we have had plenty more opportunity to hear about, and experience first-hand, the kind of problems faced by the people of Prince George.

The first prime example was Scott, the man with the breathalyser. But he had nothing on our main driver yesterday, 24-year-old Anthony, a former gang leader and drug dealer.

"I used to be a hoodlum," confessed Anthony, who is half Italian, half First Nation, and grew up in foster care.

He wore various tattoos that testified to his past life, although by the end of our journey together, we wondered just how much had changed. "YDS" was written on his neck. He told us it stood for Young Dragons Society, a gang he had created. "CASH" was scribbled on his lower forearm, a reference, he said, simply to his love of money. "Joy r" was on the other arm. He told us that, originally, he was going to have "joy ride" spelled out, but he'd ended up a few letters short.

"My friend was really drunk when he did that one!" Anthony said.

These symbols served to introduce us to Anthony's life, past and present. Later we would sit in his pick-up truck while he went out to steal from seven different shops – some clothes from Walmart; gadgets for his car at an auto trader; a pack of Cheetos and a sandwich from two food stores; and then, tellingly, three bottles of wine from three liquor stores. By the time we parted, at 10.30pm, Anthony was on to his second bottle, had been thrown out of his sister's house here in Dawson Creek, and, as such, had lost access to any means by which to pay us back the $90 we had lent him for diesel.

Oh, and he'd managed to sink his truck in a few feet of snow that had hidden an unused railway line. I guess it was the "joy r" part of the evening that led us to that moment. Two hours later, thanks to kind Farmer Joe, we had been towed out and were snow-drifting our way back to the city over the icy roads.

At one stage, Anthony suggested he could drive us to Alaska if we gave him some more money for diesel. At another, he said he'd found us a place to stay for the night with some "stoner friends". But by the time he dropped us at a motel, on his way to a backstreet to crash out for the night, both of these suggestions had been long forgotten. We worried for our new friend, as he left us, bottle in hand, and saying something about going to check on his "baby mother".

"She says she's got my baby," he explained, although we didn't quite understand. The only baby we'd heard about was his three-year-old daughter, Olivia, whom he had left the previous night after a fight with girlfriend Brandy. It was Brandy, we were told, who was responsible for the broken passenger door and lack of licence plate.

"She gets crazy when she drinks!" Anthony said.

Anthony's struggles put our own problems into perspective. We forgot all about the stresses of the previous day, and indeed about our earlier ride with Danny, 64, a dope-smoking "happy bachelor", who told us he had several girls on the go. Like I said, it seems it's true what they say about Prince George.

Jo

As we sat stuck in a snowdrift, acrid smoke wafting my way from the tyres that were spinning fruitlessly, it struck me that I was not even the tiniest bit surprised by our predicament. I could have foretold it an hour into our journey – around the moment we pulled off the highway to spin in the snow for a while, and just before the first time Steve and I paid for extra diesel, so that we wouldn't get stuck on an isolated stretch of road. If I was watching the events unfold on a cinema screen, I would have complained that the script was too predictable.

More conspicuously than most, Anthony demonstrated the complexity of the human character. He would put the car into full throttle for short bursts to show off the turbo boust, but then conscientiously put on the indicator for the (non-existent) other vehicles, and meekly turn the corner. His truck was falling apart thanks to his girlfriend's violent drunken outbursts, and yet he told us he would acquire (steal) a new air freshener every two weeks to keep it smelling sweet.

I spent much of our time together looking forward to not feeling like a 14-year-old hanging out with her bad-influence pal, but I was also aware that Anthony couldn't press the off-switch. His life was full of negativity, emotional turmoil and conflict; all Steve and I could do was hope we'd provided a little calm for a few hours.

DAY 248 (CONTINUED): 16.43
THE SHEPHERD'S INN, MILE 72, ALASKA HIGHWAY, BRITISH COLUMBIA, CANADA

STEVE

It's -7°C outside. We know this because we've been standing out there for the past three hours, beneath the falling snow. We lost feeling in our toes after the first hour. During the second, I wondered whether we should have invested in snow boots, but by the third I had grown quite used to the numbness. Anyway, it could be worse. The locals here tell us that, by rights, it should be -30°C at this time of year.

Perhaps we shouldn't grumble, but it is hard not to when vehicles are passing as if you aren't there. I'm not sure what the problem is exactly. One lady suggested we'd arrived here too late and missed the morning rush to the next town, Fort Nelson, 400km away. We were also informed that a collision between two trucks had caused the road ahead to close for several hours.

Another problem was our position. The exit at the Shepherd's Inn, a petrol-station-cum-diner, is on a downhill, so in these conditions it is unsafe for drivers to stop, even if they wished to do so. One kind gent turned around and told us he could offer us a ride 9km, but he suggested we were probably better off where we were. At least here, there would be rooms available if, as transpired, we failed to get a ride.

It is depressing to know we have wasted an afternoon standing outside in the cold, and that we travelled just 100km today, thanks to our one and only ride, with Philip, 41, a salesman of heavy machinery used in the thriving oil and gas industries here. Philip was kind enough to bring us to this Inn, way beyond his office in Fort St. John, and told us he felt confident we'd stand a good chance of meeting someone travelling on to Fort Nelson. Sadly, although it is highly likely we have been passed by a few such people, none have yet offered us a ride. It is still early, but the sun is already gone and we don't have the energy to approach every driver who stops here.

... Ah, saying that, Jo has just discovered that there are no rooms available tonight, so our day's journey may not be over yet, after all.

DAY 249: SATURDAY 22ND NOVEMBER 2014, 16.35
STEVE AND LEONA'S HOUSE, FORT NELSON, MILE 300, ALASKA HIGHWAY, BRITISH COLUMBIA, CANADA

STEVE

Sometimes it really does seem as though someone is watching over us. Last night, as we found ourselves without a ride and unable to find a room, we remembered meeting a lady who lived just two doors down from the Shepherd's Inn. When I knocked on her door, a bed for the night was offered before I even had a chance to ask. Colleen and husband John, a middle-aged couple fond of hunting (as displayed by the many "trophies" hanging from their walls), ran us a hot bath and said we needn't worry if we needed to stay an extra night.

Over breakfast this morning, Colleen told us she feared we may again struggle to find a ride. A snowstorm had hit the previous night, snow was still falling and, while the temperature gauge read -12°C, with wind chill Colleen estimated it would feel more like -30°C. With our lack of snow boots and sufficiently thick winter coats, Colleen suggested thumbing a ride was out of the question.

"You'd freeze to death!" she said.

Eager to press on, I recalled that the previous evening a waitress at the Shepherd's Inn had enquired of drivers on our behalf. Borrowing Colleen's phone, I called the Inn and asked if they could let us know if anyone came by who was heading to Fort Nelson and wouldn't mind giving a ride to two English hitchhikers.

The waitress, a different one from the night before, sounded unsure – "We don't normally ask people such things," she said – but told me she'd call if anything cropped up.

We didn't hold out much hope, but prayed someone would come to our aid and readied our bags with a plan to head to the Shepherd's Inn in person to better our chances and alleviate the pressure on the reluctant waitress.

But then the phone rang.

"Is that the gentleman looking for a ride north?"

"Er, yes it is."

"Well, there's a couple here willing to give you a ride. They're just eating their breakfast, so hurry! They'll be leaving soon."

Just like that, we were on our way. Colleen saved us a walk through the snow with a ride in her pick-up truck, and we were soon shaking hands with Steve and Leona, a couple in their sixties on their way home to Fort Nelson after a trip to a medical specialist in Fort St. John. Leona had recently been diagnosed with breast cancer. Still, they had it within their hearts to invite a couple of strangers to travel with them and then invite us to stay. Here in their home in Fort Nelson, we have each been donated a pair of snow boots and invited to join them at their church tomorrow; they've also posted a note on the town's Facebook page to ask if anyone is driving north on Monday.

A day that started with pessimism was transformed into one of the easiest, and best, of the trip in one phone call, and all because of a lousy breakfast at Steve and Leona's motel in Fort St. John.

"It tasted like plastic," Steve told us, so they had decided to splash out on a second breakfast at their favourite local joint, the Shepherd's Inn, where they were recognised by a waitress. The rest, as they say, is history.

19. THE END OF THE ROAD

DAY 253: WEDNESDAY 26TH NOVEMBER 2014, 15.24
HOMER AIRPORT, HOMER, "THE END OF THE ROAD", KENAI
PENINSULA, ALASKA

STEVE

I can't quite believe I'm writing this, but we've reached the end of the road.

One minute, we were waiting on the far edge of Fort Nelson, wondering how much longer we could survive in -17°C and whether we might struggle to find a ride 500km to Watson Lake – the next town – let alone Alaska. The next minute, Chuck, a 55-year-old American dressed in a full army surplus winter jumpsuit, had pulled over and told us he was driving to Alaska. Just like that, our journey was over.

Well, we still had the small matter of 900 miles to the border – Chuck and I shared the driving, as we drove there non-stop in 20 hours – but to all intents and purposes, our journey was over the moment we saw the Alaska plates on the back of his old pick-up truck.

To be honest, we didn't care where in Alaska he was headed. We had never set an end point; the border would do. But it has been the icing on the cake to have travelled with Chuck a farther 600 miles all the way here to Homer, the westernmost point on the Alaskan road network and the so-called "End of the Road", where Chuck just happens to live.

As we drove onto the Kenai Peninsula yesterday, the landscape was reminiscent of that first day back in Ushuaia. Giant snowy peaks were all around, as we skirted alongside the Cook Inlet south of Anchorage. We had switched the Beagle Channel, named after a pioneering ship, for a waterway named after a famous explorer. We'd come full circle. It felt so right.

As in Patagonia, the uniformity of colours was striking, even if Alaska used a different palette – white snow on the mountains and fields; a greyish green on the trees, which blended with the colour of the asphalt and, at first light, even the sky.

We enjoyed some jaw-dropping scenery throughout our journey with Chuck. Even at night, as we passed through the enormous and almost utterly barren Yukon Territory (which has a total population of just 35,000), a green haze of Northern Lights crested the mountain before us to crown the final moments of our adventure. In the daytime, it was just mountain after mountain, snow-covered pines and cedar trees, and herds of bison.

In the long hours before the border, I waited for the moment our hopes would be dashed. Perhaps the car would break down, or we'd be involved in a crash just a few kilometres short of the border. Maybe Chuck would tire of us and throw us out, or just drive off with all our stuff in his boot. But although I once thought I caught Chuck leaving a petrol station without us ("I got you worried there, didn't I!" he joked, after he'd turned the car around), he was as good as his word and his old pick-up truck hauled us safely over the finishing line. And once there, once we'd crossed that final border, we struggled to get to grips with the realisation that this was it, our journey was really over.

As we sit in the tiny Homer Airport, awaiting a flight back to Anchorage and then home, it still hasn't sunk in. I keep worrying that if we fell asleep, we might wake up back in Fort Nelson, or worse still, Prince George. The thought fills me with dread. It isn't that I've fallen out of love with hitchhiking, but the road has been long and enough is quite enough, thank you. Last week's wasted 970km round trip put our reserves of strength to a very stern test. Another blow might have pushed us over the edge.

But no, it's really, truly over! No more hitchhiking, no more worrying, no more waiting – well except for the plane, but that is one wait we can handle.

Jo

I've daydreamed countless times about the way this adventure might finish. Most of my recent projections have ended with us not finishing: deported out of Canada in handcuffs, or defeated by the weather and having to fly back to try again in the summer. The versions that have had us arriving in Alaska were somewhat limp: only reaching the border and then having to catch a bus, or finishing up in Skagway on the Alaska Panhandle (not part of the main body of Alaska).

It's lucky, then, that I'm not the author of events, as the reality has been nothing short of perfect.

"Are you cold?" Steve asked me at around 8 on Monday morning. He had just pointed to the frost collecting in the hair peeking out from under my hat, which complemented the ice crystals in his moustache. This did not strike me as a positive development.

"Yes," I said.

"Where?" he asked.

"In my soul," I responded, the kind of reply I like to give when disgruntled with life. Who on earth hitchhikes at -17°C? Oh that's right, we do.

For once I was not affronted that, despite the cold, people were driving past without acknowledgement. We had taken a tour of the area with Leona's husband Steve the night before and knew that, apart from a few houses on the periphery of Fort Nelson, there was nothing at all for about 300 miles. These drivers knew that a short ride up the road would not gain us anything; at least where we were, we could walk back into the town if we needed to.

We had chosen to stand at the entrance to the town's leisure centre, which was soon to open for the day. When an approaching car put on its indicator and the driver pointed behind me, I assumed he would turn into the car park. But then the car pulled over, rather than heading for a parking bay, and Steve shuffled over for a chat. I remained in my spot, jumping up and down to keep the blood circulating and employing my usual "don't get too excited" attitude.

"... We are too!" I heard Steve exclaim. "We've hitchhiked here from Argentina! Can we come with you?"

This was not the usual response Steve would give when in negotiations with a driver. "Oh, that's great," was usually sufficient to confirm the ride, and the whole story of our adventure would come out once we were safely ensconced inside the vehicle. But there wasn't much opportunity to consider this, before Steve was turning back towards me.

"HE'S GOING TO ALASKA!" Steve shouted, with a huge grin stretching across his cold face, and it all made sense.

This time, I made no attempt to protect myself from eventualities such as the car breaking down, or the driver deciding not to go there after all, or any other reason that would mean that at some point we were not really going to Alaska. No. It just felt too right.

And so it was that we finished the adventure while simultaneously breaking our record for the longest distance travelled with one person: 1,500 miles with Chuck Pinkerton the Hero. We saw bison charging a trio of trucks; we revelled in two days of awesome splendour, wooed and wowed by the fantastically beautiful scenery of northern Canada and Alaska; we made it to the "End of the Road".

Perfect.

Redwoods in California

The land of the freeway

The Highway of Tears

Colleen

Steve and Leona

-17°C

The last ride

Alaska

'The End of the Road', Kenai Peninsula, Alaska

Chuck Pinkerton

The best feeling in the world